Housing Microfinance

Housing Microfinance

A Guide to Practice

Edited by Franck Daphnis and Bruce Ferguson

Kumarian
Press, Inc.

Housing Microfinance: A Guide to Practice

Published 2004 in the United States of America by Kumarian Press, Inc., 1294 Blue Hills Avenue, Bloomfield, CT 06002 USA

Production and design by Rosanne Pignone, Pro Production
Copyedited by Beth Richards
Proofread by Jody El-Assadi
Index by Robert Swanson

The text for Housing Microfinance is set in ITC New Baskerville 10.5/12.5. Printed in Canada on acid-free paper by Transcontinental Printing. Text printed with vegetable oil-based ink.

∞ The paper used in this publication meets the minimum requirements of the American National Standard for Information Sciences—Permanence of Paper for Printed Library Materials, ANSI Z39.48–1948.

Library of Congress Cataloging-in-Publication Data

Housing microfinance : a guide to practice / edited by Franck Daphnis and Bruce Ferguson.
    p. cm.
    Includes bibliographical references and index.
    ISBN 1-56549-182-3 (pbk. : alk. paper) — ISBN 1-56549-183-1 (cloth : alk. paper)
1. Microfinance—United States. 2. Microfinance—Developing countries. 3. Housing—United States—Finance. 4. Housing—Developing countries—Finance. I. Daphnis, Franck, 1965– II. Ferguson, Bruce, 1951–
HG178.3.H68 2004
    332.7'22—dc22

                                2003018054

---

13 12 11 10 09 08 07 06 05 04   10 9 8 7 6 5 4 3 2 1   First Printing 2004

Contents

Tables, Figures, and Boxes

TABLES

FIGURES

BOXES

Foreword

Robert P. Christen

The private finance of low-income housing presents the micro-credit industry with one of its most dramatic challenges. The purchase of new homes, parcels of land upon which to build, or the major upgrading of a current residence all represent sums of money that require relatively long loan terms to keep payments within the reach of poor families. Yet microcredit operators have built their success on the backs of lending methodologies that keep loan terms quite short, loan amounts low, payments frequent, and that use peer-based knowledge as a basis for assessing a potential borrower's character (willingness to repay). These techniques were developed precisely to counter the fact that poor families had no collateral to back their credit requests, and that their sources of income, while potentially sufficient, were too unstable and difficult to verify for the longer terms of traditional loans.

Most low-income families would probably be interested in a long-term, lower interest rate loan that they could use to purchase or substantially improve their living quarters. This interest stems from the fact that shelter meets a basic human need and can represent a major capital asset for poor families. Further, land is almost universally seen as an important element guaranteeing old age survival. Land can have a house built upon it; elderly parents who own a house can offer shelter to income-earning children in return for their own maintenance. Or it can be rented for income that provides an old age pension.

In fact, we already know that microcredit clients use the proceeds from their loans, or increased income from their business activities, to improve their dwellings or purchase real estate property.

In addition to the informal empirical evidence familiar to loan officers all over the world, several case studies undertaken as part of the United States Agency for International Development's AIMS (Assessing the Impact of Microenterprise Services) project indicate the important role of building assets (primarily housing) to reduce the vulnerability that poor families face.

The push to bring housing finance to microclients comes from a couple of different directions. In some countries, the supply of microcredit services has grown such that a competitive market has developed. In these places, microfinance institutions or MFIs compete for clients primarily based on the attractiveness of the services they offer. Using such strategies as reducing transactions costs, eliminating the hassles associated with group lending, and holding down interest rates, some MFIs are trying to adjust the terms and conditions of their loans to make them more responsive to the liquidity needs of their clients. Some are offering clients an extensive array of loan products, each of which has its own terms and conditions, among which housing is starting to figure more prominently.

From another direction, advocates of low-income housing are discovering the microenterprise credit field and its clients. Traditional housing lenders to poor families are exploring ways to apply some of the techniques developed by microcredit organizations to extend the long-term, larger loans required for improving the housing of those poor located in the informal sector. This book reflects the ways in which these two groups and sets of technologies are coming together and challenging the deeply held paradigms of each.

Microfinance applied to housing can be quite simple. To the extent that the microfinance of housing refers to the use of loans to make marginal improvements in current housing—all that may be required is a greater degree of flexibility in current products, especially those individual loan products that already incorporate a significant evaluation of creditworthiness. Most home improvements can be carried out with loans that range from a few months in term to three years. A steady succession of repeat longer-term loans can readily finance the steady stream of home improvement that most families wish to undertake. This mirrors the normal process most families go through in building their principal capital asset, one room at a time. For those microlenders who use group-based methodologies, the transition to individual lending of the type required to make three-year loans is much more profound.

But the technology for how to engage in this transition can be found within the microcredit industry itself.

Microfinance applied to housing can also be quite simple to the extent that "microfinance" is understood by traditional low-income housing providers to refer simply to poorer families than those reached by existing programs. Microcredit, as currently practiced, serves very poor families who have independent sources of income, whether these be from microenterprises or small-scale farming. Generally, microcredit programs are not aimed at families where the principal wage earner has a stable salary from a formal sector job, although many families receive earnings derived from a member who works as a day laborer. Much of low-income housing finance, however, is directed at civil servants and others who fall on the low end of the wage scale, yet participate in the formal sector.

For low-wage, salaried clients the challenge to traditional housing programs is simply that the size of the loan is too great for the client's income. This is partly due to the fact that most formal sector housing lenders finance only new home purchases (not the upgrading of current residences; there are very few options for mortgage finance of used homes—the most commonly used types of finance in developed markets). To address this issue, many governments subsidize the construction and finance of new homes for lower-income families but give preference in these subsidies to those families that can demonstrate salary history. The challenge that traditional housing programs face with these low-income, salaried families is how to drive down the cost of new construction, or how to increase or better use government subsidy.

The greatest challenge of all lies with those who wish to make long-term, larger loans for substantial housing rehabilitation or new home purchase for microenterprise clients whose income flow is variable and uncertain.

Any successful lending technique must be able to sort out potential borrowers according to their willingness and ability to repay. This process is called borrower selection. Normally, banks rely on secondary information to establish a client profile. They get copies of paycheck stubs, tax returns, rental agreements, titles to major property items, and any number of other documents that certify the underlying financial information on which the decision is to be based or guarantees constituted. In microcredit, due to the informal nature of clients' sources of income and lack of assets that can be collateralized, lending methodologies rely on group mechanisms and incremental approaches. Microlenders gather information about clients' character through peer group mechanisms and build credit relationships through a series of short-term loans that increase over time, depending on the timeliness of the client's repayment. Microlenders who make individual loans still rely on the incremental approach and other indicators of prior credit history that can be gleaned from that person's community or from a credit bureau.

In addition, successful lending methodologies must enforce repayment. The strongest pressure to repay comes from the ability of a lender to cut the borrower off from future access to credit. In developed financial systems, this is done through a credit bureau, a system that collects information on the indebtedness and repayment history of anyone having financial relations with banks and consumer debt organizations. In the early stages of development of a microlending market, pioneer MFIs operate in a virtual monopoly, and the incentive to repay is simply the continued access to further loans from that same MFI. As a competitive market evolves, borrowers have more options for obtaining loans and, unless MFIs share information about their risky clients, this incentive dramatically weakens.

So the challenge of housing finance is to overcome two issues: 1) the lender's lack of familiarity with the microclient who wishes to take out a very large loan for a very long time, and who can not provide sufficient information, and 2) the housing lender's inability to prejudice the defaulting client's ability to access future loans (from that same lender in that it is unlikely the same borrower would want to borrow again to purchase another house, and from others in the system due to the weakness of credit information reporting systems). Although low-income housing loans are collateralized, these guarantees are virtually never enforced due to their political sensitivity. Therefore low-income housing lenders must rely upon the very same mechanisms used by microenterprise lenders to enforce their contracts.

Cooperatives engaged in housing finance, and some other types of organizations, have addressed this problem by requiring potential credit clients to save for a number of months, or even years, prior to obtaining a loan. This regular pattern establishes the client's willingness and ability to repay. Other mechanisms used to overcome these two issues are explored in this book.

Housing finance can be quite an attractive product line, especially for microlenders. Housing loans can represent relatively large operations when compared to the normal working capital loans. Even at lower interest rates, a housing loan can be quite profitable. It requires little follow-through, and the cost of making the initial loan is not much higher than for the working capital loan. For MFIs concerned with financial sustainability, and even profitability, housing loans can be quite tempting.

Housing microfinance can also be quite risky if the MFI does not find adequate ways to perform the borrower selection or cannot enforce repayment incentives. These are the critical elements of product design. Furthermore, housing loans can be quite risky, especially for MFIs that add them to the product mix offered to preexisting microenterprise clients. The MFI runs the very real risk of increasing the total indebtedness levels of its clients beyond any prudent norm. This risk increases dramatically in those competitive microlending environments from which much of the interest in housing finance comes. Large housing loans granted as parallel loans to clients already repaying working capital loans are cited as the key causes of deteriorated loan portfolios in both Finansol/Corposol in Colombia and Grameen Bank in Bangladesh.

The reasons for this are quite straightforward. The tendency of clients, when providing information to loan officers, is to overstate income and understate other credit obligations or indebtedness. In addition, many loan officers expect clients to use the proceeds of their working capital loan to pay off other obligations, and therefore restructure total indebtedness. But all too often this doesn't happen, or its effect is only temporary, and total indebtedness simply increases and diversifies. And finally, to the extent that the loan is not tied directly to the purchase of a new home, it can encourage gamesmanship on the part of clients who simply seek a larger, longer-term loan to suit their general purposes. This forces the housing loan to compete internally with other products. Such competition wouldn't be so bad, except that the housing loan is usually the most attractive for clients in terms of interest rates, term, and amounts—while at the same time it can be the highest risk.

Subsidy is likely to remain a part of the low-income housing picture for a long time to come. Societies have very important reasons for subsidizing home ownership among poor families. The design of subsidy, and the manner in which it relates to housing finance, is a topic that the microcredit field can and should profitably engage. One of the notable achievements of the microcredit industry has been to clarify the importance of subsidizing institution building through operating grants, not reduced interest rates. It has also clarified the importance of subsidizing targeted client groups through grants in lieu of reduced interest rates or high default levels, as a way to maintain healthy financial systems based on credit discipline and sustainable institutions.

The intersection of housing and microfinance challenges the way we see clients, their financial requirements, the way we design products, and the way we think about the kinds of institutions that do microfinance. We are undoubtedly seeing a blurring of the line between the low-income household and the microenterprise as the primary target of microcredit. Savings is an important element in many housing finance schemes, which further blurs the line between saving and credit. Housing finance, especially large, long-term loans, challenges everything we think we have learned about how to extend credit to the poor whose income is variable and informal. It represents a relatively high risk for institutions that are either taking on a new product, as in the case of the traditional MFIs, or a new target group, as in the case of the traditional housing lenders. Yet the desire for improved shelter is one of the most universally recognized basic human needs, and it is manifest every day in the financial decisions poor families make with their limited resources. Thus, designing financial products that can more directly respond to the desire for improved shelter represents one of the most interesting challenges we face in the world of development finance.

Preface and Acknowledgments

Franck Daphnis and Bruce Ferguson

Housing microfinance is an emerging practice that applies key lessons learned from the microfinance revolution to the field of habitat financing. As such, housing microfinance intersects housing finance and microfinance, and incorporates elements of both. At the same time, the new practice has evolved strong distinguishing characteristics of its own, and the breadth of experience is such that a comprehensive survey and analysis of these characteristics is in order.

Housing Microfinance: A Guide to Practice seeks to answer a number of key questions:

- What is housing microfinance, and what differentiates it from microenterprise lending and more traditional forms of housing finance?
- What are the institutions involved in housing microfinance and what can we learn from their successes, trials, and errors?
- How do we assess demand for housing microfinance and what are the financial and nonfinancial services that appropriately meet that demand?
- How do microfinance institutions deal with issues that are not a part of the enterprise lending tradition—land and construction assistance, for instance?
- As microfinance begins to develop a foothold in places like the United States, is there also a potential for *housing* microfinance in developed economies? And if so, what form can it be expected to assume in a place such as the United States?

- What can policy makers and donor institutions do to capitalize on and nurture the momentum generated by the emerging practice? How do we bring housing microfinance to scale?

The book focuses both on what has been done (documenting the state of the practice and lessons learned), and on what should be done—and how (proposing standards for market assessments and product design and suggesting a policy agenda). As the title suggests, the book seeks to provide answers and guidance to practitioners as housing microfinance comes into its own and emerges from the shadows of traditional housing finance and microenterprise lending.

The book is a joint effort. It includes the work of seventeen authors, all practitioners, researchers, and policy makers with a diverse blend of perspectives to make it, we hope, a worthwhile contribution to the development finance literature.

In chapter 1 Franck Daphnis defines housing microfinance and traces its early evolution out of the shadows of microenterprise lending and traditional housing finance. In chapter 2 Bruce Ferguson discusses the reasons for the recent rise of housing microfinance and its usefulness to the housing finance and microfinance communities. He argues that the emerging practice lies at the intersection of microfinance and housing finance and is a natural, potentially high-demand extension of both. Chapter 3, by Alejandro Escobar and Sally Merrill, surveys the state of the art for housing microfinance services in Asia, Latin America, and Africa and presents summary data on the characteristics of key housing microfinance programs worldwide.

Chapters 4 through 7 look at a range of specific issues facing microfinance institutions (MFIs) and housing finance providers. Mayada Baydas examines market assessments for housing microfinance programs. Franck Daphnis looks at crucial elements of product design, including pricing for financial viability, optimal loan maturity, affordability, loan security requirements, and capital adequacy considerations. Kimberly Tilock (in a chapter based partially on unpublished papers from Michel Holsten and Juan Buchenau) considers the question of whether to provide construction services alongside housing microfinance loans and reviews the types of construction services that can be offered to housing microfinance clients. Irene Vance examines issues related to land availability, land tenure, and land security and their legal and programmatic implications for housing microfinance product design. She also analyzes and compares alternatives to formal collateral, including cosigners.

Chapters 8 through 11 focus specifically on housing microfinance and its potential in the United States. Kenneth Temkin, with Bruce Ferguson, provides a comprehensive overview of the current state of affordable housing innovations that may fall within the category of housing microfinance. Recognizing that housing microfinance as such is not a widespread field of practice within the U.S., chapter 8 also discusses how these innovations incorporate key elements of the emerging field of practice.

In chapter 9 Kil Huh and Lopa Kolluri look at the current and potential market for housing microfinance in the United States, focusing on three possibilities: colonias, native lands, and the owner-occupied rehab market. In chapter 10, Bruce Ferguson and Michael Marez present original research about affordable home ownership and progressive housing development on both sides of the U.S.-Mexican border. They assess the potential of progressive housing microfinance for increasing the U.S. home ownership rate in an era of mass immigration from developing countries where this practice is widespread. They also explore the use of this practice in high-cost U.S. metropolitan areas where home ownership rates are low, for special populations (for instance on Native Land), and for nontraditional households. Finally they suggest lessons for U.S. developers, local and national governments, and lenders.

In chapter 11 Sohini Sarkar and Kate McKee look at the potential future of U.S. housing microfinance. They build on the preceding three chapters to explore what the emerging practice could mean within the U.S. context, its relevance within that context, and what decision makers can do to foster the practice in the next few years.

Mohini Malhotra's chapter 12 is an international counterpart to chapter 10. It summarizes the key operational lessons learned from housing microfinance in the developing world and proposes programs and policies for international donors, national governments, and microfinance institutions to expand the new practice.

The editors would like to thank the United States Agency for International Development and the Fannie Mae Foundation for their generous support. We are also grateful to CHF International and to the Inter-American Development Bank, our employers, for providing the professional setting for many of the ideas explored in this book.

Tara Panek deserves a special mention for her diligent copy-editing and formatting of an early version of the manuscript. Kate McKee and Monique Cohen encouraged us to pursue our original idea for an anthology on housing microfinance. This book would not have been possible without their support. Finally, this book would not be what it is without the work of Guy Bentham and of Kumarian Press.

Acronyms

AMEEN	Access to Microfinance and Enhance Enterprise Niches (program of CHF)
CARD	Center for Agricultural and Rural Development (Philippines)
CBFI	Community-based financial institution
CDBG	Community development block grants
CDC	Community development corporation
CDFI	Community development financial institution
CEPAL	UN Economic Committee for Latin America
CGAP	Consultative Group to Assist the Poorest
CHBP	Community Home Buyers Program
CHF	Cooperative Housing Foundation
CLTV	combined loan to value ratio
CRA	Community Reinvestment Act
ECLOF	Ecumenical Church Loan Fund
FFIEC	Federal Financial Institutions Examination Council
FHA	U.S. Federal Housing Administration
FHEFSSA	Federal Housing Enterprises Finance Safety and Soundness Act
FICO	Fair Isaac and Company score
FUCVAM	Federation of Housing and Mutual Aid Cooperatives (Uruguay)
FUNHAVI	Foundation for Habitat and Housing (Mexico)
GDP	gross domestic product
GSE	Government Sponsored Enterprise
HILP	Home Improvement Lending Program
HMDA	hmda data
HMF	housing microfinance
HRTC	Historic rehab tax credits

HUD	Department of Housing and Urban Development (United States)
HUDCO	Housing and Urban Development Corporation (India)
IADB	Inter-American Development Bank
IDA	International Development Association
IFC	International Finance Corporation
LMI	low and moderate income
LTV	loan to value (ratio)
MFI	microfinance institution
MSA	Metropolitan Statistical Area
NAFTA	North American Free Trade Agreement
NGO	nongovernmental organization
NSDF	National Slum Dwellers Federation (India)
OFHEO	Office of Federal Housing Enterprise Oversight
PMSA	Primary Metropolitan Statistical Area
REMIC	Real Estate Mortgage Investment Conduit
SAHPF	South African Homeless Peoples' Federation
SDFN	Shack Dwellers Federation of Namibia
SELVAP	Servicio Latinoamericano y Asiatico de la Vivienda Popular (NGO)
SHF	Sociedad Hipotecaria Federal (mortgage finance, Mexico)
SMLV	minimum legal salary
SMSA	Standard Metropolitan Statistical Area
SPARC	Society for the Promotion of Area Resource Centers (India)
UNCHS	United Nations Commission for Human Settlements
UNIAPRAVI	Iberoamerican Union for Housing

Housing Microfinance: Toward a Definition

Franck Daphnis

Housing microfinance has come into its own.

Filling a void created by the limitations of traditional housing finance and building on the lessons of the recent microfinance revolution, housing microfinance is now a discrete area of practice that intersects housing finance and microfinance. The emerging practice holds ambitious promise for microfinance institutions, housing finance providers, and commercial banks the world over: It shows how the shelter needs of the poor can be financed in a way that is economically viable, affordable, and consistent with tested methods of delivering microfinance services to the poor. The situation in the United States is somewhat different, as we shall see later in this chapter, but there are applicable lessons from developing country experience.

DEVELOPING ECONOMIES

In developing countries, historic constraints in the supply of traditional housing finance and recent demand opportunities revealed by the successes of microfinance underlie the recent rise of housing microfinance.[1]

From a supply perspective, traditional housing finance has not succeeded in addressing the needs of poor people around the world. Bertrand Renaud defines the housing finance problem as "the need to reconcile three partially conflicting objectives: affordability for the households, viability for the financial institutions, and resource mobilization for the expansion of the sector and the national economy" (Renaud 1984). Until recently, housing finance providers, governments, and donors understood that problem as the need to finance a complete dwelling under terms that are affordable to poor families, attractive to the commercial sector, and on a scale large enough to register an impact on national housing shortages. More often than not, in poor and very poor countries, this simply proved impossible. Mortgage lending and a supporting secondary mortgage market never materialized as financially viable options in addressing the housing needs of the poor. Poor people could not afford to borrow enough money at real interest rates to finance a completed home, unless repayments were stretched over long periods of time. This created two problems: (1) few sources of funds existed that could match repayment periods spanning ten to thirty years, creating a severe asset/liability mismatch for commercial institutions interested in housing finance; and (2) when these sources were found (government pension funds for example) poor borrowers could not sustain repayments over long periods of time. Understandably, outside investors did not place their money in securities backed by such loans. Currently no reliable secondary mortgage markets for housing loans targeting poor people exist outside the Western World. Mortgage lending, while a part of commercial lending in middle income and poor countries, generally focuses on rich and near-rich clients. Housing banks created with the help of donor agencies over the past thirty years have gone bankrupt or moribund, evolved into full-fledged commercial banks (such as Capital Bank in Haiti), or become real estate focused banks with very few poor clients (the Housing Bank of Jordan).

To be sure, many governments in poor countries have developed noncommercial schemes to help poor people finance a completed basic home. These schemes include, for instance, mortgage loans financed by the country's national social security fund (RAP in Honduras and Infonavit in Mexico) and even group-based national subsidy programs (in South Africa). These programs, while sometimes useful in a specific national context, tend to be excessively bureaucratized and have never come close to offering a promise for worldwide replication.

Although mortgage lending has not supplied low-income families with viable means of financing their housing needs, promising developments in microfinance suggest that demand does exist for alternative forms of housing finance. In many parts of the world, the home is the most important asset poor people will ever own. Sometimes it can be a productive asset, for instance in the case of home-based microentrepreneurs. Even in cases where the home is not systematically used as a place of business, microfinance institutions (MFIs) have long observed that clients use loan proceeds to improve their living conditions.[2] Microfinance clients make the economically rational choice of subverting the use of business loans in response to the lack of widespread access to housing finance (or of more flexible consumer finance, for that matter). A microenterprise loan offers much better repayment terms than do informal sources of money lending (loan sharks), and such a loan can be a supplement or alternative to saving toward habitat improvements. This suggests that a fundamental expectation of microfinance—that economically active poor people can finance their needs incrementally, affordably, and under conditions that allow the financing provider to cover all associated costs—has potential beyond income-generating (enterprise) uses and can apply to personal asset building (housing).

Indeed organizations as diverse in size, client focus, and service offerings as Grameen Bank in Bangladesh, CARD in the Philippines, SEWA Bank in India, Banco ADEMI in the Dominican Republic, Financiera Calpia in El Salvador as well as several institutions affiliated with Accion, CHF, and IPC, currently offer financial services purporting to fit under the housing microfinance tent. In addition, providers include commercial banks and suppliers of construction materials who offer up to twelve-months worth of credit for home improvements to low-income customers throughout Asia, Africa, and Latin America. Reflecting the diversity of these organizations, the housing services they offer elude easy classification. In Mexico, CHF International and FUNHAVI have developed a home improvement loan that features an average loan amount of $1,800, a repayment period of eighteen months for first-time borrowers, and a 54 percent effective annual interest rate. The Grameen Bank's housing loans typically are repaid over ten years. They are offered at an interest rate that is 10 percent below rates assessed for microenterprise loans, and first-time clients are not eligible for such loans. If microfinance in its own right defies precise categorization, the intersecting housing dimension does not render the task any easier.

Still, a discussion of the range of services covered under housing microfinance is a necessary prelude to any serious analysis of it. In the interest of inclusion rather than selectivity at this early stage in the research, a useful definition should allow a reasonable range of ongoing initiatives to rise to scrutiny. A subsequent analysis would consist of sifting the useful from the less useful and, ultimately, in suggesting key elements of best practice that define successful housing microfinance services. For this to happen, a reasonably inclusive attitude should serve as context for the question at hand: What is housing microfinance?

Current practice and a survey of the emerging literature suggest two paths toward a preliminary answer: a microfinance *product*-centered definition, and a *provider*-centered definition of housing microfinance.

From a microfinance product perspective, housing microfinance encompasses financial services that allow poor and low-income clients to finance their habitat needs with methodologies adapted from the microfinance revolution. These methodologies rest most notably on the following principles: (1) Loans are for relatively small amounts and are based on clients' capacity to repay; (2) Repayment periods are relatively short (especially compared to mortgage lending) and are on par with mid- to high-end microfinance individual loans; (3) Loan pricing is expected to cover the real, long-run costs—operational and financial—of providing the service; (4) Loans are not heavily collateralized, if at all, and collateral substitutes are often used; (5) Loans tend to finance habitat needs incrementally, a function of the purchasing power of loans with short repayment periods and relatively low monthly payments; and (6) If the provider is an MFI, credit services for housing can be linked to prior participation in savings or more traditional microenterprise loan services.[3] In summary, from a product-based perspective, housing microfinance is the "microfinancing" of housing needs: the application of a microfinance-based approach to housing finance.

An alternative way to proceed is to define housing microfinance from a provider-based, rather than a product-based, perspective. Housing microfinance, according to this viewpoint, would include all explicitly recognized housing-focused financial services that microfinance institutions offer—even when the conditions under which these services are offered appear to deviate from microfinance orthodoxy. This is a literal rather than a methodological interpretation: Housing microfinance services are housing services offered by microfinance institutions. This definition, less rigorous than a methodological or product-based definition, is nevertheless useful given the desire for inclusion. It allows a range of services not otherwise fitting a recognized microfinance spectrum to come to scrutiny and guide our emerging understanding of housing microfinance. It also helps bring to light an important issue in housing microfinance: MFIs sometimes find it compelling to offer their clients housing products that deviate from their traditional product offerings.

The product-based and provider-based filters complement one another, albeit with ample areas of overlap. The product-based approach reaches outside the realm of microenterprise-centered organizations by focusing on the distinguishing characteristics of the financial services rather than on the types of institution that offer these services. It brings to the fore housing finance providers, NGOs, and commercial institutions that have developed innovative housing-related financial services based on microfinance best practices. The provider-based filter allows the consideration of housing innovations that do not appear to fit the expected confines of traditional microenterprise lending products—but nevertheless constitute an important part of current MFI housing portfolios throughout the world. Together the two approaches define the current universe of activities classified under housing microfinance. They also provide a point of departure for more refined analyses.

If the two-pronged approach helps define an inclusive universe of current housing microfinance services, what are we to make of that resulting universe? Specifically, what are the basic clusters of products that—allowing for expected variations—demonstrate some level of consistency in how MFIs and other providers offer housing microfinance services to their clients?

A survey of current housing microfinance initiatives suggests that one answer to this question lies in analyzing the distinguishing characteristics of financial services (loan amounts, repayment period, and pricing strategy) in relation to the client's history with the service provider. Using this framework, housing microfinance providers fall into two clear categories: (1) those that make housing financing available on a stand-alone basis to all eligible clients, including first-time clients; (2) and those that extend such financing on a linked basis and only to clients who have a prior history with the provider.

Stand-Alone Housing Microfinance Services

MFIs, banks, and NGOs currently deliver stand-alone housing microfinance services alongside but independent of other microfinance or
housing finance products. Some organizations, such as FUNHAVI in
Mexico, have built their entire organizations around a single housing microfinance loan. As the name suggests, stand-alone housing
microfinance products do not rely on a prior history with the
provider as a proxy for capacity to pay. The eligibility criteria, loan
term, and loan uses are designed to qualify potential borrowers on
the merits of their current financial profile and habitat needs.
Loans are extended to individuals (rather than to groups of individuals), tend to be for relatively small amounts ($1,000–$5,000),
and carry a relatively short repayment period compared to traditional housing loans (1 1/2 to 4 years). Consequently, loans typically—though not always—allow borrowers to finance their home
incrementally (Daphnis and Tilock 2001, 5).

Table 1.1 illustrates basic features of stand-alone housing microfinance services for three organizations that have developed such
services.

ADEMI, Calpia, FUNHAVI, BancoSol in Bolivia, MiBanco in
Peru, Genesis Empressarial in Guatemala, and CHF International
(in Central America and the Middle East) are among the dozens
of organizations that deliver stand-alone microfinance services to
their clients. CHF provides the following rationale for its own version of housing microfinance (the Home Improvement Lending
Program, or HILP):

> CHF's approach is rooted in the observation that the working poor in
> developing countries build and improve their homes incrementally.
> As mortgages are typically not available, low- and moderate-income

Table 1.1 Examples of Stand-Alone Housing Microfinance Products

Organization	Average Loan Size	Maximum Repayment Period	Security Collateral	Required Time with Program	Savings Required	Solution Type	TA to Clients
ADEMI	$4,000	36 mos.	Loan is collateralized	None	No	Variable	No
FUNHAVI	$1,500	20 mos.	2 cosigners	None	No	Variable	Yes
CHF/Gaza	$4,800	36 mos.	2 cosigners	None	No	Variable	Yes

Source: IFC, HIID, Daphnis/CHF MFT Course Survey

earning individuals rely on their disposable income and savings or borrow money from informal sources to finance their home improvements. Traditionally they begin with a basic core house and gradually improve the structure by increasing its size and adding amenities such as sanitation connections as funding becomes available. The [housing microfinance service] provides access to credit based on how people build, their building needs, and what they can afford (Daphnis and Tilock 2001, 5).

For MFIs offering stand-alone housing microfinance services, the benefits are multiple. Stand-alone products can help MFIs diversify their client base beyond microentrepreneurs, assuming salaried employees who do not operate a microenterprise can become eligible for financing. Housing microfinance products can also help MFIs manage default risks by spreading these risks over an increased number of financial services. Finally, housing microfinance services offered on a stand-alone basis should help with client satisfaction (and retention) by providing clients with a fuller range of financing options under one roof.

Stand-alone housing microfinance products make sense for organizations looking to respond to a perceived demand for housing finance services that is independent of other credit or saving services they offer. Future clients, whether they are microentrepreneurs or not, will have the financial capability to take on a new loan, given current income and debt circumstances. For instance, CHF International will allow clients to use only 25 percent of their disposable monthly income toward loan repayment. CHF will not accept a monthly debt burden (including housing loan repayment) that exceeds 40 percent of monthly disposable income (Daphnis and Tilock 2001, 17). The repayment period for housing microfinance loans is relatively short as providers attempt to mitigate the risks of repayment fatigue, uncertainty over future income, asset-liability mismatch, and the absence of a repayment history as proxy for repayment capacity.

Linked Housing Microfinance Services

Many MFIs, especially in Asia, have developed housing microfinance services that are linked to prior participation in microenterprise or savings services. The Grameen Bank, SEWA Bank, and CARD are among the best known MFIs linking housing microfinance to other products they offer. A survey of these MFIs shows that clients access linked loans at interest rates that are often lower than what they would have to pay for microenterprise loans. The repayment periods for these loans appear, on average, to be longer than for stand-alone products.

Linking eligibility for housing loans to clients' performance on prior services seems to accomplish several objectives. Housing microfinance loans, especially for organizations involved with poorer clients and with solidarity or other group-based lending, do not constitute business as usual. Housing loans are usually provided on an individual basis; they tend to be for higher amounts than group-based loans or individual loans targeting the very poor; as a result, they require longer repayment periods than these more established loans. MFIs offering linked housing loans use their credit or savings services as a performance filter, a form of internal credit bureau that allows faithful and reliable clients to rise and become eligible for the different, seemingly riskier, loan.

Table 1.2 illustrates some basic characteristics of linked housing microfinance services as offered by three well-known MFIs.

MFIs that link housing microfinance to more traditional microfinance services subordinate housing finance to their other products. From a risk standpoint, this suggests a much more cautious approach than that of MFIs following the stand-alone approach—perhaps a function of the targeted clientele. Indeed, many among the MFIs currently offering housing microfinance as linked services have clients at or near the poverty level. Assuming that microentrepreneurs have financing needs beyond their business

Table 1.2 Characteristics of Linked Housing Microfinance Services

Organization	Average Loan Size	Maximum Repayment Period	Security Collateral	Required Time with Program	Savings Required	Solution Type	TA to Clients
Grameen Bank	$100–$600	120 mos.	5 cosigners and center guarantee	Two years minimum	Yes	Fixed (incl. Latrine)	No
SEWA Bank	$300	60 mos.	One year savings as lien, 2 cosigners	One year minimum	Yes	Variable	No
CARD	$359	12 mos.	5 cosigners	One and a half years	Yes ($39)	Variable	No

Source: IFC, HIID, Daphnis/CHF MFT Course Survey

needs, the promise of a housing loan is a powerful incentive to perform on first-tier loan and savings programs. As a consequence, housing microfinance, when tied to other MFI services, has the potential to enhance the MFI's overall financial performance and client retention rate.

Linked housing microfinance services, to the extent that they only benefit current MFI clients, do not necessarily lead to an expanded client base. If, however, housing loans are linked to a savings program open to nontraditional clients, diversification is possible.

Many MFIs offer linked housing loans at a lower interest rate than they charge for microenterprise loans. A possible explanation is that these MFIs price housing products to account for a reduced default risk from clients with whom they already have a relationship. Another explanation is that MFIs view housing loans more as a reward to faithful clients than as a profit center. As such, housing loans would not be expected to generate the returns anticipated for other loans. It is tempting to compare this discrepancy in pricing with the fact that commercial mortgage loans typically carry annual interest rates that are lower than business or consumer loans. This is not, however, a useful comparison. Mortgage loans are priced lower than other loans because the risk to the financing provider is lower: Mortgages are highly collateralized by the resale value of the home being financed. In the case of linked housing microloans, the house does not always serve as collateral for the loan. In many countries where MFIs operate, housing resale value is often doubtful and the MFI's ability to repossess the home in the first place may be even more problematic. Uncertainty surrounding land tenure in these countries can also prevent large segments of the housing stock from becoming transferable assets, especially when owners are poor people building in marginal areas. Whatever the reason for the differences in interest rates, it does appear that many MFIs linking housing products to other services engage in some form of cross-subsidization. MFIs will be able to sustain this practice in the long run only if the benefits of running housing microfinance operations outweigh the opportunity costs from the unearned income.

Construction Assistance

A defining characteristic of some housing microfinance programs is the provision of construction advice or supervision to clients.

Some institutions view this form of technical assistance to the client as an important part of any housing microfinance loan. Others do not perceive any particular value added in providing construction assistance services.

One way to approach construction assistance is to view it in the context of institutional attitudes toward the concepts of due diligence and follow-up. To the extent that institutions believe that pre-loan due diligence on a business microenterprise loan is necessary—to assess whether a client's desired loan amount is appropriate to and can be used for the purpose declared on the loan application—they may want to extend the practice to housing microfinance. This could entail helping with basic construction design, budgeting, and guidance on materials and labor procurement. Similarly, if an institution's practice is to follow up, post-loan, to ensure that the loan was used for the intended purpose, construction oversight may make sense.

If construction assistance is not an option, then housing microfinance becomes in effect a consumer loan whose declared purpose is housing but whose ultimate use cannot be determined with certainty. The proposed construction project provides a rationale for assessing the required loan amount; repayment performance determines the client's future standing with the institution.

If housing microfinance includes construction assistance, responsible providers with no outside subsidies should include that service in the pricing of the loan. This suggests that the product line will be viable in the long run only if rational clients determine that the cost/benefit ratio to them—including the added value of technical assistance—is favorable. If the pricing is prohibitively high, clients will look elsewhere for alternative sources of housing financing. They may, as a consequence, choose to access microenterprise or other loans for that purpose.

If a housing microfinance loan is a flexible consumer loan using housing for marketing appeal or as a gauge for the loan amount, the loan could compete with other products the organization offers. Clients will shop around for the loan terms that best suit their various needs. They may access a housing loan for enterprise and other purposes, depending on the level of flexibility the housing loan offers.

Construction assistance in the context of housing microfinance does not appear to be a predictor of financial performance. FUNHAVI and ADEMI, for instance, have developed housing microfinance programs that are polar opposites in their attitude toward such assistance but similar in many other ways. Both report repayments rates approaching 100 percent. FUNHAVI sees its non-financial services to clients as a cornerstone of its mission. ADEMI managers have publicly stated that such assistance is contrary to their operating philosophy; clients, they believe, must decide for themselves how best to use their own money. No empirical evidence currently suggests that one approach is correct and the other is not.

Product and Market

A survey of current practice in developing economies shows that housing microfinance loans are extended to low-income-earning individuals or households, under terms that reflect the lessons learned from microenterprise lending. Loans can be for minor home improvements (such as a paint job, a door, or windows) or major home improvements (a room addition, a new roof). Less typically, a loan can finance a new home. Housing microfinance loans are typically extended to a single party, rather than to a group. Unlike microenterprise lending, however, housing microfinance explicitly includes among its targeted clientele salaried workers, in addition to self-employed entrepreneurs. Interest rates for housing microfinance loans should reflect the long-run operational and financial costs of providing the service. This often means that interest rates should be close to those a given organization would charge on individual microenterprise loans with comparable loan maturity. Cosigners provide the most common form of loan guarantee. Some organizations do use hard collateral including, in a few cases, the property being financed.

THE UNITED STATES

At first blush, the potential impact of housing microfinance in the United States seems much more limited than in developing countries. After all, housing microfinance (indeed, microfinance) is emerging as a powerful force in places where a vast, underserved, and bankable market exists beyond the reach of the formal finance sector. This is, a priori, not the case in the United States. Over the past fifty years, the United States has developed a sophisticated and far-reaching housing finance industry that would appear to serve most eligible households. As Huh and Kolluri point out (see chapter 9), 67.8 percent of American households own the homes in which they live. Very large government-sponsored enterprises, such as the Fannie Mae Corporation and Freddie Mac, have flourished by focusing on creating "more affordable loan products and underwriting experiments" and fostering a secondary mortgage market. These institutions, in partnership with an extensive network of retail level private institutions, have ensured that most households that present an acceptable credit risk have access to long-term financing for home ownership at affordable interest rates. Other government-sponsored initiatives such as the Community Reinvestment Act (CRA) have created additional incentives for commercial banks to service underserved communities and contributed to increased financial access for the working poor. To the extent that such a product makes sense in the United States, it is more suited to a niche market, albeit one with a growing and still relatively untapped potential.

As currently defined in the context of developing economies, housing microfinance involves relatively small housing-focused loans, targeting economically active poor households with limited access to more traditional forms of financing, and with terms that are affordable to these households and financially viable for the lending institution. As Temkin points out, however, families that would be prime candidates for housing microfinance loans in the United States do not necessarily qualify as underserved:

> [F]amilies that, in other countries, benefit from housing microfinance programs [. . .] have one or both of the following characteristics: (1) wealth- and/or income-constrained and (2) lacking a satisfactory or formal credit history. [For these families] home ownership rates increased without a large housing microfinance component; rather, lower-income home buyers benefited from affordable mortgage products introduced in the 1990s that allowed home buyers to qualify for 30-year loans despite having little or no equity for a down payment and imperfect or no formal credit histories. Such products obviated the need for microfinance loans, which typically do not allow for high loan-to-value ratios and have shorter terms (Temkin 2002, 3–4).

Temkin goes on to acknowledge that "innovations introduced into the mainstream housing finance system in the 1990s may be approaching their limits in increasing service to lower-income families" and suggests that housing microfinance techniques may help meet a demand from "markets that are beyond the reach of current affordable lending product" (Temkin 2002, 4).

In developing economies, housing microfinance can be a gateway to home ownership by providing poor working households with incremental financing to build a home over time. In the United States, the high cost of construction—as much a function of comprehensive enforced building codes mandating minimum standards for construction, safety, and comfort as it is a function of material and labor costs—and the policy focus on home ownership suggest that the housing microfinance market in the United States may be substantially different. Huh and Kolluri (see chapter 9) suggest that demand for housing microfinance products is likely to arise from those low- to moderate-income households in need of short-term, affordable home rehabilitation loans that do not have access to the formal financial sector.

The capacity of housing microfinance to increase housing finance options for specific niche geographically-based U.S. populations is particularly promising. Ferguson and Marez (see chapter 10) suggest that housing microfinance could be an important tool in helping U.S. financial institutions "greatly increase the production of and choice among a wide range of entry-level housing products" along the U.S.-Mexico border in the emerging communities commonly referred to as *colonias*.

CONCLUSION

Housing microfinance is emerging as an important tool in the struggle to help meet the housing needs of poor people around the world and is becoming a standard product for many MFIs in Latin America, Asia, the Middle East, and Eastern Europe. At present its most useful and widespread application consists of a series of incremental loans allowing poor households to build according to established microfinance strategies. MFIs interested in offering housing services to their clients must carefully assess whether they have the administrative and technical capacity to do so. They should also ensure that housing microfinance fits their strategy from an institutional and financial perspective (liquidity, opportunity cost of capital, and interproduct competition).

The emerging practice is finding its place as an attractive and practical alternative to traditional housing finance and an economically viable complement to more established microfinance services. In most cases, MFIs and housing finance providers should be able to provide housing microfinance services that are affordable to their clients and financially sound from an institutional perspective. Successful strategies from practitioners suggest that such services build on the lessons of the recent microfinance revolution and adapt these lessons to housing lending. Pricing, loan maturity, affordability analyses, pre-loan due diligence, and post-loan financial follow-up closely reflect accepted best practice for microfinance individual lending. Strategies for land security and construction assistance capitalize on decades of work in affordable housing finance. Finally, emerging approaches to land security (as a factor in the overall credit analysis) appear to be uniquely suited to the specific needs of housing microfinance.

Housing microfinance believes that the shelter needs of the poor can be financed in a way that is affordable, economically viable, and consistent with established methods of delivering microfinancial services to the poor. As MFIs, NGOs, and commercial institutions begin to scale up their efforts and learn important lessons from one another, housing microfinance is showing tremendous potential for following in the footsteps of micro-enterprise lending—and for having a long-lasting impact on the lives of tens of millions of people in the decades to come.

NOTES

1. Documented most notably in Harvard University 2002; Ferguson and Haider 2000; and Daphnis and Tilock 2001.

2. As much as 20 percent of MFI business lending goes "de facto" for housing, according to Ferguson and Haider 2000, 9.

3. See Daphnis and Tilock 2001 for a more detailed discussion of these principles.

2

The Key Importance
of Housing Microfinance

Bruce Ferguson

Housing microfinance grew steadily during the last two decades of the twentieth century. A 2000 Harvard study profiled forty housing microfinance programs mainly in Asia and Latin America but also in Africa. Hundreds of others existed but functioned on a relatively small scale.

Since 2000, the practice has expanded explosively. In Latin America, in particular, the bulk of established microfinance lenders now have or are developing a housing product. Housing microfinance has also proved quite profitable when launched by well-managed, established institutions, and it enjoys immense effective demand. Not surprisingly, some large microfinance lenders (such as MiBanco in Peru) project that housing credits soon will come to dominate their portfolio.

The recent dramatic expansion of housing microfinance reflects recognition of the importance of this practice. This evidence suggests that housing microfinance is not a fad or the novelty du jour in international housing. On the contrary, the evidence demonstrates that housing microfinance can have great positive impact on the lives of the low- and moderate-income household majority, can operate without subsidies, and, hence, is financially sustainable. The bulk of this chapter examines why housing microfinance is so important and why it fits the context of developing countries so well. The conclusion briefly reviews some key challenges that the practice must overcome to realize its promise.

HOUSING MICROFINANCE VS.
TRADITIONAL MORTGAGE FINANCE

A striking but unappreciated reality underlies most housing programs, policies, and discussions in emerging countries: *Only a small share of the population can qualify for a traditional mortgage to purchase the least expensive commercially built unit.* Typically, this share is less than 20 percent of households and, often, less than 10 percent. Even more amazing and catastrophic from a developmental perspective, some of the most important and dynamic middle-income countries virtually lack a market-rate mortgage finance sector.

Mexico serves as a particularly important example. Because of the North American Free Trade Agreement (NAFTA) and a thriving national economy, more households than ever have reasonably paid, formal-sector jobs. But the bulk of families lack adequate housing and the ability to build wealth through property ownership. A relatively high share of Mexican families—above 80 percent—own the property in which they live ("owner-occupants"). However, 60 percent of these owners lack full legal tenure to their lot, although most of this group has paralegal rights that secure their occupancy. In 2000 less than half (300,000) of newly formed Mexican households (750,000) received a mortgage. Of these 300,000 mortgages, more than 95 percent received a large subsidy from the government, with the remainder extended at what could be considered market terms. This subsidy, which is conveyed in myriad forms,[1] costs the government around five billion dollars each year—a large expenditure that burdens the Mexican economy and taxpayers as a whole but that gets transferred largely to middle-income households rather than low- or moderate-income families. Without this large subsidy, only about 25 percent of the Mexican population could afford a market-rate loan (even when initial loan payments are lowered through the double-indexed mortgage widely used in Mexico) for the least expensive commercially built unit (about U.S.$12,000).

The remaining households must build their own homes without formal-sector support. Hence, housing for most people throughout the developing world is quintessentially progressive. The low- to moderate-income majority buys or invades land, then constructs their homes incrementally over a period of five to fifteen years. Families typically construct a makeshift dwelling, then substitute permanent for temporary materials and expand the unit (upwards

on, ideally, a concrete roof or horizontally in less dense environments), and band together to lobby government for basic services.
This progressive housing builds the majority of developing country cities (housing accounts for three-quarters of urban development). However, it receives little institutional support. In particular, institutional credit for home improvement, to refinance
homes, and for purchase of existing homes is virtually unavailable.
Consequently, households cannot easily fix up or sell their homes
to move to areas of greater economic opportunity. Less than one
home in ten in the Mexican housing stock has a mortgage. Taking
out equity to start an enterprise or for any other reason is virtually unheard of. Largely as a result of this lack of home finance
and poor savings instruments, 70 percent of Mexican families have
no relationship with a financial institution, not even a checking or
savings account. Once families succeed in occupying property or
buying a home, households tend to stay there for life and pass it on
to succeeding generations. As a result, one Mexican government
official quipped that "we build coffins," because purchasing families
never leave their government-subsidized housing and die there.

The housing finance situation is worse in most other developing countries, which lack the resources of Mexico to subsidize traditional mortgage finance. Typically, mortgage finance funds less
than 20 percent of new homes (compared to 45 percent in Mexico) and no existing home purchase or home improvement.

Thus, the syndrome that characterizes Mexican housing and
housing finance tends to recur throughout developing countries:

- The small amount of mortgage finance available goes for
  the purchase of new, commercially built units of upper-class
  and some middle-income households. Most households cannot afford the debt service on even the smallest commercially built unit. Sometimes the central government attempts
  to bridge this affordability gap by creating a large subsidy
  system[2] to drive mortgage finance downmarket. But these
  subsidies end up going disproportionately to middle- and
  upper-income households.
- The remainder of the population must build and finance
  their own homes incrementally. Without support and guidance, this process generates enormous public costs. In particular, the reordering and extension of basic infrastructure
  (water, sanitation, roads, drainage, common facilities) to

informal settlements typically costs three times the amount
of extending infrastructure to formal-sector settlement.
Thus, governments usually end up behind the curve of
housing and urban demand and try to catch up at enormous public cost. Governments lack the subsidies to bridge
the affordability gap necessary to satisfy new household formation, thereby creating great pent-up demand that households satisfy through informal settlement (land invasion and
informal subdivisions) and unsupported progressive housing, whose costly regularization further depletes government resources—thereby aggravating this vicious cycle.

- No significant amounts of institutional debt finance go
  to support the progressive housing process of the low- to
  moderate-income majority (three-fourths of the population), to rental housing, or to development finance (land/
  infrastructure) or construction finance of formal-sector
  housing. For this and other reasons, housing fails to fulfill
  its economic function—in particular, that of building household wealth and assets—and falls short in its social function,
  as too few and too low-quality units get built to house an
  expanding population.

The poor fit between traditional mortgage finance and the needs of
the majority lies at the crux of these interrelated problems. This
poor fit derives from three drawbacks that housing microfinance
can address: (a) a highly limited market; (b) mismatch of the terms
of liabilities and assets; and (c) underwriting requirements unsuited
to the conditions of low- and moderate-income households.

Highly Limited Market

Mortgage finance involves relatively large loans for long terms, typically fifteen to thirty years. In developing countries, most mortgage lenders extend credit only for purchase of a commercially
constructed new unit. These characteristics poorly suit the needs of
low- and moderate-income borrowers and greatly limit the effective
demand for these loans. This is because these households must
build their homes progressively in order to afford them.

In contrast, housing microfinance funds the steps in the progressive housing process: acquisition of a lot, building a small core
unit, and expanding and improving the core unit. Households can

afford a series of such small, short-term loans. As a result, the effective demand for such home improvement lending is large. A market study of microfinance demand based on interviews of one thousand households in three Mexican cities along the U.S.-Mexico border—Tijuana, Matamoros, and Juarez—found that 14 percent of all households both wanted and could qualify for a housing microfinance loan under the most rigorous of assumptions.[3] Interestingly, the effective demand for housing microfinance in these three cities ($122 million) exceeded that for microenterprise finance by six times ($20 million).

The market for housing microfinance represents a substantially higher share of the population in lower-income countries. For example, a pilot housing microfinance program in Nicaragua operating only in four medium-sized cities outside the capital city of Managua currently originates more loans (1,200 per year) than all mortgage finance lenders in the country combined.[4] In Nicaragua, as elsewhere, the institutional and technical capacity of microlenders is the chief bottleneck for expanding housing microfinance—not effective demand, which is many times that of existing loan volumes.

Even when low- to moderate-income households can afford a traditional mortgage loan, many do not want one. Traditional mortgages require fixed payments over long periods of time. However, for people in developing countries the radical uncertainty of wipeouts (disease, unemployment, highly fluctuating income) and windfalls makes such a payment scheme highly dangerous. If they run into problems, these households risk losing their most precious asset, their home, which is a refuge from this instability and in old age. In contrast, these families can realistically plan for and commit to the short-term payments of microloans.

Studies also show that low- and moderate-income families highly prefer improving their existing home to purchasing a new home elsewhere, where the social capital from relationships with their friends, family, and neighbors in their old neighborhood lies largely out of reach. However, traditional mortgage lenders usually fund only the purchase of such new commercially built subdivisions.

The immense social value of home ownership in developing countries as well as distortions that stunt rental markets cause families to make extraordinary sacrifices for a place of their own. An indicator of this great benefit is that a common method of lot acquisition, group land invasions, often carries serious risks of physical harm and even death as well as extreme hardship. As a result, home ownership rates in many developing countries substantially exceed those of advanced industrialized countries. Home ownership rates are 86 percent in Mexican cities, 85 percent in Bangladesh, and 80 percent in Nicaragua compared to the current all-time high of 67 percent in the U.S. and 69 percent in Canada.

Thus, most families "own" something. Home ownership in developing countries, however, usually refers to having rights—often paralegal rights—to a lot with a structure requiring substantial improvement and, often, missing some basic services (such as sanitation). As a result, small credits to acquire the lot, regularize tenure, acquire an adequate sanitation solution, expand the unit, and improve its quality have tremendous potential for improving housing.

Mismatch of the Terms of Liabilities and Assets

The characteristics of traditional mortgage finance pose some other serious problems for lenders. Deeply rooted characteristics of the economies of many emerging countries—such as macroeconomic instability, fluctuating inflation, and, thus, foreign exchange risk—combine to raise real interest rates and shrink the terms of the liabilities available to financial institutions. Lenders typically fund their loans very short term, with liabilities of a maximum of one to three years. Hence, lenders engage in serious term mismatch when they make traditional mortgage loans of fifteen to thirty years. This term mismatch often goes unmonitored by financial institutions and represents a hidden, potentially explosive problem for many.

One way to deal with the mismatch without much analysis is to lend only a small share of an institution's assets in mortgages. As a result, building societies, mutual associations, and other supposed mortgage lenders (that often enjoy tax breaks and other legal and regulatory advantages for home lending) frequently place a high proportion of their assets in government bonds and short-term commercial loans or auto loans rather than mortgages. Of course, this tactic further shrinks the already small supply of mortgage lending.

In contrast, housing microcredit has much shorter terms—typically two to eight years. These short-term assets better fit the short-term liabilities available in developing countries and substantially reduce, although do not eliminate, the risks of term mismatch.

Such microloans also greatly reduce the risks of systemic crisis. The collapse of many banks that contributed to the Asian economic crisis of 1997 and 1998 came mainly from problems with large commercial and corporate loans. In contrast, microfinance institutions (MFIs) in Asian countries such as Bank Rakyat Indonesia had relatively few problems with their portfolios while other financial institutions failed.

Increasingly, developing country governments attempt to avoid the high real interest rates and short-term liabilities implicit in macroeconomic instability and exchange-rate risk by dollarizing in one form or another. Calls for a new international financial architecture and regional currencies have a similar purpose. The housing sector would be, perhaps, the main beneficiary of such reforms, which have the potential to drive traditional mortgage lending downmarket. Even if such currency reforms were successful—a heroic assumption—a substantial share of the bottom half of the income distribution would still fail to qualify for a loan for the least expensive commercially built new unit, and would prefer a microloan for progressive housing.

Unsuitable Underwriting Requirements

Mortgages typically require payments every month for a long period, demonstrable credit, a stable and verifiable source of income (typically salaried, formal-sector employment), and full legal title to the property. Low- and moderate-income households have difficulty with all of these underwriting requirements. Many have fluctuating incomes from a variety of family members and sources, usually informal. Few have any credit record. Depending on the country and the city, many also have paralegal title to land, rather than full legal title.

One of the greatest issues for traditional mortgage finance is that of property rights and the ability to collect through foreclosure. Paralegal title embraces a wide range of traditional and formal rights, depending on the society and legal code. In much of Latin America, households gain rights by paying property taxes and other governmental fees for a period of time. In Indonesia and some other Asian countries, imported Western legal property rights structures coexist with traditional property rights structures, with many nuances, levels, and combinations of rights, and much confusion. In some countries—such as Haiti and Venezuela—colonial land claims and poor property registrars make virtually the entire territory contestable and no one, not even the wealthy, can be absolutely sure of full legal title. In other countries such as Nicaragua and parts of Eastern Europe a war or radical regime change has thrown property rights of a substantial part of the population into limbo.

Foreclosure is also often problematic. Countries vary tremendously in their legal codes and the ability and speed of foreclosure. Most of Mexico's states have passed laws that allow lenders to use more rapid, extrajudicial foreclosure. However, the local police often will not enforce the new law!

In principle, small home loans for short terms have greater flexibility for dealing with these underwriting and collection challenges than traditional mortgage lending. In practice, many of the technical issues of housing microfinance concern how to deal with underwriting a borrower's credit and securing the loan, at a cost that makes the transaction sufficiently profitable. For example, an axiom of home microlending is that alternative forms of collateral—such as cosigners—demonstrate better value in securing a small loan than a lien on full legal title. As the amount of the construction and the loan increases, however, securing a lien on full legal title may become cost effective and essential.

The cost of servicing loans is a core issue for housing microfinance. It costs mortgage servicers about $10 per month to service a loan in the United States, and $15 in Mexico. But payments affordable to low- and moderate-income households on home microloans typically range from $20 to $80 per month. Thus, it appears to traditional Mexican mortgage lenders that servicing housing microfinance loans costs too high a share of the monthly payment to be feasible. In contrast, MFIs and Popular Savings Banks (Cajas Populares) in Mexico use different methods for servicing loans with a substantially lower-cost structure more suitable for housing microfinance. The shorter term of housing microfinance credits (typically two to eight years) compared to the long terms (fifteen to thirty years) of mortgage loans also reduces the servicing cost challenge.

MFIs' ROLE IN
EXPANDING HOUSING MICROFINANCE

Housing microfinance helps overcome key difficulties encountered by traditional mortgage finance in developing countries and much better suits the housing needs of the low- to moderate-income majority—which consists, essentially, of small short-term credits for steps in the progressive housing process. This technical fit has always been the case, although it has only recently been clearly recognized in the development literature (Mitlin n.d., Ferguson 1999, Ferguson and Haider 2000, Merrill et al. 2000).

The key element that gives housing microfinance much greater appeal and feasibility today compared with twenty years ago is the rich network of MFIs and the development of this field. Microenterprise lending has developed from pilot projects in the 1970s into an industry. This event deserves to be called a "lending revolution" as it succeeded for the first time in extending large numbers of loans to low-income households in developing countries on a sustainable basis.

In this context, housing microfinance holds great appeal for two reasons: (a) microfinance lenders are, in effect, already in the business of extending loans for housing and this business resembles their microenterprise lending business in many respects; and (b) housing microfinance represents a huge new market for MFIs.

MFIs and Housing Microfinance

Microenterprise lenders already extend credit de facto for housing. Fundamentally, microfinance supports the household economy of microentrepreneurs. The home typically provides the physical plant for business. Although loans are ostensibly for the enterprise, households often also spend funds on emergencies and ongoing households needs such as housing improvement. Many microenterprise lenders—such as FIE in Bolivia—estimate that around 20 percent of their loans actually go for housing. In turn, roughly 20 percent to 30 percent of homes in low-income neighborhoods house small businesses. Thus, considerable overlap exists between housing and microenterprise in the living situations of low-income households and in the credit extended to this group.

The business of individual microenterprise lending also strongly resembles that of small credits for home improvement.[5] The clientele of both consists of low- to moderate-income households. Loan terms are short, often three to twenty-four months for microenterprise and twelve months to five years for small home improvement loans. Loan amounts are small, from fifty to several thousand dollars for microenterprise in low-income countries, and

$300 to several thousand for home improvement. Underwriting and collateral are similar, joining a maximum debt-to-income ratio with cosigners or coborrowers.

Overall, then, MFIs enter a quite similar business in making small loans for home improvement. In contrast, traditional mortgage lenders must make a much more radical shift, from upper- and middle-income clients to low- to moderate-income households. The similarity between housing microfinance and microenterprise lending breaks down as the loan amount and the construction size grow. Hence, lending for a new basic unit—as opposed to a small loan for home improvement—may require considerable technical innovation for most MFIs.

It is occasionally asserted that microenterprise is "economic" and housing is "social," and that lending for housing violates the mission of NGOs and donors dedicated to economic development. A large body of theory and practice, however, supports the view that microenterprise and housing are both strongly economic with important social components. Housing—not microenterprise—represents the main means used by households in developed capitalist societies to accumulate wealth. In the United States, for example, forty-two percent of the net equity of households with net equity between $100,000 and $250,000 (i.e., the center of the middle class) consists of equity in their residence, compared to only eighteen percent in the stock market. The housing industry usually accounts for 15 percent to 20 percent of gross domestic product in most countries and is frequently the sector that catalyzes economic expansion or maintains an economy out of recession, as it did in the United States for much of 2001. See below for more information on the critical economic function of housing and how its economic power can be unleashed in developing countries.

A Huge New Business for Many MFIs

Housing microfinance represents a huge new market for MFIs. The scale of the market can be estimated in various ways. Demand studies are the most useful (see Chapter 3). A simple comparison, however, gives an idea of the relative scale. In Mexico, a detailed market study of microfinance in three cities on the U.S. border calculated the effective demand for housing microfinance at six times that for microenterprise finance.

This potential market holds particular importance for MFIs operating in saturated microfinance environments, such as those of Bolivia and El Salvador. Not surprisingly, MFIs in these countries have been the first to develop solid housing microfinance programs in Latin America.

In general, housing microfinance can provide essential scale and diversification not only to MFIs but also to microfinance programs. Programs are often operated by second-tier institutions established by governments and donors that purchase loans or make liquidity advances to first-tier lenders that originate loans directly to households. Such global microcredit facilities, as they are sometimes called, can operate in a state or province, a country, or a group of countries. Adding housing microfinance to microenterprise for these global facilities can greatly increase their volume and reduce cost per loan. Adding housing microfinance, however, may well require the second-tier institution to go beyond its normal stable of originators—typically MFIs—to explore innovative home lenders and popular finance institutions such as credit unions as first-tier lenders.

A microloan for their home can also serve as a reward to good microenterprise clients. Many MFIs take this path on first entering the housing credit business, including SEWA Bank in India, which still restricts its home lending to its microenterprise clients. Connecting a housing credit to faithful payment on a previous microenterprise loan is one form of what we call linkage.

Linking housing microfinance to a previous microenterprise credit or to another factor outside of standard underwriting can greatly enhance the soundness of the loan at low cost to the originating institution. In South Africa, for example, housing microlenders have used borrowers' pension fund contributions as collateral for housing microfinance credits. In Juarez along the U.S.-Mexican border, FUNHAVI has developed relationships with a number of manufacturing assembly plants (*maquiladoras*) to lend to their employees, while the firm provides some extra assistance and allows deduction of the debt service directly from the borrower's salary.

Creating such links offers perhaps the best way to enter the housing microfinance field and a low-cost method of credit enhancing the loan. Such linkage (which is more common in Asia) compares with the stand-alone approach (more common in Latin America) in which a housing microfinance lender deals with and lends to the public at large with no additional relationship or factor credit enhancing the loan. Chapter Seven further investigates the nature of stand-alone versus linked housing microfinance lending.

HOUSING MICROFINANCE: THE MISSING LINK IN SOCIAL HOUSING PROGRAMS

A brief history of government housing policies puts the relative importance of housing microfinance to housing programs in perspective. Many governments in highly industrialized as well as developing countries first dealt with housing problems partly by building and financing units directly. With some exceptions, this method has proved highly inefficient, generated government-induced slums in some contexts, and delivered subsidies mainly to the middle class in others.

Influenced by the failure of direct building and finance, many governments have shifted to channeling funds at below-market interest rates through private-sector financial institutions for private-sector building of social housing. In Latin America, the money for these programs has traditionally come from social security schemes that in practice resemble salary taxes. By the mid-1980s, most countries in the region had these programs, and some still persist. Extant examples include the Ley de Politica Habitacional in Venezuela, the National Housing Trust in Jamaica, the Fundo de Garantia de Tempo de Servico in Brazil, and INFONAVIT and FOVISSSTE in Mexico. Although somewhat better than direct government finance and building, these programs have involved large per-unit subsidies, continued to deliver units mainly to the middle class rather than the low-income families to which they are intended, and decapitalized the social security component of the scheme. The subsidized interest rates have undermined the development of private-sector, market-rate primary and secondary home lending.

In response donors and governments in Latin America and elsewhere have shifted from these below-market interest rate, social-security-cum-housing finance schemes to direct-demand subsidies. These subsidies are upfront grants allocated to qualified low- and moderate-income families. Households then match them with a down payment and, in theory, a market-rate mortgage loan to purchase a new home, typically a core expandable unit. Chile started the first such direct-demand subsidy program in 1977. Since then, direct-demand subsidy programs have spread to the bulk of Latin American countries, South Africa, Indonesia, and elsewhere.

Direct-demand subsidies and other social housing programs in developing countries, however, suffer from two key problems that housing microfinance can help overcome.

First, private lending institutions generally have little interest in extending market-rate mortgage financing to low- and moderate-income families under these programs for all the reasons previously discussed. Hence, the credit piece of the tripartite financing (subsidy/down payment/credit) necessary for these households to afford adequate shelter is missing. Programs often try to compensate for the lack of private credit by increasing the subsidy amount—a poor and financially unsustainable solution. Alternatively, government extends credit directly, which usually turns into a grant in disguise as households have few incentives to pay back a government loan. Housing microfinance would fill this gap and make a tremendous difference to the operational feasibility of these programs.

Second, the purchase of a new unit—the typical goal of these programs—ends up requiring relatively large subsidy amounts per unit which are impossible for most countries to provide to a significant share of their population. Bridging the affordability gap between the amount that low-income households can save plus the amount they can borrow and the purchase price of a commercially built unit ends up costing many thousands of dollars: $6,000 in subsidy per unit in Venezuela, and $4,000 to $7,000 under PROSAVI (a program of FOVI) in Mexico. The high per-unit subsidy means that the program can serve few households relative to the need.

Instead, programs ideally finance a wide range of low-cost housing solutions reflecting the steps in progressive housing—a serviced site, basic services, home improvement and addition, and replacement of a unit on a lot a family already owns—rather than just the purchase of new commercially built units. This is, in effect, the definition of housing microfinance, debt finance of a step in the progressive housing continuum.

HOUSING MICROFINANCE PROVIDES
LIQUIDITY TO BUILD HOUSEHOLD WEALTH

Home ownership fulfills a critical economic function in advanced, industrialized countries; it is one of the three pillars of the middle-class (along with education and reasonably remunerated employment). The United States illustrates this reality. A highly sophisticated network of mortgage lenders, secondary market institutions, title companies, infrastructure providers, and others support housing markets. Many of these functions are rapidly being automated (underwriting, appraisal, refinancing, etc.).

The depth and liquidity of U.S. housing markets extends not only to home owners but also throughout the housing development process. Loans for land purchase, for subdivision and infrastructure (development finance), and for construction (construction finance) make possible a highly articulated and flexible housing development industry. Despite the stock market rise of the 1990s, U.S. households still hold the largest share of their wealth as equity in their home, which represents much of their nest egg for retirement as well as a residence.[6] Many means exist for leveraging this equity to build wealth. Many small entrepreneurs capitalize their start-up companies by taking out equity in their home through refinance loans. U.S. households sell their homes on average every seven years, making real estate markets deep and fluid. Home construction employs substantial numbers of semiskilled workers, has a high multiplier effect (estimated at about 3), and can serve as a key locomotive to help keep economies out of recession (as it did for much of 2001).

Thus, fluid markets for land and housing play a crucial role in economic development, particularly in building household wealth and a middle class. In *The Mystery of Capital,* Hernando de Soto (2000) argues that the key difference between successful and unsuccessful capitalist societies is the ability to build wealth through property ownership, mainly that of land and housing. De Soto focuses on regularization of land title—which is typically largely informal—as the key to building a middle class and household wealth, although finance is just as critical. De Soto's case has compelling elements. De Soto estimates the total value of real estate held but not legally owned by the poor of developing countries at $9.3 trillion, more than all the foreign direct investment in these countries in the last decade, and forty-six times as much as all World Bank loans of the past three decades.

tudies of housing microfinance by Cities Alliance (a
ed program housed in the World Bank) and the dissem-
this knowledge through microfinance networks such as
d CHF International is beginning to solve this problem.

NOTES

nly through the below-market interest rate of INFONAVIT.
ically through channeling below-market interest rate loans to home
d developers, but sometimes now through up-front grants to first-
e buyers (called direct-demand subsidies), discussed later in this

cluding a highly positive interest rate—35 percent per annum nom-
15 percent real—at the time of the study (1998), and a short tenor
three years. Since then, mortgage interest rates have declined to
2 percent.
nder PRODEL, which is funded by Swedish Assistance.
lthough some differences exist even between small home improve-
ans and microenterprise loans. For example, housing microfinance
uses solidarity groups. Housing microloans may also require technical
e in planning construction work. The following chapters go much
eeply into these technical challenges.
U.S. households with $100,000 to $250,000 in net worth hold 43 per-
their wealth as equity in their primary residence, compared to 17 per-
the stock market. Cited on CNN 6:00 P.M. news, July 15, 2001.

Real property also forms the basis of a healthy financial system, both internationally and within countries. In the United States, mortgage loans represent about a third of all assets held by financial institutions. Mortgages on owner-occupied homes, in particular, have proved the soundest, most secure private debt, with correspondingly low risk weighting (and, thus, low capital requirements for financial institutions that hold them).

Unfortunately, housing and home ownership fail to fulfill their economic potential in developing countries. Mortgage finance is typically available only for a small sliver of all housing transactions—the purchase of new commercially built homes by the upper-middle class. Households in developing countries have virtually no access to institutional credit for purchasing an existing home, for home improvement and the steps of the progressive housing process, or for refinancing a home to start a business, and the majority lack access to financing for the purchase of a new home. Once households manage to secure a house, they tend to live in it the remainder of their lives. As a result, housing markets tend to be very thin.

Developers and builders face similar problems in developing countries. Development and construction finance is either missing or restricted to certain government programs. Only well-capitalized firms that can invest substantial funds of their own in a housing project for long periods can succeed in this context. In the United States and other advanced industrialized countries, different firms often develop the infrastructure and subdivision and build the houses. Customarily, each gets separate financing from commercial institutions and is reimbursed the cost of their investment on the sale of their product. In developing countries, the functions of developer and builder are often joined. The one firm must commit funds for a long time—often two to three years—until the houses are finally sold. Most would-be housing developers and builders lack financing, and produce at very low scale.

The lack of assets backed by housing has highly negative consequences for the development of the financial systems of these countries. The short supply of such assets makes banking and the development of the financial system a perilous enterprise. Without the ability to invest in home owner mortgages, banks have had to place much of their money in much more risky enterprises, including commercial real estate and corporate expansions, which contribute greatly to the recurring financial crises in emerging markets, such as that of the Asian meltdown in 1997–98. Property ownership is also critical to good governance and helps create an internal mass market that serves as an alternative to export-dependent development.

From this perspective, housing microfinance can help turn home ownership in developing countries into an economic asset and unleash the economic power of housing. In particular, housing microfinance injects liquidity into the progressive housing process, the method used by the majority of households in developing countries to afford home ownership.

CONCLUSION:
THE CHALLENGES TO EXPANSION

If housing microfinance is so important and well-suited to developing countries, one might ask, why is it not more widespread? The dramatic expansion of housing microfinance over the last three years is gradually turning this question into a moot point. Housing microfinance is, indeed, spreading widely. However, housing microfinance is still miniscule relative to the size of its market and to the housing problems of developing countries. The remainder of this chapter quickly reviews some key barriers and pitfalls to expansion of this practice.

Lack of Funding and Institutional Weakness of Many MFIs

Although immense effective demand exists for housing microfinance, MFIs—rather than home lenders—represent the key vehicle at this moment for expanding this practice. MFIs understand how and want to lend to make small loans to low- and moderate-income households and most traditional home lenders and banks do not.

However, many MFIs lack access to the funding (liabilities) necessary to expand. National banking regulations prohibit MFIs—the bulk of which are unsupervised institutions—from accessing funds from the public through savings accounts and other measures. Many MFIs have become accustomed to funding from donors on terms substantially softer than those of the internal markets of their countries. This dependency allows high operating costs inconsistent with accessing private markets. These in turn result in high prices (interest rates and other charges to borrowers)

that greatly reduce the effective
MFIs, thus, get stuck in a low-le
ther the means nor the incentiv
field has focused on solving thes
more successful MFIs are becomi
ulated institutions and are begin
and improve their efficiency.

Confusion Surrounding Housing Subsi
in Developing Countries

Governments throughout the worl
considered a merit good. However,
sidies in international development c
erable confusion concerning the me
the strategic role of housing subsidie
governments have abandoned inter
which suffer from many vices (Ferguson
alternative in international work has be
subsidies—essentially vouchers delivere
However, the attempts to make direct-d
low-income households have largely fail
consensus exists on the subsidy amoun
unit) that should be delivered.

Perhaps most problematic, housing
placed within a strategic plan to gradually
toward market (i.e., and the gradual re
Housing subsidy programs that are well d
their funding over a decade can make an in
to stimulating credit (including housing m
larly joined with other actions that increase
However, governments sometimes fail to pa
prerequisites for achieving the development
ing subsidies to expand market mechanisms,
vention as a stopgap measure. In such cases, h
grams can undermine credit.

Limited Knowledge of Best Practice

Finally, the limited knowledge of best practice
finance has, until recently, impeded its growth.

detailed s
U.N.-fund
ination o
Accion a

1. Ma
2. Ty
buyers an
time hom
chapter.
3. In
inal and
of one t
around
4. U
5. A
ment lo
seldom
guidan
more
6.
cent o
cent i

3

Housing Microfinance: The State of the Practice

Alejandro Escobar and Sally Roe Merrill

During the 1980s and 1990s, major structural reforms took place in many developing countries that paved the way for increased liberalization of internal and external markets. Major economic sectors, which had been state controlled for many years, experienced strong levels of growth and dynamism. Trade also expanded for most developing nations in the 1990s and the financial and labor markets became much more flexible and dynamic. The housing markets have been no exception to this increased dynamism, and amid continued growth in urban populations, the demand for housing has also grown significantly. However, unlike some of the other sectors, traditional housing finance has not been able to respond adequately to the intense growth in demand for basic housing. This remains a challenge for policy makers and the private sector who are often limited not only by the stock of capital within their own economies, but also by adequate mechanisms to deliver financial services to the lower- and middle-income populations.

One restrictive factor is institutional. In most developing countries access to long-term mortgage finance has been limited to high-income groups. Formal housing finance institutions have simply not developed, or been able to access, adequate mechanisms to expand shelter finance to the needed scale. Commercial financial institutions, for example, have consistently avoided lending to low- and moderate-income families because of the perceived high risk of this market segment. Low- to moderate-income families often lack sufficient collateral to meet the bank requirements for larger, longer-term loans. These families are usually not engaged in the formal economy and therefore have not been able to build an adequate credit history that could be established or tracked in local credit bureaus. Underwriting many of these households is not straightforward and requires flexible approaches to assessing income potential and conducting transactions, including consumer education. Low-income families often own property for which they have no legal documentation or appropriate title, which combined with the above-mentioned factors, leads to a perceived high risk. Credit enhancements and legal infrastructure widely used in developed markets, such as mortgage default insurance, title insurance, and efficient foreclosure, for example, are not available. Competitive pressure to help force banks to go downmarket has generally been insufficient. Finally, balance sheet management issues have often favored a conservative approach and limited the scope of lending; thus, lucrative investment alternatives in many countries, such as holding high-yield government paper, has limited the formal sector's progress in expanding its horizons.

Another restrictive factor is structural. Many low-income families require relatively small and short-term financing for incremental building or home improvements. Commercial banks and public financing organizations do not have an organizational structure that can work cost effectively with the large number of small loans characteristic of this market segment. Working with small loans and large numbers of clients becomes too costly compared with the average transaction costs of larger loans and more easily underwritten customers.[1] This is an area where at least some microfinance institutions (MFIs) and community-based lenders have succeeded in providing more appropriate financial services on a reasonable scale.

The field of low- and moderate-income shelter finance has emerged as a confluence of interests from various sectors, including public policy makers, donors, MFIs, and financial institutions with a community focus, all of whom believe the above-described situation must have some solutions. From the perspective of the public sector, newly elected governments and housing authorities are faced with the challenge of modernizing their housing institutions. Long considered instruments of political interest, the housing programs and agencies of the public sector have expanded and grown, but often have little to show in terms of sustainable results and outreach. An example of this growing interest is the recent publication of a series of studies sponsored by the United

Nations Economic Committee for Latin America (CEPAL) that focuses on improving the efficiency and impact of public policy and housing programs (Szalachman 2000).

Less well documented but still relevant is the interest from the private financial and construction sectors of many countries that are beginning to look at low-income populations as a potential market for their products. Recent conferences in Central America have focused on developing strong primary and secondary mortgage markets, given the increasing demand for housing from low- to moderate-income groups, the growth in sources of local currency liquidity, and the rapid standardization of mortgage underwriting techniques among major banks. Institutions such as the World Bank and the International Finance Corporation (IFC) have been instrumental in forging this kind of debate and are continuously looking to attract private sector players, such as banks and development companies, into the discussion.

Finally, the donor community maintains a strong interest in supporting creative mechanisms that can address the need for shelter finance. One area of interest for this group is the emergence of the microfinance sector as a possible venue for shelter finance. Increasingly, MFIs are successfully reaching the poor with sustainable financial services on a greater scale. Of particular importance is that many MFIs have found that a large percentage of their portfolios were actually being invested in housing. Growing evidence of this practice has been documented by several studies.[2] Private and public organizations are now starting to look at this sector as one that may hold important lessons, particularly in underwriting technologies and portfolio management. A large amount of the work in this study is centered on the impact and importance of MFIs and the recent evolution of their practice to deliver shelter finance. Understanding how they have entered the housing finance sector may lead to the identification of good practices that could be promoted, enhanced and replicated. In addition, in some emerging markets, shelter efforts sponsored by nongovernmental organizations (NGOs), especially for the very poor, are evolving from a focus on projects to one on larger and more sustainable financial models. Finally, partnerships among a variety of players—banks, MFIs, NGOs, and community lenders—offer yet other avenues for employing the comparative advantage of each type of institution, in funding, outreach, consumer assistance, or other transactions.

INSTITUTIONS

There is a very broad spectrum of institutional types and market focus among the low-income housing lenders including MFIs, government programs, NGOs, community-based financial institutions (CBFIs), and formal financial institutions. Given the heterogeneity of institutions involved, and the diversity of roles they play, no single typology for a shelter finance institution exists.[3] A broad categorization of these institutions is presented below in Table 3.1, with a brief description of their main focus and some examples.

Microfinance Institutions

MFIs, which traditionally finance small businesses and microenterprises, have started to enter the shelter finance sector and are becoming important players. Some MFIs are entering the housing sector in order to provide additional services to their original client base while others are extending this service to a new client base.

One of the main advantages of MFIs becoming involved in housing is their ability to offer financial services that reach low-income households in a sustainable manner. MFIs often engage in shelter finance for one of three reasons:

1. *Disaster:* Some MFIs have started housing loans to respond to natural disasters that have affected a large number of their clients, such as CALPIA in El Salvador and Caja Arequipa in Peru.
2. *Diversification:* For many MFIs, housing loans are another form of product diversification in their portfolios. The emphasis on diversification may come from the need to spread portfolio risk or cross-subsidize products for overall improved financial health. This is the case of BancoSol in Bolivia, SEWA Bank in India, and Financiera CALPIÁ in El Salvador. Grameen Bank in Bangladesh offers housing loans at below-market interest rates to customers who have successfully completed microenterprise loans.
3. *Increased competition:* Many MFIs have started offering housing loans in order to maintain their microentrepreneur clients and not lose them to other MFIs or banks that can offer larger and longer-term loans. Longer-term loans also guarantee longer relationships with clients and the opportunity to

Table 3.1 MFIs Involved in Housing Microfinance

Type of Institution	Area of Focus	Examples
MFIs – Large-scale MFIs – Mid-scale	Large-scale MFIs with more than 100,000 clients Housing portfolio often born out of a disaster situation or as diversification May be a reward for successful completion of a micro-enterprise loan	Grameen Bank (Bangladesh, specialized bank), SEWA Bank (India, cooperative bank), BRAC (Bangladesh, microfinance NGO), BRI (Indonesia)
	Medium-scale MFIs with 10,000–100,000 clients Most have already achieved best practice in microfinance field Similar principles are applied to housing products (short terms–low amounts) Some have taken government funds for expansion Commercial funding usually not available for these loans, resulting in funding mismatch	CALPIA (El Salvador, specialized Finance Company), BancoSol (Bolivia, bank), ADEMI (Dominican Republic, bank), MiBanco (Peru, bank), CARD Rural Bank (Philippines, specialized bank)
North American/ European NGOs	Capacity to transfer technologies across affiliates in diverse countries Limited focus on technical assistance for housing products Currently working at commercial funding for traditional microenterprise portfolios Could leverage financing for housing Some are direct lenders and some are wholesale providers of credit	Accion, CHF International, Habitat for Humanity, FINCA, Plan International, Homeless International
Cooperatives, Mutuals, and Municipals	Locally owned and often locally started housing programs Good experience and best practice Usually part of networks that enable cross-experience sharing	Jesus Nazareno (Bolivia, S&L co-op), Mutual La Primera (Bolivia, housing co-op), Mutual Imbabura (Ecuador, S&L co-op), Caja Arequipa (Peru, municipal S&L)
Government Housing Programs	Some are professionally run; others are very political and/or not market-based Major source of second tier financing for housing but with limited outreach Demonstrated outreach to low-income clients	HUDCO and HDFC (India), MiVivienda (Peru), ex-FONVIS (Bolivia), Uganda National Housing Finance Co., FONAVIPO (El Salvador)

(continues)

Table 3.1 Continued

Type of Institution	Area of Focus	Examples
Commercial Banks	Some downscaling to housing faster than to microcredit Security is a major issue Have the capacity to expand and compete Could mobilize large amounts of commercial financing if mechanisms are in place	Banco de Desarrollo (Chile), Banco de Pichincha (Ecuador), Banco Caja Social (Colombia), CashBank/BoE (South Africa), African Bank (South Africa)
Local NGOs	Mainly involved in housing from a community development perspective Some involved in housing at very small levels (less than 1,000 clients)	Life in Africa/UMU (NGO in Uganda), SPARC (India), SPDB (NGO in Samoa), and FUNDAP (NGO in Guatemala), People's Dialogue/SAHFP (South Africa)

offer other products and services to them. Caja Los Andes in Bolivia is an example of this trend.

MFIs employ a wide variety of mechanisms and institutional forms for providing their services. Some authors suggest that housing microfinance services can be classified as either stand-alone programs or linked programs (Daphnis and Tilock 2001). Stand-alone housing microfinance products do not rely on a prior loan history with the provider as a proxy for capacity to pay. The eligibility criteria, loan term, and loan uses are designed to qualify potential borrowers on the merits of their current financial profile and habitat needs independently of their existing relationship with the provider. Loans are extended to individuals rather than to groups; the loans tend to be for relatively small amounts ($1,000–$5,000) and have a relatively short repayment period when compared to traditional housing loans (1.5 to 4 years). Consequently, loans typically, though not always, allow borrowers to finance their home incrementally (Daphnis and Tilock 5). It is important to emphasize that in many cases, unlike conventional mortgage finance, these loans are not mortgage loans—that is, the loan is not collateralized by the property.

On the other hand many MFIs, especially in Asia, have developed housing microfinance services that are linked to prior participation in microenterprise or savings services. The Grameen Bank, SEWA Bank, and CARD are among the best known MFIs linking housing microfinance to other products they offer. A survey of these MFIs shows that in some cases, such as Grameen, clients access these linked loans at interest rates that are often lower than what they would have to pay for microenterprise loans. Also the repayment period for some of these loans appears, on average, to be longer for stand-alone products.

Even though microfinance methodologies and products often have been able to be replicated across regions and countries, when it comes to housing, a significantly larger set of issues and factors makes replication more challenging. Some of these issues and factors, which vary by country, include:

- Restrictions and regulations on financial institutions and MFIs in relation to mortgage and assets-backed financing;
- The level of government involvement in the housing sector. Housing is still a political issue in some countries and while many governments have scaled back their presence in the local financial markets, some are still quite active in the housing sectors;
- The level of penetration of government subsidized housing in the housing microfinance market, or the presence of private and quasi-public mechanisms providing subsidized housing finance. This denies a level playing field to institutions offering market-based finance, which may be counterproductive in the long run;
- Varying levels of access to basic infrastructure for housing development; and
- Varying levels of access by MFIs to medium- or long-term financing for housing.

Cooperatives and Mutuales

Cooperatives and mutuales in Latin America play an important role in providing shelter finance in the region. Many of these institutions have some experiences to share in underwriting techniques, housing regulation, municipal restrictions, and construction codes. Some examples include the Mutuales de Ahorro y Préstamo para la Vivienda in Bolivia (Mutual La Primera), Mutualista de Ahorro y Crédito para la Vivienda in Ecuador (Mutualista Imbabura), Asociación de Ahorro y Préstamo S.A. in Honduras, and Asociación de Ahorro y Préstamo para la Vivienda in Dominican Republic.

Government Housing Programs

Most public housing finance institutions are targeting subsidies at the client level, in other words, focusing on the demand side of the problem. Subsidizing interest rates, transaction costs, and access are means by which government institutions directly assist potential clients. Public institutions like FOGUAVI, the housing finance institution of Guatemala, which used to finance the construction of large housing projects, are now channeling funds through local banks and MFIs. Although this is primarily limited to formal financial institutions or regulated MFIs, in some cases NGOs and community organizations have received funds, such as CODEP in Colombia. Targeted subsidies through NGOs are particularly common where natural disasters have occurred. The shifting focus of public institutions will be an important trend to monitor as shelter finance issues come to the fore in many developing countries.

In Peru, MiVivienda, the state housing finance authority, is channeling housing funds to some thirty financial intermediaries. Over two thirds of these institutions are MFIs, many of which are relatively small. Some cajas municipales, the municipal saving and loan cooperatives, and MiBanco, a large, specialized microfinance bank, are also using these loans. With banks in Peru downscaling aggressively and competing with traditional MFIs, MiVivienda must consider issues of efficiency and long-term sustainability. Would MiVivienda be better off working with fewer intermediaries and concentrating its efforts in larger, more efficient financial intermediaries?

Commercial Banks (Including Community-based Lenders)

Traditional banking practices do not easily support the housing finance needs of low-income households, and the housing finance sectors of many emerging nations are relatively undeveloped. In the lower-income countries, housing finance lending by commercial banks may be extremely limited, even for upper-income households. Lack of competition, combined with lack of advocacy (or moral suasion) and little experience with the types of outreach and transactions necessary to conduct microfinance for housing, greatly limits the downmarket horizons of traditional banks. However, some financial organizations and companies with similar

clients and products as MFIs and that already have housing portfolios, such as Banco de Desarrollo in Chile and many mutualistas
and cooperatives that have specialized in housing for many years,
are now slowly entering the market segment initially targeted by
MFIs. Similarly, CashBank/BoE and African Bank, both in South
Africa, have targeted the low- to moderate-income market and
offer a variety of housing loan products. Such institutions are perhaps best labeled CBFIs to distinguish them from commercial
banks focused strictly on the upper-income formal sector.

**Box 3.1 Lending Downmarket:
Banco de Desarrollo, Chile**

Banco de Desarrollo, a private commercial bank, formed in 1983
with a mission to serve microentrepreneurs throughout Chile, has
more than 60 branch offices and has served more than 200,000
clients. Banco de Desarrollo has also financed more than 95,000
housing loans since 1983 and is the leader in housing finance in
Chile with 18 percent of the market. However, housing loans com-
prise only a small percentage of its total portfolio; the microenterprise program had more than $14 million in loans at the end
of 2000. The program, which started in 1991, has some 15,000 loans
outstanding, an average balance of $1,200, and an average term of
twelve months at a monthly interest rate of 2.6 percent. The types of
loans for microenterprise include working capital, investment capital, housing, and solidarity lending. The housing microfinance portfolio is still small, at $1,892,855. However, there does seem to be a
trend by similar banks in other countries in trying to target the
lower-income groups with financial products for housing.

Nongovernmental Organizations (NGOs)

There are a number of microfinance activities being started by
housing NGOs, and microfinance NGOs engaging in housing.
Such is the case of Servicio Latinoamericano y Asiático de la
Vivienda Popular (SELAVIP), which has built more than four million square feet of housing for the poor, and Habitat for Humanity, which is starting to engage in microfinance as part of its housing activities worldwide.

The traditional NGO approach to low-income housing development focused less on finance and credit than on sites and services projects, incremental housing, and a host of related issues:

land acquisition, mutual self-help building techniques, slum clearance, and so forth. Thus, generally, NGOs involved in housing and community development work have had a project focus—that is, improvement of an existing neighborhood or developing a greenfield site, often addressing issues of land, land title, or infrastructure as well as housing. However, just as microenterprise lending has strengthened its financial functions, NGO microfinance for housing has begun to do the same. BancoSol in Bolivia, which grew out of the microenterprise lending of the NGO, PRODEM, is one of the best known cases.

SEWA Bank and Society for the Promotion of Area Resource Centers (SPARC) are major forces in the development of low-income housing in India and are examples of NGO-based microfinance for housing that have both made a major transition from a project focus to one seeking sustainable finance at a larger scale. SEWA Bank is an example of a decision by an NGO to facilitate finance in a formal manner as a crucial adjunct to its other activities. In contrast, SPARC did not create a financial institution but rather has sought credit and savings facilities in a variety of approaches, beginning with small savings groups. SPARC works within an association of NGOs and has pioneered philosophies regarding communities as stakeholders, the core importance of savings groups, women as borrowers, and group lending and guarantees. SPARC has in recent years become one of the best known urban NGOs working on housing issues for the poorest of the poor—pavement dwellers and slum dwellers in India. SPARC's sole focus is supporting housing, infrastructure, and community development. Land and sanitation are also important elements of this holistic approach to urban development.

Finally, the South Africa Homeless Peoples' Federation (Box 3.2) is an example of a partnership among savings associations, an NGO, and a government- and donor-supported housing development fund, which targets the very poor.[4]

Other International Housing Microfinance Actors: Developers and Networks

The importance of land and housing developers in the provision of shelter finance cannot be overlooked. Three examples of private developers involved with financing housing are worth mentioning: Argoz, a developer in El Salvador discussed in detail by

---

Box 3.2 South African Homeless Peoples' Federation

South African Homeless Peoples' Federation (SAHPF) is a national network of grassroots savings and credit collectives called *nsukuzonke* ("every day" in Zulu). It is supported by a small NGO, People's Dialogue on Land and Shelter. The SAHPF has approximately 110,000 member households in 1,500 savings schemes across South Africa, primarily in urban and peri-urban areas. Its membership is 85 percent women, with an average household monthly income of under R850 (about U.S.$100). Since 1994, the alliance of SAHPF and People's Dialogue has jointly operated a national finance institution called uTshanti Fund ("grassroots"). The uTshanti Fund gives collective loans for housing, land acquisition and servicing, and income generation. Loans are given only to members of SAHPF (i.e., the uTshanti Fund is not available to the general public). Housing constitutes 90 percent of uTshanti Fund lending. The remainder is mostly bridge finance for land acquisition and servicing. A very small proportion is for income generation. The share of housing is decreasing somewhat, as the uTshanti Fund restructures to focus on land acquisition and servicing.

Ferguson and Haider (2000); the Roda Group in Santa Cruz, Bolivia, a major developer and construction company that is partnering with BancoSol; and a group of developers in Guatemala, who are venturing into the lower- to mid-income bracket. A review of these examples highlights several unique characteristics that developers bring to the shelter finance field:

- Often developers have the financial capacity to finance lot purchases and construction;
- Developers often address many factors related to housing development, including subdividing land and financing utilities and infrastructure (water, sewage, and lighting systems);
- Due to size and business approach, developers can reach significant numbers of clients;
- Most important, developers are able to work within this sector on a for-profit basis.

Although most of these characteristics describe Argoz in El Salvador, further research should be conducted to test these assumptions for developers elsewhere. Developers in other countries seldom have sufficient capital to embark on a financing campaign similar to that of Argoz. Nonetheless the interaction and relationship of these two sectors in the delivery of services to low-income groups is certainly worth monitoring in the future.

An alternative to corporate developers in some advanced countries has been the role of cooperatives. In Uruguay, the Federation of Housing and Mutual Aid Cooperatives (FUCVAM), which has been in operation for almost thirty years, has a division of housing development and construction. Not only do the federation's members offer savings and loan services for housing, they also engage in cooperative construction and infrastructure development for groups of families and communities. Through this process, cooperatives can generate savings of up to 40 percent when compared to the cost of structures of developers. Again, this example is limited to the countries where the cooperative movement has shown its financial and administrative strength.

Networks play an important role in supporting many of the financial institutions that specialize in housing. Several types of networks are worth mentioning. International NGO networks such as ACCION, Plan International, and Habitat have the capacity to move resources and experiences across their different country programs. They are also better able to articulate and experiment with common strategies and methodologies. Regional housing networks have great potential to share experiences and replicate methodologies. Although finance is not the only component of their agenda, it does play an important role, and often finance organizations are part of the network. One case in point is UNIAPRAVI, the Iberoamerican Union for Housing, which brings together state banks, housing authorities, construction chambers, financial cooperatives, and housing credit unions. Through such networks, the potential for exchange and formulation of best practice is significant.

FUNDING LINKAGES:
FINANCING THE HOUSING SECTOR

In most developing countries, the banking and financial sectors are still underdeveloped. According to some studies, stronger financial sectors will enable the development of larger local capital markets, attracting institutional investors that could play an important role in financing the housing sector.[5] Along these lines, there is evidence that some Latin American countries, such as Peru and El Salvador, are starting to develop the legal framework to allow pension funds to invest assets in long-term housing finance. This appears to be a growing trend, which some claim could help expand financing for low- to mid-income housing.

Many MFIs face a currency mismatch since their portfolios are mainly in local currency, and they are limited in their capacity to access long-term financing in foreign or local currencies. This is particularly the case in countries with less developed financial markets. In Chile, for example, the private pension fund industry is highly developed, and as Ferguson (1999) suggests, it could be a future source of long-term financing for low-income housing. However, this is not the case for most of the other Latin American countries. ADEMI, for example, in the Dominican Republic, expressed concern over their inability to tap into long-term sources of capital because current regulations prohibit them from borrowing in foreign currency, and there are no local sources of long-term debt. Many MFIs, like ADEMI, do not have the resources to hedge their currency risk, and therefore are limited to the type of product they can offer in local currency.

Shelter finance institutions are constrained by access to long-term financing. Cooperative Jesus Nazareno, BancoSol, CALPIA, ADEMI, and Diaconía, among others, expressed a serious limitation in expanding their housing portfolios, which often have longer terms than their traditional portfolio because of the mismatch in terms between their assets and liabilities. Most MFIs have limited options to finance their intermediate- to long-term financial needs. In addition to an MFI's own funds, options are typically as follows.

Savings

The financial success of many of the best known housing microfinance lenders, including SEWA, SPARC, CARD, Grameen, and People's Dialogue, depends on their emphasis on savings. SEWA Bank's savings exceed its loans by a considerable margin. This is also true of BRI, although the savings accounts are not mandatory. For SPARC, while savings cannot meet the funding needs for its housing loans, they do cover the demand for its short-term emergency loans.

Commercial Bank Lines of Credit and Partnerships

As noted above, SPARC and SEWA rely to some extent on funding from mainstream banks; this approach has not been notable as a major source of liquidity, however, for these housing lenders. CARD's relationship with the People's Credit and Finance Corporation appears to be fruitful, however.

Donor and Foundation Funds

The People's Dialogue/SAHPF is the most heavily subsidized of the groups analyzed here, as about 95 percent of its funds come from European and North American donors, with the remaining 5 percent from the South African government. Grameen Bank is next in line in terms of the proportion of funding obtained from foundation and donor funds. Both of these groups offer heavily subsidized housing loans.

Innovative Credit Enhancements in Microfinance for Housing

The use of credit enhancement mechanisms in housing microfinance in emerging markets is a new field of endeavor for most housing microlenders. We cite two recent examples: the use of donor and charitable funds by SPARC as a guarantee fund, and the attempt, now stalled, to develop a secondary market for moderate-income housing loans in South Africa.

A guarantee fund to leverage lending. SPARC has recently forged a new financing structure, involving both grant funds and a guarantee fund from Homeless International and a local currency "loan" from Citibank, India. First, SPARC has joined the numerous savings groups that work with the NGO partners into a Federation of Savings Groups, which is able to leverage much greater credit. The origination, underwriting, savings, and servicing functions are handled through systems developed by the Federation. Second, Citibank, India has provided a loan to SPARC at the prime rate. Clearly this rate is too low to cover the necessary risks and costs; SPARC and Citibank note that it is partially philanthropic. Third, SPARC's guarantee fund from Homeless International takes the top 20 percent of the risk on Citibank's loan.

Secondary market funding for low- and moderate-income (LMI) loans. A number of developing countries have initiated efforts to develop secondary mortgage markets. The explicit and unique goal in South Africa was to broaden access to low- and moderate-income housing finance. Gateway Home Loans, a subsidiary of the National Housing Finance Corporation in South Africa, was designed to fund LMI loans through a secondary market process. Gateway represents an example of both underwriting using pension funds as collateral and credit enhancement from a parastatal in an attempt to access wholesale funds on the secondary market for a well-defined LMI loan product. At the moment, however, the Gateway process has been much slower than expected. Gateway finds itself at a crossroads and has been reabsorbed into the National Housing Finance Corporation, South's Africa's parastatal for assisting low-income housing lending. In fact, successes of secondary market development in emerging nations are extremely limited. Malaysia's Cagamas, a very successful secondary market funding institution, is a clear exception. In South Africa, as Porteous (2000) notes, the choice is not currently clear: should it abandon the low- to moderate-income approach to a secondary market in favor of first building a secondary market in upper-income loans?

Group Asset Mapping

Asset mapping is a tool being developed by Homeless International (a U.K.-based NGO) in its research project—Bridging the Finance Gap in Housing and Infrastructure—as a means of identifying the range of resources that organizations of the urban poor have created for housing and infrastructure projects. Among other things, asset mapping helps quantify the positive impact that strong organizations can have on repayment rates, either on group loans or group guarantees of individual loans. The mapping exercise also helps explore options for risk management and mitigation. Homeless International has found the process useful to support credit assessment by financial institutions considering lending to community driven initiatives (McLeod 2000).

In Africa and Asia, housing microlenders have approached the funding problem in a variety of ways. Most of the microlenders and banks offer competitive rates on various deposit accounts. In addition, savings accounts from the mandatory savings programs are especially important to some lenders. SEWA Bank's financial success depends on its original and continuing emphasis on savings accounts. Its savings operations exceed its loans by a ratio of 10:1 in both number and value. Deposits plus shares contribute 83 percent of the Bank's capital, and excess savings are invested in financial instruments. SEWA offers secured loans, using savings deposits as collateral (the loan can equal up to 85 percent of fixed deposits). BRI's savings deposits also exceed its outstanding loans.

Other approaches include the use of credit enhancement facilities (guarantees for example) as well as financing from international development–focused investors, such as the IFC. Table 3.2 illustrates some of the funding strategies of select MFIs in Asia and South Africa.

MFIs often use a mix of funding sources to meet demand for housing microfinance services:

- SEWA's savings accounts, for example, leverage funds from the private and public sectors, including its headquarters city (the Ahmedebad Municipal Corporation), HUDCO (India's public sector infrastructure and housing fund), and HDFC (India's premier private sector housing lender);
- Savings provide 60 percent of CARD's funds with another 30 percent provided through a credit line with a bank, the People's Credit and Finance Corporation. The remaining 10 percent is provided by foundations—Catholic Relief Services and the German Savings Bank Foundation;
- Grameen, more heavily subsidized than most of the lenders, relies on its savings deposits, but the bank also receives

Table 3.2 Funding Strategies of Some Asian and South African MFIs

	SEWA Bank	SPARC	CARD	BRI	Grameen Bank	People's Dialogue	Cash Bank/BoE	African Bank
Mandatory savings	X	X	X		X	X		
Deposits		X	X	X	X		X	X
Bank funding/ partnerships		X	X				X	X
Donor funds	X	X	X		X	X		
Foundation funds	X	X	X		X			
Public funds	X	X				X		
Credit enhancement		X						
International investors/IFC					X		X	

funds from both donors and foundations. Major donors include SIDA (Swedish Aid) and NORAD (Norwegian Aid) as well as IDA funds. Foundation lenders are organized via the Grameen Foundation, which received over $3.2 million in 2000, up from $1.8 million in 1999. Grameen also borrows from the Central Bank of Bangladesh at 10 to 12 percent (rates for 2001). By comparison, commercial bank lending rates have recently been about 15 to 20 percent;

- SPARC funding sources include its savings accounts, foundation funding (the Rashtriya Mihila Kosh, for income generation loans only), public funds from HUDCO, and recently, credit from a major investment fund (UnitTrust of India). An innovative credit enhancement is discussed below;
- CashBank, prior to being bought by BoE, worked hard to raise funds on the South African capital market and also received two loans from the IFC.

LOAN PRODUCTS, METHODOLOGY, AND FINANCIAL VIABILITY

The international field of housing microfinance is still quite young, and most MFIs have only recently entered the housing sector. Many of the shelter finance institutions reviewed and documented have fewer than five to ten years' experience in the field. Particularly in Latin America, most MFIs have not faced major challenges associated with macroeconomic instability, as was common in the hyperinflationary 1980s. Nonetheless, a review of the recent literature and direct contacts with many of the lenders have allowed us to compile current trends in this field. Table 3.3 highlights the key findings and current noteworthy practices among MFIs implementing shelter finance.

Loan Products

Increasingly, MFIs are seeking to differentiate housing as a separate loan product. Some of the MFIs surveyed have a separate product package for housing loans. Although many MFIs are lending to the housing sector de facto through their traditional lines, it seems that the best practice is to market the housing products as a separate line of business. Many MFIs are even differentiating between the government-sponsored program and their own. This is the

Table 3.3 Summary of Current Practice in Housing Microfinance

Current practice	Rationale	Examples
Clearly differentiated products	Many MFIs are starting to have a separate product package for housing loans.	Mutuales and cooperatives, MiBanco in Peru.
Relatively short loan terms	Most land purchase or construction loans were for two to five years. Home improvement loans and additions had terms of three months to two years. Longer-term loans, five years or more, were usually associated with government-backed loans.	Co-op Jesus Nazareno, max. loan of $30,000 with a five-year limit.
Mixed interest rate policy	Some MFIs who have traditionally used mortgage-backed loans have had an easier entrance into the housing sector, as they have been operating within the regulations and legal framework of mortgage-backed assets. These MFIs often offer lower interest rates for housing than for traditional microcredit loans. Others offer the same rates for housing and microenterprise products.	Financiera CALPIA Genesis Empresarial BRI, SEWA Bank
Individual loans	Most of the housing programs use individual lending, and this seems to be the growing trend. Only a handful are using the group lending or solidarity model for housing.	BancoSol, SEWA Bank
Client history	For most MFIs exploring the housing sector, the best assurance of repayment with a new product is client history, as demonstrated by credit history with the organization and time of involvement.	Grameen, Jesus Nazareno
Mandatory savings and savings groups	Using demonstrated savings ability as an underwriting tool is extremely common among microhousing lenders. Some require membership in a savings group.	SEWA Bank, SPARC, CARD, Grameen, People's Dialogue, UCDO (Thailand)

(continues)

Table 3.3 Continued

Current practice	Rationale	Examples
Home or land ownership	Many experienced MFIs require formal home or land ownership, even if the loan is not secured by a mortgage. Some even provide technical support and financing for speeding up the ownership process.	CALPIA, BancoSol
High transaction costs for securing title and registration	Most of the literature discussing collateral and registry points to the fact that enforcing and implementing these procedures is very costly; therefore, smaller loans are not attractive to lenders.	Guatemala, Bolivia, El Salvador
Simple enforcement of loan contract	Some organizations are using simplified procedures for enforcing loan contracts. For example, an MFI in Honduras uses personal guarantees for smaller housing loans in addition to a contract that enables the creditor to seize personal assets in case of default.	Fundación para la Vivienda Coopertiva, Honduras
Counseling and borrower education	Training programs and counseling are widespread and cover a variety of issues including consumer education on loan terms and repayment, housing design, and construction techniques.	SEWA Bank, SPARC, Grameen, CARD, People's Dialogue, CashBank
Women borrowers	Some MFIs in Asia lend only, or primarily, to women, who have proven to be better credit risks.	SEWA Bank, SPARC, CARD, Grameen
Lack of standard ratios	Loan to Value (LTV) and Debt Equity (D/E) ratios are not standard. LTV and D/E ratios vary significantly among MFIs. Access to funding via secondary markets would produce more conformity.	Widespread

Box 3.3 Grameen Bank: Financing Prototype Housing

Grameen Bank was started in 1976 in Bangladesh as a specialized rural bank designed to provide financial services to poor women, using a solidarity group approach. In 1984, Grameen Bank started a housing program, as a response to demand from its clients and a perceived improvement in their income-generating capacity. By 1999, more than 500,000 houses had been financed by the housing program. Grameen offers five types of housing loans: Housing, Basic Housing, Pre-basic Housing, Homestead Purchase, and House Repair. While the housing loans range from $101 for the home-repair up to $600 for the larger standard housing loan, Grameen proposes a prototype home with standard specifications. The "basic" house measures 12' by 18' and has a two-sided tin roof, four cement and concrete pillars, one wooden door, and two windows. The "standard" house is larger, but with similar specs. Providing housing loans through this prototype methodology has enabled Grameen to expand its housing program to reach a portfolio of about $185 million by 1999. In addition, borrowers are responsible for the design of the house, but standardization has allowed Grameen to require minimum construction standards, including having a pit latrine. The benefits of implementing these requirements were evident during the flood of 1987, in which it was clear that houses built under these guidelines fared much better than those that were not.

case with MiBanco in Peru and many mutuales and cooperatives. FUSAI in El Salvador has differentiated housing loan products such as community housing (housing for newly organized settlements, lots with service, and home construction), home improvement, and reconstruction loans. The Grameen Bank has three different types of housing loans: new construction, rebuilding, or the purchase of land following a natural disaster.

MFIs often engage in home improvement, upgrading, and incremental loans, as opposed to home purchase or new construction. This is the case of many MFIs that do not have explicit housing products, but who are lending from their traditional lines of credit to improve the dwelling or finance additions or enhancements. The smaller size of home improvement or incremental loans is a better match for many of their customers. BRI, Indonesia's largest bank, offers only one general loan product targeted for microenterprise activities that is used for housing-related purposes. African Bank, which lends in the moderate-income market, provides home improvement loans, in part because the cost of new "standard" housing exceeds the repayment capacity of many of its customers.

In practice, MFIs are starting to develop differentiated products for self-employed, salaried, and disaster-affected clients. For example in Bolivia, BancoSol has a specialized housing product targeted to salaried employees (see Table 3.4). Although the amount of the loan is still somewhat small, $3,000 to $10,000, this market segment has not been BancoSol's traditional focus.

However, limited information is available on the actual clients being served with shelter finance. Few studies have provided an in-depth analysis of the housing clients served by MFIs. Both micro and macro studies are needed. Recent micro case studies, sponsored by the Cities Alliance, have started to look more closely at clients of shelter finance programs and organizations. For example, Banco Caja Social clearly tailors its products to clients with a certain income level. For home purchase loans, Banco Caja Social requests that borrowers earn at least the minimum legal salary (SMLV), or U.S.$125. For progressive housing loans, clients must earn at least one but no more than four SMLV.

For the macro picture, as discussed below, neither the level of effective demand worldwide nor the relationship of effective demand to currently available funding sources has been addressed.

Table 3.4 BancoSol Housing Loans

Requirements for Salaried Clients	Requirements for Microentrepreneurs
• One year minimum in the current job • Work certificate and pay stub • Notarized declaration of assets and loan request • Personal documentation • Monthly payment shall not exceed 25 percent of monthly income or 65 percent of monthly expenses	• One-year minimum of experience in the trade and six months minimum of work in the current business • Proof of ownership of the business • Proof of stability in the current trade • Notarized copy of declaration of assets • Personal documentation (for both owner and spouse), foreign immigrant documents, and proof of residency for non-Bolivians. • Monthly payment of loan shall not exceed 80 percent of the net profit of the business. • Clearing from the credit bureaus

Source: BancoSol Product Brochure

Box 3.4 Moving into Housing: BancoSol, Bolivia

BancoSol is a microfinance leader in Bolivia with almost ten years' experience serving the financial needs of microentrepreneurs. Since 1997 the bank has ranked among the top three banks in Bolivia based on solvency, liquidity, and capital adequacy. In 1998 BancoSol was the second most profitable institution in the Bolivian banking system. With an investment grade credit rating, BancoSol is the lowest risk MFI. This bank has achieved impressive outreach as it is now the largest bank in the country, with 61,393 clients and 35 percent of all borrowers in the banking system in Bolivia. 57 percent of its clients are women, and it has thirty-three branches in five major cities: La Paz, Santa Cruz, Cochabamba, Oruro, and Sucre.

BancoSol launched a housing program in July 2000, having identified a strong demand for credit to finance home purchases, improvements, construction, repairs, and anticretico. (Anticretico is a loan for an agreed-upon amount between a renter and owner paid up front, similar to a deposit that must be returned to the renter, without interest, upon termination of the agreement. No regular rental payments are required. It is an alternate source of credit for property owners who are usually entrepreneurs and use these funds to finance their business activities.) Cooperatives, commercial banks, and private financial funds also offer credit for the purchase of homes, and to a lesser extent home improvements, but credit for property legalization and anticretico for renters are products unique to BancoSol.

Housing loans currently account for approximately 7 percent of the total portfolio, but BancoSol is currently preparing an advertising and publicity campaign to inform the target population of these new housing products to increase the housing portfolio. The housing program is completely unsubsidized, financed from savings and credit lines from second-tier banks. For the line to be more profitable, bank officials claim they need access to lower-cost capital and to streamline their administrative costs.

Loan Terms and Sizes

Housing microloans have relatively short terms but are often longer than traditional microfinance loans. Access to long-term sources of financing is a major constraint for shelter finance organizations and MFIs alike, which tends to limit possible loan terms. In Latin America, most land purchase or construction loans are for two to five years, as in the case of DIACONIA in Bolivia,

---

Box 3.5 Community Housing Program:
The Case of FUSAI in El Salvador

FUSAI, a locally-run NGO originally established in 1987, has developed a market niche in housing. It is a pioneering institution in the development of mutual help projects offered in the housing program, in which self-construction considerably reduces the costs of progressive development housing. Within the credit program, housing finance products are subdivided based on three distinct uses, each category having its own requirements and loan process.

1. Individual loans for housing improvements, lot purchases, and the construction or purchase of a home.
2. Community loans for families involved in FUSAI's self-construction and mutual help housing program.
3. Emergency reconstruction housing to help clients with the reconstruction of their homes affected by the earthquakes in early 2001.

In addition to providing credit, FUSAI performs all the paperwork for property and lot registration and provides assistance in filling out application forms and constructing financial statements for micro- and small-enterprises. These services are covered by commission fees charged to the clients.

While the loans for FUSAI's community housing program are to individual families, there is significant community involvement. On the one hand, clients must have resided in the same geographical area where the housing project is to be carried out, and have an income less than four minimum salaries (equivalent to U.S.$580). On the other hand, a feasibility study of the housing project to be executed is performed, prior to which there is an entire social and technical process to measure the feasibility of the project—search for land, purchase of land, design, approval of legal aspects, etc. With the technical aspects of the project decided upon, the beneficiaries start a savings account for six to nine months. At the end of the process of paying these "primas" and appropriate approvals are received for the project, each client is submitted for credit approval, which involves an analysis of the client's payment history in the prima process and the actual capacity to pay.

---

which offers housing loans for a maximum of three years. Home improvement loans and loans for additions generally have terms of three months to two years. FUNDAP in Guatemala provides mortgage-backed loans for twenty-four months. Longer-term loans, five years or more, were usually associated with government-backed loans, as in the case of FUSAI, which has terms of up to ten years. Experienced home lender Cooperative Jesus Nazareno, has a maximum loan of $30,000 for a five-year period. Financiera CALPIA also lends with terms not surpassing three years. The average balance of BancoSol's microcredit loans was $1,100 and for housing was close to $10,000.

The terms and sizes of housing microloans in Asia, Africa, and South America exhibit a very wide range (see Table 3.5). CARD in the Philippines, for example, provides housing loans of twelve to twenty months with loan sizes similar to its microenterprise loans. In South Africa, African Bank's loans are a maximum term of thirty

Table 3.5 Loan Terms for Housing Finance Products

Institution	Average/Maximum Loan Size and Term
Diaconía, Bolivia	$800 3 years
FUNHAVI, Mexico	$1,400 20 months
FUCAC, Uruguay	$50,000 2 years
Mutual La Primera, Bolivia	$3,000 15 years
Banco de Desarrollo, Chile	$23,000 12 years
ADEMI, Dominican Republic	$5,000 5 years
BancoSol, Bolivia	$10,000 5 years
BancoSol, Ecuador	$1,095 15 years
Grameen Bank, Bangladesh	$600 10 years
SEWA, India	$300 3 years
CARD, Philippines	$350 3 years
Rural Finance Facility, South Africa	$15,000 7.5 years
People's Dialogue, South Africa	$1,200 15 years
CashBank, South Africa	$8,000 15 years
African Bank, South Africa	$2,500 2.5 years

months and loan size of about $2,500; as noted, this is not large enough to purchase conventional, standard housing, and, thus, improvement loans are featured. BRI's microhousing loans range from three to thirty-six months and do not differ from microenterprise loans, since housing loans are not distinguished.[6] On the other hand, Grameen, SEWA, and CashBank offer much longer-term loans: SEWA's housing loans can be up to five years, Grameen's up to ten years, and CashBank's loans up to fifteen years. Thus, some microloans for housing are nearly the same duration as conventional mortgage finance (CashBank mortgage loans carry a maximum of twenty years). However, relative to conventional mortgage loans in these countries, the microloans for housing are much smaller. The largest loan is offered by CashBank, which now provides a conventional mortgage loan with a minimum size of R65,000 (currently about U.S.$7000).

Progressive loans, repeat lending of additional small loans, are common. This approach is used by those who lend to poorer households, such as CARD, SPARC, SEWA, and BRI. This approach was also previously used by the institutional predecessor to Cash-Bank, which relied on the small, repeat approach during its early years as a finance company. This approach fits the construction profile of incremental housing and the preferences of the low-income borrowers.

Interest Rates

Interest rates for MFI housing loans may be lower, higher, or the same as for microenterprise loans (see Table 3.6). Some MFIs who

Table 3.6 Examples of Housing vs. Microenterprise Interest Rates for Selected MFIs

MFI	Microfinance Loan (APR)	Housing Loan APR
BancoSol, Bolivia	32.11%	23.02%
Cooperativa Jesus Nazareno	20.5%	18%
Financiera Calpia	32%	23%
FUSAI	24%	23%
Grameen Bank	20%	8% (subsidized)
BRI CARD	same	same
SEWA Bank	same	same
People's Dialogue	24%	12 percent (subsidized)

have traditionally used mortgage-backed loans have had an easier entrance into the housing sector, as they have been operating within the regulations and legal framework of mortgage-backed assets. These MFIs may offer lower interest rates for housing. Others, who still rely on individual guarantees or other collateral mechanisms, have higher interest rates or rates equal to their microcredit portfolio. Of its nine loan products, Financiera CALPIA's second-to-lowest rate is for housing: 21 percent for dollar-denominated loans. Genesis Empresarial's housing loan interest rate was almost ten points below its microenterprise loan. Some MFIs also seek low-cost funds (donor or philanthropic) explicitly for housing loans. Grameen Bank housing loans are heavily subsidized, offering an interest rate of only 8 percent in contrast to the market-based interest rate of 20 percent on microfinance loans. Similarly, People's Dialogue/HPF uses a heavily subsidized approach; the rates for their housing loans are roughly one-half the lending rates for conventional mortgage loans. It is important to note, however, that the majority of these lenders use rates that are market based or "commercially viable.

Fixed rates are nearly universal. Exact knowledge of repayment responsibilities has proved to be an important approach to reducing payment shock for low-income households. CashBank/BoE in South Africa, however, uses variable rate loans linking its interest rate to the prime rate, as discussed below. Although fixed rate lending introduces a certain level of risk for the lender, it is by far the preferable approach for low-income borrowers. This approach to pricing is in marked contrast to conventional mortgage lending, where various types of variable rate loans are the norm in the emerging markets of Asia and Africa.

Risk-based pricing is an essential tool for being able to offer higher-risk products in higher-risk markets and at the same time cover costs and spread risk across a variety of clientele. While risk-based pricing has long been conventional in microfinance, it has been difficult in microfinance for housing, as lenders were typically looking for affordable funds, especially for the very poor, and numerous governments used interest rate subsidies for housing. Setting interest rates at sustainable levels for housing loans, thus, seems to have faced greater barriers than in microenterprise lending. Furthermore, microfinance for housing has a heavily transactions-based operational focus, for example, manual application procedures, valuing nonhousing collateral, and securing rent payment receipts.

For long-run viability, lending rates must obviously reflect risks and administrative costs, and the market-based approach has now gained much more acceptability. Practices vary, however. While some microlenders charge a markup over their cost of funds adequate to cover costs through commission, service, and other charges, others seek donor and grant funds to keep rates lower.

Methodology

While many shelter finance institutions are trying to develop innovative technologies for their clients, there is little evidence that these methods and techniques have much in common or are standard even within a country or region. For example, key ratios such as loan to value and debt equity are not defined or standard across shelter finance institutions within a country; loan documentation varies significantly by institutions within a country; and although most shelter finance institutions have property appraisal processes in place, these processes and the external agents involved in the process do not appear to follow particular standards or guidelines with much rigor.

Group versus Individual Loans

The issue of group versus individual loans is complex, and experience presents a mixed picture. However, with a very few exceptions, housing loans are predominantly individual. In dealing with the poorest of the poor, and in microenterprise lending, group loans have a proven appeal: SEWA, SPARC, CARD, and Grameen, for example, all use group loans for microenterprise lending. For housing lending, however, group loans are markedly less popular. During the evolutionary phase of developing housing lending, CashBank (and PROA/Mutual La Paz in Bolivia) concluded that group loans were not viable for housing; both often found the failure rates for group loans too high. CashBank also found that group loan products exhibited term sensitivity; those of a year's duration or less had a very good recovery rate, but the default level rose extremely rapidly thereafter, increasing to 69 percent of the five-year group loans. One reason for this was individual repayment ratios in the group environment could quickly become overextended. Similarly, following a pilot project in 1997, African Bank also rejected group loans.

Although the group approach has proved less tenable, a few MFIs use the group lending or solidarity model for housing including Cooperative Jesus Nazareno in Bolivia, Fundación Pro Vivienda in Argentina, Genesis Empresarial in Guatemala, CARD in the Philippines, People's Dialogue in South Africa, and community-based new construction loans from SPARC in India. SPARC has found that groups "swapped" repayments for individual loans to cover the 20 to 30 percent of households who in any given month could not meet their repayments. A tentative conclusion may be that, for the poorest households, group lending may continue to be used. For Cooperative Jesus Nazareno, the group lending methodology served primarily as an alternative to the costly process of creating a mortgage lien. Where transaction costs and settlement fees for mortgage loans are high, group lending may be an option.

Underwriting Linkages

Given the considerable constraints facing housing microfinance, lenders have developed an impressive array of nontraditional approaches to both underwriting and collateral, including the use of mandatory savings, personal guarantees, payroll deductions, pension fund collateral, cosigners, and training programs (see Table 3.7). Flexible underwriting based on various requirements, or linkages, is one of the hallmarks of housing lending in emerging nations, responding to the informal sources of income and lack of credit information.

Client history and track record with the same organization is paramount. Mechanisms to assess creditworthiness among potential shelter finance clients are still underdeveloped. Most developing countries still do not have fully integrated or computerized credit bureaus. They often have to rely on recent history to assess a potential client's capacity and willingness to pay. In some countries, private companies that track consumer and credit card history are emerging, and offer one way to track credit history. Only a limited number of institutions reviewed used credit scoring to analyze their potential shelter finance clients. However, for institutions exploring the shelter finance sector, the best assurance of repayment with a new product like housing is the client's history with their own organization.

Table 3.7 Examples of Collateral Used to Secure Housing Loans

Institution	Collateral Required
BancoSol, Bolivia	Mortgage and personal guarantees
Cooperative Jesus Nazareno, Bolivia	Mortgage
Financiera CALPIA, El Salvador	Mortgage, fixed assets, deposits, and mixed
FUSAI, El Salvador	Mortgage, solidarity depending on the size of the loan
Banco de Desarrollo, Chile	Personal guarantees (loans less than $5,000) Fixed assets (loans greater than $5,000)
CashBank/BoE	Pension fund collateral
SEWA Bank, Grameen Bank	Cosigners
SEWA Bank, BRI, CARD, Grameen	Previous microenterprise loan
Caja Social, Colombia	Personal, guarantor, and mortgage. For progressive housing second mortgage is accepted.

Most MFIs require clients to: (1) have membership with the institution for a number of years; (2) demonstrate previous microfinance history; (3) show a positive savings history, and/or (4) show acceptable records as a past customer. Even in the case of loans for disaster relief, recipients are predominantly existing MFI clients. The Grameen Bank views their emergency housing loans as a reward for faithful microenterprise borrowers, who must have at least a three- to five-year track record of successful borrowing. Most cooperatives and savings and credit unions follow this practice, as is the case with Cooperative Jesus Nazareno. These types of MFIs also require a number of years or months of savings before approval for a housing loan.

According to Klinkhamer (2000), many of the multipurpose organizations that provide loans for housing as well as for business or other purposes, demand good credit history on a business loan prior to disbursement of the housing loan. This establishes a proven source of income and knowledge of previous loan behavior. Such is the case with SEWA in India, the Grameen Bank, CARD in the Philippines, and the Women's Thrift and Credit Cooperative in Sri Lanka.

Family income estimates are used to assess housing affordability. Only a few organizations used monthly income estimates to calculate the amount and term of the housing loans, at least in the traditional manner in which various debt and income ratios are used in formal mortgage finance. Although the traditional approach appears to be a practice among the more established financial organizations, the practice was not evident in many of the institutions reviewed. Many organizations provide housing as part of their overall microfinance portfolio, which suggests that the criteria developed for housing loans is an adaptation from their microcredit portfolio, and not specially designed to adapt to housing affordability.

Client ownership of the home or land is preferred. It is against the policy of some lenders to provide credit for housing on squatted land, and paralegal title for "legitimate" owners may or may not suffice. Many of the experienced MFIs require ownership, even if the loan is not secured by a mortgage. Some even provide technical support and financing for speeding up the ownership process, as in the case of BancoSol. Cooperative Jesus Nazareno retains the documentation of the ownership, not as collateral but as pressure for repayment. SEWA Bank requires the title of the asset used as security to be put in the name of the female borrower, based on solid experience with women's higher repayment rates.

Many organizations that accept land title as collateral do not necessarily use it due to high implementation costs, complex registry systems, and the myriad procedures involved in foreclosure. Adequate property registry institutions are lacking in most developing countries, and property rights issues remain a key constraint for financial institutions to engage in shelter finance. An additional problem of using land title is that, for a variety of social as well as legal and administrative reasons, the collateral, the land, and the dwelling may not be realizable, either at all or on a timely basis. If the housing loan cannot be foreclosed lenders are forced to seek other ways of underwriting. This has a direct impact on the cost of the loan transaction for low-income families. Properly registering a title or house in most developing countries can involve many months and high costs to the client. The high transaction costs associated with the enforcement of contracts is a major obstacle for housing microfinance to reach the poorest sectors.

This is particularly true for the Bolivian MFIs surveyed, all of which indicated that the costs of using title as collateral were a major challenge in extending housing loans. Although most Bolivian MFIs require ownership and title as part of the qualification process, the element of psychological pressure—that is, holding their title—was more useful than the actual security it provides.

Technical assistance for housing is offered directly by a limited number of organizations, often NGOs. The most developed MFIs do not offer any kind of service, with the exception of their own appraisal of the property, for larger-size loans. Other organizations like FUNHAVI in Mexico, FUSAI in El Salvador, and Genesis Empresarial in Guatemala offer additional services, such as support and assistance in legal documentation and construction standards, in an effort to ensure clients meet basic requirements. The literature suggests that most of the other technical services such as appraisals, legal documentation, registry compliance, and valuation are often outsourced to specialized agencies. There is little research that analyzes whether these technical assistance services are provided with no subsidy.

Training programs are widespread in Asia and Africa and address a variety of credit risk issues, including appropriate housing design, construction techniques, consumer education in loan terms and repayment, and consumer budgeting education as well as traditional microenterprise training. SEWA, CARD, SPARC, and People's Dialogue all undertake various housing-related training efforts, and in some cases they are mandatory.

According to Ferguson and Haider (2000), in order to avoid the challenges involved in seeking a mortgage lien, some organizations, like Fundacion para la Vivienda Cooperative in Honduras, use personal guarantees and a contract that gives the creditor the legal right to seize personal assets and retain wages in case of delinquency. However, these procedures, which are also applicable to microenterprise loans, are seldom used for housing finance.

Savings accounts are used as a method to make payments. Savings are often a crucial aspect of housing microfinance. Proven savings ability is used in underwriting as proof of ability to pay; mandatory deposits are sometimes used as alternative collateral. The terms for mandatory savings vary. SEWA Bank, for example, requires a minimum savings period of one year, and CARD requires a minimum of eighteen months. Most groups require regular payments—monthly, weekly, or daily—with minimum amounts established. Some organizations offering savings products request that clients use their savings account to make payments on housing loans. This practice is seen particularly among banks such as Banco Caja Social in Colombia but also in some cooperatives such as Mutual Alajuela in Costa Rica and Cooperative Jesus Nazareno in Bolivia. This practice is seen as another mechanism to reduce the possibility of default or late payments.

Payroll deductions are used as a payment method for salaried workers. Payroll deduction is now common in lending in South Africa, where social and political turmoil has led to repayment boycotts and prevented realization of mortgage collateral. While payroll deduction offers benefits for underwriting and reduces transactions costs, it clearly limits the participation of those with informal income which, in many of the emerging markets, is the main form of livelihood for most lower-income households. In addition, payroll deduction has reportedly been abused by some microlenders in South Africa, as they greatly overextended the repayment capacity of borrowers who lacked experience with budgeting and debt management. Abuses of the practice have led to government regulations providing tighter controls and pricing parameters to attempt to balance the benefits and risks of this underwriting approach.

BRI in Indonesia also offers payroll deduction loans; unlike BRI's income generation loans, these loans are less stringent with regard to their stated purpose and are among the types of BRI loans that are in fact used for other purposes, particularly housing and education.

Pension and provident funds are used as collateral. Pension-backed loans are an alternative arising out of the unique circumstances in South Africa, where the ability to realize mortgage collateral has been severely impaired. CashBank pioneered the approach and still relies upon it heavily. African Bank, on the other hand, had decided not to pursue pension-backed loans, as it is now a highly competitive methodology, with mainstream banks such as Standard Bank becoming big players. As with payroll deduction, pension fund collateral raises difficult policy concerns, in this case focused on retirement.

Financial Viability

MFIs generally start with a pilot program that may be limited to home improvement. Most MFIs start with a pilot project, risking limited amounts of assets in the process. This restricted entry into the market is preferred over starting with large-scale housing loans. Often MFIs enter the housing sector with home improvement loans before offering financing for the purchase or construction of a new home. Most MFIs have less than 20 percent of assets in the housing category, with the exception of specialized agencies such as Mutual La Primera.

The loan-to-value (LTV) ratio is not a key factor for housing loans. The literature reveals that LTV varies according to specific conditions and the individual MFI. The values for LTV range from 40 to 90 percent. Client history, credit analysis, liquidity, and collateral all play an important role in determining the LTV.

High default levels do not generally appear to be a serious problem. Grameen's default rate has exhibited a wide range over the years, from 1 percent to nearly 7 percent. BRI's default rate (as of March 2001) was about 2.5 percent. Some microlenders seem unduly risk averse; CARD, for example, currently has no loans in default. As noted, group loans have tended to have higher default rates than individual loans.

Most public housing finance institutions are targeting subsidies at the client level, in other words, focusing on the demand side of the problem. Subsidizing interest rates, transaction costs, and access allows government institutions to reach the client level directly. Public institutions like FOGUAVI, the housing finance institution of Guatemala, which used to finance the construction of large housing projects, are now channeling funds through local banks and MFIs. Although this is primarily limited to formal financial institutions or regulated MFIs, in some cases NGOs and community organizations have received funds, such as CODEP in Colombia. Targeted subsidies through NGOs are particularly common where natural disasters have occurred. The shifting focus of public institutions will be an important trend to monitor as shelter finance issues come to the fore in many developing countries.

In Peru, MiVivienda, the state housing finance authority, is channeling housing funds to some thirty financial intermediaries. Over two-thirds of these institutions are MFIs, a good number of which are relatively small. Some Cajas Municipales, the municipal saving and loan cooperatives, and MiBanco, a large, specialized microfinance bank, are also using these loans. With banks in Peru downscaling aggressively and competing with traditional MFIs, MiVivienda must consider issues of efficiency and long-term sustainability. Would it be better off working with fewer inter mediaries and concentrating its efforts in larger, more efficient financial intermediaries?

Examples of public funds channeled through MFIs are wide-spread. CORDEP, in Colombia, is an NGO subsidiary of Ecumenical Church Loan Fund (ECLOF), based in Switzerland. CORDEP received public funds after a 1998 earthquake for reconstruction. The National Slum Dwellers Federation in India began receiving funds from the Housing and Urban Development Corporation (HUDCO) in 1990. This was the first time HUDCO engaged in lending to a community organization that was guaranteed by a European NGO. With the success of this first loan, HUDCO channeled further loans through community organizations, including SEWA Bank and the NGO Sri Padmavathy Mahila. In Peru MiBanco, a local bank, and Edyficar, a regulated nonbanking institution for microcredit, both originated from the work of international NGOs (ACCION and CARE). MiVivienda, the Peruvian state agency, channels housing loans to low- and middle-income families through these two agencies.

Legal and regulatory issues. Selecting the appropriate legal and regulatory structure remains a problem for many microlenders. Lenders must balance such factors as the cost of capital requirements, the desirability of deposit-taking authority, formality of structure, and ability to maintain relations with the community. SPARC, for example, has assessed this problem rigorously, together with the quest for more funding without becoming a bank, which is very expensive in India because of capital requirements. This dilemma absorbs an enormous amount of energy. There continues to be policy discussion about formalizing alternative, less formal financial structures that might have less demanding capital adequacy requirements. Improved intermediation by the low-income lenders is another issue, such that lower-income savers can save in local institutions rather than in mainstream banks, which tend not to lend to these same groups.

Scale, capacity, and sustainability are still major barriers to effective microfinance for housing. Issues include increasing deposit mobilization, finding sustainable lines of credit, determining the best institutional/legal

structure for engaging in microlending for housing, and undertaking partnerships with formal sector banks or other institutions.
The most pervasive and limiting is probably the quest for sustainable funding. In any event, given the balancing act among affordability, the need to cover costs, and the search for adequate funding, the ability to take low-income lending to scale is a serious and
pervasive problem. Furthermore, the institutional structure and
skills required for outreach, organizing savings associations, training new borrowers, servicing low-income loans, and so forth may
be at odds with the institutional structure most able to obtain
funding on a large scale. Does becoming a more formalized institution mean abandoning the very poor or losing flexibility and
legitimacy as a community force?

Housing Microfinance as Part of an Integrated Development Process

It is important to stress that microlending for housing stems from
a much broader context than that for either conventional housing
finance or microenterprise finance. Housing for the poor in many
emerging nations is inextricably entwined with access to land.
Infrastructure follows. In large urban areas, single-family housing,
with its large appetite for land as well as building materials, may
not be cost effective. Thus, obtaining financing may also include:

- forming community groups for planning and land acquisition,
- developing community savings mechanisms,
- convincing the relevant authorities to finance infrastructure,
  or at minimum to provide sanitation, and
- obtaining bridge financing for land, multifamily dwellings,
  and so forth.

Three of the low-income lenders discussed in this chapter are
part of an NGO–finance partnership, with each having a particular role to perform in this holistic context. The roles of SEWA,
SEWA Bank, and Mihila Trust speak to the fact that there are
many more low-income housing needs than funding. Peoples' Dialogue, the Homeless People's Federation, and the uTshanti Fund
form a similar coalition, while SPARC and its savings federations
provide a different sort of coalition, but one with the same goals.

NOTES

1. This is a major issue in South Africa, where low-income housing is a national priority. The large banks, however, that must compete internationally, argue that their necessary ROE (return on equity) profile is not compatible with such high transactions costs. See Tucker, R.S., "The Retail Dimension: Rethinking the Provision of Retail Banking Services to Low-Income Communities," *Housing Finance International* (December 1999).

2. SEWA Bank in India was among the first to recognize the importance of shelter investment in its portfolio nearly two decades ago. Bank Rakyat in Indonesia has conducted a number of formal studies on the disposition of its "untied" loans and has continued to address the role that housing should play in its portfolio.

3. Given the marked differences that often prevail in developing lending for the poor and for moderate-income households, Merrill distinguished LMI (low and moderate income) and microlending for shelter (see, for example, Merrill March 2001). We have not attempted to distinguish these groups here, however.

4. See Baumann 2000.

5. See, for example, Renaud 2001.

6. Studies currently being undertaken by BRI on its loan portfolio may change this stance.

4

Market Assessment
for Housing Microfinance

Mayada Baydas

Despite donor and government efforts, there is little in the development literature about the financial structure of micro- and small-scale entrepreneurs, minimum wage employees, the working poor in general, or microfinance clientele. Although the microfinance sector moved from the supply-driven approach led by targeted credit to a market-oriented, demand-driven approach, responding to client demand has been addressed without a thorough understanding of who the clients are and without identification of the underlying factors that explain their demand. Research efforts have largely focused on the growth and graduation of this clientele (Mead and Liedholm 1998) and on the microfinance organizations and their sustainability (Rhyne and Otero 1992). Many institutions, particularly those who adopted the group lending technology while they focused on institutional development have used standard microfinance products. Impact studies provided donors with indicators that relate to poverty alleviation measures when examining the clientele group.[1] Who are included in our clientele group, who are not, and what is their demand for various services are questions that have been recognized only lately (Park and Ren 2001, Rhyne 2001, Navajas et al. 2000). Understanding the financial structure of the economic agents or microfinance clientele and their effective and potential demand for the alternative financial services has been analyzed in a number of market assessment reports (Baydas 1993, Baydas, Graham and Valenyuela 1997).

Market research in general is the study of existing markets, the existing and potential demand, the adaptability of products, and the exploration of new markets. Market assessments can provide us with a better understanding of our existing and potential clients and their demand. In the microfinance world, informal and formal markets provide alternative channels for clients to draw upon. Identifying the characteristics of these markets, segmentation, niches, suppliers, economic agents, and household units who transact in these markets yields significant insight into the nature of these markets and clientele. Entering new markets or expanding in existing markets with new products requires meeting the clientele's demand with a product mix that responds to the existing met and unmet demand.

Market assessments can be tailored to provide information about clients in a number of ways. The main objectives for conducting market assessments in the microfinance sector are to assess the overall demand for microfinance services, profile the current and potential clientele, gather information about the most appropriate technology by which to reach the clientele, and document details about the nature of the financial products demanded. Entering new markets, creating institutions that provide financial products, and expanding the scale or scope of existing financial products needs to be based on information about the nature of the existing environment and the predominant set of relations that exist. Economic agents fulfill all or a part of their demand for various types of financial services given the available supply options in the informal or formal sector. Identifying and understanding the nature of these contracts, their terms and conditions, and their limitations allows identification of the gaps in meeting the potential demand and consideration of ways to improve the efficacy of meeting effective demand.

The shelter needs of the urban and rural working poor have been met in a variety of ways in different regions in the world. Organizations that focus primarily or solely on meeting this demand have delivered these services through a number of traditional methods, whether for basic construction or for home improvements. More recently, many microfinance organizations have begun to incorporate housing microfinance as one of the services they offer their clients. Recent research efforts have documented a number of housing microfinance initiatives with the main focus on the choice of financing methodologies, methods of capitalization, and mechanisms for expanding outreach (Center for Urban Development Studies 2000). Research on housing microfinance clientele, however, is still relatively limited.

The rationale to undertake a market assessment for housing microfinance, therefore, lies mainly in the fact that it is important to understand the market and potential clients before a new product is designed and offered. Designing the terms and conditions of this product, the method of delivery, and how it fits within the overall financial structure for the clientele will be based on information derived from the market assessment. It is as critical to conduct market assessments for housing microfinance products as it is when designing and launching a microfinance program initially or at considering a new product.

The following sections will present, first, the objective for conducting market assessments and their particular application for housing microfinance. Second, a detailed discussion of the components of a typical market assessment will be offered and, third, a review of the market assessment methodology encompassing housing microfinance data collection will be described. The fourth section will discuss the results generated from the survey and the estimation of the effective and potential demand. The final section will highlight the significance of conducting market assessments as well as point to their limitations. This chapter is aimed at the general microfinance audience, with a particular application to the housing microfinance providers, to guide them through a step-by-step approach to conducting market assessments.

OBJECTIVE FOR CONDUCTING A HOUSING MICROFINANCE MARKET ASSESSMENT

The primary objective of this chapter is to describe and detail the purpose, methodology, and various components of undertaking a market assessment for housing microfinance. The various steps will be reviewed to reflect how information on the effective and potential demand as well as on existing suppliers can be gathered. Information on existing suppliers of housing microfinance products can be gathered from both clients and existing informal or formal providers. Information on potential clientele is obtained directly from clients mainly through a baseline survey supplemented with case studies and information collected at various community levels.

Prior to conducting the market assessment, important information can be gleaned from existing organizations providing housing microfinance services to the target market. These organizations should be visited and officials interviewed regarding their programs. Information about existing formal organizations is typically documented or available through publications, flyers, and the general distribution network through which these organizations operate. Information about informal suppliers of housing microfinance products is less readily available. Identifying these providers is also less obvious. In principle, investigating the current effective demand for microfinance services in general (and housing microfinance in particular) as well as the sources of funds that are used to satisfy home improvement needs allows proper identification of the suppliers. This information is typically documented from the potential clientele survey. In effect, some of the informal suppliers, as will be discussed in subsequent sections, are the same providers of general microfinance products. Given the fungibility of funds, targeted credit does not serve its intended purposes and is often channeled to other uses (Adams, Graham, and Von Pischke 1984). Some home improvements are funded from informal sources or general microfinance loans.

Market assessments at the community level involve gathering information from a number of sources. Information is collected primarily at the clientele level, largely through the potential clientele survey. This includes documenting clients' demographic, socioeconomic, and business characteristics as well as their financial profile. This information allows for a depiction of the potential clientele group, identification of the appropriate technology to deliver the service, and formulation of the suitable product. Most important, market assessments allow for estimation of the effective and potential demand for microfinancial services, including housing microfinance. Further, market assessments can allow for estimation of the potential market size in any given region or country.

COMPONENTS OF MARKET ASSESSMENT

Market assessments for housing microfinance at the clientele level consist of four main components, which are discussed below. Each of these components has to be carried out and completed in this sequence.

Designing the Survey Instrument

The first component of the market assessment is the design of the survey instrument or questionnaire—one of the most important steps in the study.[2] Table 4.1 provides a summary of the main variables or questions in the survey instrument. Housing microfinance market assessment should provide an overall profile of the potential clientele through detailed information on the client's demographic, socioeconomic, and business characteristics as well as details on the effective and potential demand for financial services, debt burden, and repayment capacity.

The first questionnaire section begins with questions that provide general information about potential client location, type of

Table 4.1 Summary of Key Questions in the Market Assessment Questionnaire

Category	Main Questions
I. Basic information	Type of Business, Location, Sector, Age, Gender, Education, Home Ownership, etc.
Current Household Income	Income, number of dependents, etc.
Current Expenses	Rent, food, medical expenses, utilities, etc.
II. For Entrepreneurs Only	Basic financial information, number and type of employees, cost of labor, expenses, etc.
Contractual Relations with Suppliers	Material produced or purchased, etc.
Form of Payment	Cash, credit, advanced, consignment
Contractual Relations with Clients	Type of clients, sales, etc.
Form of Collection	Cash, credit, advanced, consignment
Problems and Constraints	Labor problems, financial constraints, etc.
III. Formal and Informal Demand	
Informal Borrowing	Participation, size, term, price, type, etc.
Formal Borrowing	Participation, size, term, price, type, etc.
If Loan is Currently Received	Current repayment status and basic loan information
IV. Potential Demand for Microloans Through Banks and NGOs	Loan size and type, collateral, interest, etc.
V. Savings with Banks	Participation, interest, number of accounts, etc.
VI. Bank or Nonbank Services	Credit cards and ATM, insurance participation
VII. Informal Groups	Participation, terms and conditions
VIII. Most Significant Informal Group Participation	Number of members, women's participation, type and size of contribution, etc.
IX. Potential Demand for Group Loans	Contribution and repayment information, loan size, etc.
X. Request for Home Improvement Loans	Number of people in-house, type of home, roof type, kitchen, bathroom, rooms, improvements in past 5 years, etc.
XI. Current Improvements	Building, repairing, painting, electrical, cost, source of funds, etc.
XII. Potential Improvements	Building, repairing, painting, electrical, cost, size of needed funds (material and labor), repayment period, etc.

employment, sector, age, gender, education, and home ownership structure. The second section inquires about household income sources and details of family expenses, including debt burden, leading to an estimation of current repayment capacity. The third questionnaire section documents the business activities of the entrepreneur (if the individual being interviewed has a private business) the relationships with input suppliers and customers, and the financial transactions involved in purchase and sales contracts.

The next section explores the overall effective demand for financial services from the informal and formal sector, probing details of the terms and conditions for loan contracts currently in use by clients or those that have been used over the past couple of years. Questions in this section focus on the loan amount, term, interest and fees paid, and collateral used as well as the time it took to receive the loan from the time of application and the transaction costs involved. In addition, this section examines the degree of participation in Rotating Savings and Credit Associations (RoSCAs), as well as the practice of savings with informal collectors. This information indicates the savings potential and the demand for group loans through indigenous group structures. Questions about the terms and conditions of the potential demand for individual and group loans—in contrast to the previous set of questions on the effective demand—explore interest and willingness to borrow and pay for these services. The later questions on potential demand probe potential clients by asking whether they are interested in individual or group loans, the loan amount, term, interest and fees they are willing to pay, and collateral they can provide.

All of the above questions regarding the demand for alternative loan contracts consider the demand for the various types of loans (i.e., working capital, fixed asset, and consumer loans). This information leads to various inferences. On the one hand, loan size, term, price, and collateral used reflect a borrower's preference for the type of lending technology, for example, individual versus group loans, and current repayment capacity as indicated by the debt burden being serviced. On the other hand, questions regarding the use of the loan signal that while working capital and fixed asset loans are used for the business, by default personal loans encompass a variety of consumption purposes including, in some cases, home improvements.

The above information alone, however, is not sufficient for designing a home improvement loan product or a general housing loan. The demand for home improvements is additionally investigated in a section that reviews the type and condition of the house, number of inhabitants, types of improvements made over the past few years, costs of these improvements, and the sources of funds. This reveals the existing sources that meet the demand for home improvements. Potential clients are also asked about their interest in undertaking home improvements, their willingness to borrow to service these needs, the estimated cost of these improvements, and the different components of these costs, such as input material versus labor as well as the time it would take them to be able to pay back the amount if it was taken on loan (Daphnis and Tilock 2001, 18–26).

Appropriate pretesting of the questionnaire and modification of questions to fit the local environment should be the last step in designing the survey instrument. Additionally, the information documented through the survey should be supplemented with information from the community about overall housing stock status and costs of home improvements from specialized contractors and input dealers. Information on the overall housing stock in the surveyed communities can be documented through reconnaissance visits to these areas. This step is actually undertaken prior to conducting the client survey. The purpose of this step is to confirm the overall apparent need for home improvements in a particular community. Estimate of home improvement costs, in contrast, are undertaken after the client survey results. Types of home improvements implemented over the past few years, and the ones potentially in demand if loans were to be available, can be identified as a result of the client baseline survey. Hence, experts in the field should be consulted to verify the average figures provided for home improvements as reported in the survey.

Selecting the Sample

The second component of a market assessment is selecting the sample, that is, identifying the potential client group, geographic area, and representation. If the organization is launching its activities, then the sample would randomly include observations from the universe of the working poor in all regions that will be immediately reached as well as those that will be targeted in the near future. The working poor includes all micro- and small-entrepreneurs across all sectors of the economy and low-income employees whether in private or public institutions. If the organization plans to expand its scope of financial services, the sample should include, in addition to the above group of random observations from the working poor universe, a subgroup of randomly selected clientele from microfinance organizations from different regions.

Sample selection should attempt to control for variables that can skew the survey. The distribution of the various sectors of the economy and their relative shares in the gross domestic product (GDP) is one factor that should be taken into account—modified, however, by the general distribution of the various sectors in the informal market where many potential clientele often operate. Controlling for gender distribution is also an important issue. Again, the representation of women in the labor force typically does not accurately reflect their true participation, as many of them operate in the informal sector. Geographic representation must also reflect the population distribution and work force (formal and informal) concentrations in the country. Relative shares that are representative of the above factors, or any other factor that plays a significant role of categorizing the population, shape the percentages of the subgroups in the sample in each region, by gender, and by sector.[3]

A random walk method of selecting the observations is typically the most feasible method to accommodate the informal sector economic and household units. Whether for an informal micro- or small-scale enterprise or an informal housing structure, the random walk method takes into account those businesses not registered in the chamber of commerce or licensed by the municipalities as well as clients who do not hold registered title deeds. Moreover, the overall sample size has to ensure that it is representative of the population and provides an adequate size of the various factors that make up each subgroup.[4]

Conducting the Survey

The third component in the market assessment consists of conducting the baseline survey and the actual gathering of information. Data collection is a very crucial step in the market assessment. The survey instrument or questionnaire could be very well designed and the sample selection method could be very well outlined and planned; however, these steps are not sufficient for ensuring a good market assessment. If the actual gathering of information is not appropriate, the market assessment results will not reflect the environment or client demand. Adequate enumerator selection, training, and supervision are steps, discussed in the following section, that generate good quality, reliable primary data.

Analyzing the Reporting Data

The fourth component in the market assessment is data analysis and results reporting. Completing the data collection and entering the data into a spreadsheet or program readily available for statistical analysis is the last step before the results can be interpreted and reported. Data entry is typically the responsibility of the information technology specialist who can input it in a format based on the researcher's preferences in using a particular statistical analysis package. A very simple approach to data entry is to input the information into a spreadsheet (for instance, Excel) with the variable names or question codes in the top row and the observation numbers in the first column. This would generate a data set with the number of variables being the number of questions in the survey instrument and the observation number being the sample size. This file can then be read or transformed into a format that is readily accessed by a number of statistical packages, including the widely used Statistical Analysis System (SAS), allowing for the required statistical analyses. Other statistical packages (such as Statistical Package for the Social Sciences or SPSS) can also perform the required data entry and analysis. No matter what software is used, the researcher needs to identify the parameters by which the data should be analyzed and the variables within each category that are most important to review.

The overall descriptive statistics of all the variables or questions detailed in the survey instrument need to be generated to provide an overview of the sample and of the data set characteristics. The most basic statistical analyses provide means, medians, modes, and frequency distributions for all the variables or questions in the survey instrument. Mean, median, and mode, or univariate analysis, is appropriate for variables with continuous response, while frequency distribution is appropriate for variables with categorical responses. This analysis allows for a basic classification of the data and generation of the following:

- a profile of the potential clientele, including demographic and socioeconomic characteristics;

- potential client sources of income, summary of average levels of household income expenses, and estimation of current repayment capacity;
- detail of potential client business characteristics with a depiction of relations with suppliers and customers as well as accompanying financial contracts;
- an overall sketch of the informal and formal financial contracts that exist as well as those that may be demanded by clients.

MARKET ASSESSMENT METHODOLOGY

The market assessment methodology entails carrying out all the components discussed in the previous section. Figure 4.1 illustrates this method and the sequences involved. Designing and pretesting the survey instrument needs to be detailed carefully to ensure that the information required to develop the housing loan will be obtained. Selection and training interviewers involves finding people, preferably with previous experience in data collection, and conducting a training program that allows them to understand the objective of the survey as well as the nature of the questionnaire. Several sessions may be needed to review all the sections of the questionnaire and the various potential answers. Data from the pretesting phase can be used to simulate potential answers and discuss how interviewers should pose the questions to reach this information. Information gathering is not always a clear-cut method and may require several approaches to questioning the interviewees. Field supervision and random monitoring of data collection is also important to ensure that no inaccurate data are being generated.

Careful review of randomly selected, completed questionnaires is essential to control for inconsistencies in the data collection. This can be done through verification of actual questionnaires or through a review of the outliers generated from the overall data entered in the spreadsheet. An overall printout of all the data entered at the end of the data collection allows for quality control and verification of any data entry errors or data collection inconsistencies. Providing guidelines for statistical analysis and cross-tabulation of variables is the last step that allows researchers to read the data and form an overall representation of clients characteristics clientele as well as their effective and potential demand.

Figure 4.1 Methodology for Market Assessment

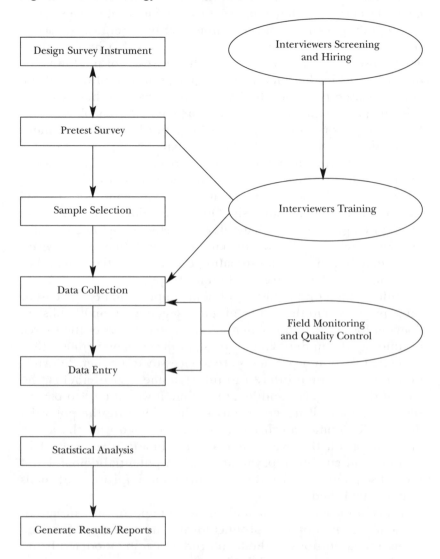

POTENTIAL AND EFFECTIVE DEMAND ESTIMATION

Market assessment can identify potential clients and their demand for various financial services. Information on financial contracts with suppliers and customers as well as with informal and formal lenders, maps the financial landscape. This serves a number of purposes, most immediately allowing for a representation of this clientele's effective demand structure for financial services. Estimating the percentage of the sample that have requested formal financial services, and examining the reasons that have discouraged those who have not, indicates the outreach of microfinance organizations in these markets. The terms and conditions of the contracts used by those who have actively accessed these services over the past couple of years signals the current available options. Moreover, information regarding debt burden and repayment capacity is contrasted with the calculated repayment capacity derived from the family income and expense levels. This analysis illustrates the effective demand for financial services.

Exploring the potential demand terms and conditions follows the effective demand analysis. Questions addressing loan size, term, pricing, available collateral, and preferred method of delivery can sketch the potential demand for overall financial services. This analysis is crucial in estimating overall potential demand of the sample and later dissemination to the population.

Information on the history of home improvements, the cost of these projects, and the source of funding generates an established demand for home improvement services. Regardless of the source of funding, the undertaking of these projects demonstrates effectively that such improvements are a necessity to be met. Information about potential interest in future home improvements, the cost of these projects, and length of time it would take to pay off such an amount if it were given as a loan indicate the potential demand for home improvement loans. Coupled with the above information on the overall demand for financial services, debt burden, and current repayment capacity, potential demand and the subsequent effective demand for home improvement loans can be established.

This information in turn allows for an appropriate design of the housing microfinance product for the institution to offer. The terms and conditions of the loan product can be modeled based on the potential clientele's demand. First, the average loan amounts reported under the potential loan demand should be contrasted with the costs to clients of undertaking the various home improvement projects, and from the home improvement estimation reported by the specialized contractors. An established range for home improvement loans can, thus, be defined based on factual information derived from the market assessment.

Second, loan terms can be designed based on the suggested time frame needed to pay off the loan, coupled with effective debt burden service payments and calculated monthly repayment capacity. Third, while the suggested pricing structure indicated by potential clients is useful, the organization should estimate and use the interest rates and fee percentages that will allow it to cover its costs and be sustainable in the future. Fourth, the use of the alternative collateral substitutes is also derived based on the available collateral the potential clients possess. Finally, the delivery mechanism or ending technology preferred by clients most often leads to adopting individual loans that are more suitable to meeting clients' demand and tailoring each loan according to the particular home improvement project needed.

The information generated regarding the effective and potential demand is not limited to the boundary of the sample under study. This sample is hypothetically a representative segment of the population from which it was drawn at random with particular consideration to the factors that characterize this population. Inferences from this sample, therefore, are possible. The percentage of interviewees using formal loans, the size of the population, and the average loan amounts accessed can be extrapolated to indicate the overall size of effective demand for formal loans in the market. Similarly, the percentage of interviewees in the sample who have conducted home improvements, the size of the sample, and the costs of these home improvements yield the overall effective demand for home improvement projects over the past period under study. The percentage of interviewees in the sample interested in future home improvement loans, the size of the population, and the average loan amounts or costs of these improvements generate the potential demand for home improvement loans. The organization can realize this potential demand and turn it into a subsequent effective demand if it adopts the preferred terms and conditions and succeeds in reaching this clientele and servicing their demand.

In June 2001, the Cooperative Housing Foundation's Access to Microfinance and Enhance Enterprise Niches (AMEEN) program undertook a market assessment of microfinance in Lebanon. The program performed an initial market assessment at the end of 1998 during the start-up stage of the program. The rationale for conducting the second study after two years of operations was twofold. First, the assessment was a tool to gather information that would enable the team to work on new product design. Second, the assessment provided information that would enable the team to evaluate current program services. The research effort allowed the AMEEN team to better understand the economic status of current and potential clients and assess their demand for alternative financial services, including the current AMEEN program services.

The market assessment involved a countrywide demand survey that entailed interviewing more than a thousand entrepreneurs and low-income employees throughout the country, including all economic sectors and a gender mix. The survey revealed significant differences between those respondents who were part of the AMEEN program and those who were not. It also provided important information about demand for individual loans, demand for home improvement loans, and sources of financing for current home improvements. AMEEN was able to identify a strong potential demand for home improvement loans, which led to a successful expansion of its range of loan products to include general microfinance and home improvement loans; AMEEN also increased the loan ceiling for repeat borrowers and revised the loan repayment period based on this data. The results also indicated that AMEEN clients found current financial products satisfactory in meeting their needs.

SIGNIFICANCE AND LIMITATIONS

Market assessment is a critical tool for estimating effective and potential demand for microfinance products in general and for home improvement loans in particular. Examining demand for the overall spectrum of microfinancial services allows an understanding of the financial landscape and the economic agents' repayment capacities. This information is a significant element in the design of new products. However, its importance does not dissolve once the housing microfinance product, or overall microfinancial product, is designed. The importance of the initial market assessment can be extended and built upon periodically to generate information regarding customer satisfaction, new product development, and even impact assessment. Impact assessment in this context examines the degree to which the new products have been competitive and have exhibited a substitution effect rather than a complementary role in the financial landscape.

The limitations of the market assessment include the ability to generate high quality and reliable primary data that reflect the effective and potential demand as accurately as possible. The representation of the sample of the population or universe of potential clientele is a very important element in the sample design. Minimizing bias at the interviewer level again is a relatively difficult task that requires due attention and a high investment in training. Data quality control and data checking for inconsistencies allow for major outliers to be detected, however, some mistakes may still occur. At best, market assessments reflect to a large degree the status of the market and general demand trends. If successful, market assessments analyze and identify market niches and, thus, help meet the mainstream demand of the majority of the population.

NOTES

1. AIMS research, see www.mip.org, Hulme 2000.

2. An example of a market assessment questionnaire is appended at the end of this chapter. See Table 4.1.

3. Other factors may play a significant role in shaping the sample in some environments (displaced populations, immigrant workers, etc.) that should be taken into account as well.

4. Large samples are those with at least 120 observations.

5

Elements of Product Design for Housing Microfinance

Franck Daphnis

This chapter discusses some of the most important issues related to the design of financially viable housing microfinance services in the developing world. It also explores some nonfinancial issues that microfinance institutions (MFIs) must consider when developing these services. It does so with a healthy appreciation for the fact that product design is an approximate exercise. Ultimately, the success of a particular microfinance loan or savings service will be a function of whether a large number of clients choose to access the service under terms that foster the provider's long-term financial viability. As MFIs, nongovernmental organizations (NGOs) and commercial institutions continue to develop increasingly refined tools for projecting demand from microfinance clients, they will find themselves asking:

- What information is most useful to the design of financially viable housing microfinance services?
- How does an MFI go about using that information to formulate a cogent hypothesis for what these services should look like?

This chapter attempts to answer to these questions. It is written for the benefit of organizations interested in adding housing microfinance to their current product lines, for institutions interested in building an operation exclusively around housing microfinance, and especially, MFIs interested in developing a service that responds to specific demand for housing-related financing. Specifically, the chapter discusses the following key elements of housing microfinance product design: clients' capacity to pay, loan repayment period, pricing, affordability, construction assistance, security requirements, land issues, and capital adequacy.

TERMINOLOGY

For the purpose of this chapter, product refers to a financial instrument (a loan or a savings service) and to its basic characteristics, including interest rate, repayment period, and security requirements. Methodology encompasses the principles, rules, and processes that define the manner in which the product can be delivered. Program is a unifying term describing the actions resulting from applying human, technical, and financial resources in support of a methodology (Daphnis and Tilock 2001).

As previously stated, product design is an imprecise exercise. Its purpose is to help the MFI formulate a working hypothesis for what successful features of a proposed product—in this case, a housing microfinance loan—might be, given available information. Ideally, product design builds on client- and market-based demand studies and precedes the real-life "roll-out" of the loan. As clients begin to access the loan, the MFI is in a position to evaluate the soundness of its hypothesis and to revise it as appropriate. Figure 5.1 illustrates the product design process.

Figure 5.1 The Product Design Process

What happens after an MFI has acquired a basic understanding of what its clients want? MFIs can use this understanding to devise a range of financial services that contribute to the key microfinance objective of financial self-sufficiency, while expanding the reach of microfinance beyond enterprise lending and into housing-related services. The resulting products must be tested through the marketplace and adjusted on the basis of client response, fluctuations in key design assumptions (for instance, operational and financial costs, macroeconomic conditions), and a changing competitive environment.

DEMAND ESTIMATES
FOR HOUSING MICROFINANCE

MFIs attempting to estimate potential client demand and market-place opportunities for housing microfinance—or for any proposed microfinance service, for that matter—face a tenuous task. Presumably, a key purpose of demand studies is to generate information that will guide product design. Such information should notably include assessments of the potential market size and composition, client preferences, and competitive environment. In the case of housing microfinance, current experience suggests that demand studies will yield useful information only when the MFI already possesses a basic vision for the types of products and methodologies it plans to offer.[1] It is almost a given that poor and low-income earning families the world over will express a need to improve their housing conditions. Client surveys that adopt an expansive, scattershot approach to understanding client preferences may highlight the extent of that need. These surveys, however, can fall short of reasonably projecting demand for a service provided under microfinance principles.

Current experience suggests that MFIs interested in housing microfinance are well advised to consider a range of services they would be willing to offer their clients and to test client preferences within that range. PLAN International's housing finance surveys showed that economically active but very poor PLAN families in nine countries around the world tended to consistently overstate housing needs and understate income.[2] Only when PLAN asked clients about specific amounts for affordable monthly payments and narrowed the types of housing intervention to home improvements did it generate information that proved useful in the ultimate design of the housing loan. In those instances, PLAN had decided before conducting the surveys that it would offer some type of home improvement loans with a short repayment period, as opposed to the long-term, high-value loans its clients invariably wanted but could not realistically afford.

Even though assessments of potential demand are not perfect, client and marketplace surveys can still provide critical inputs into the design of financially viable housing microfinance services. In this discussion, we assume that potential demand for housing microfinance stems from a positive determination that affordability, need, and willingness to borrow coexist within the marketplace.

Affordability is a function of a client's capacity to pay, the projected cost for a proposed housing intervention, and the loan terms. The MFI should also assess whether enough clients are willing to borrow funds (and under what conditions) in order to finance their housing needs. That willingness to borrow could eventually be expressed as a percentage of the total target clientele (e.g., 75 percent of clients surveyed say that they would take on a three-year home improvement loan carrying a 35 percent interest rate). Finally, the MFI should identify the range of housing needs potential clients are interested in financing. Figure 5.2 summarizes this approach.

Client surveys, MFI records, and focus groups are useful tools an MFI can use in assessing potential demand. CHF International also suggests that MFIs interested in matching housing need with demand for financially viable loans conduct at minimum a Potential Client Baseline Survey, a Housing Stock Assessment, and a Housing Cost Estimate (Daphnis and Tilock 2001, 18–27).

CLIENTS' CAPACITY TO PAY

Capacity to pay is an important component in the overall affordability analysis. For a housing microfinance loan, a client's capacity

Figure 5.2 Estimating Potential Demand for Housing Microfinance Services

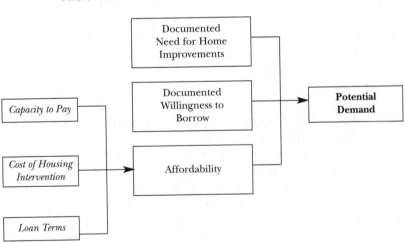

to pay should always be a function of the client's income *before* the loan is issued. If the home is the place of business, housing improvements could increase business productivity and generate increased earnings. In many cases, however, housing microfinance loans help clients improve the condition of a personal asset, without necessarily improving short-term income prospects. This is a self-evident proposition if MFIs extend housing loans to salaried employees (who do not work inside the home). The eligibility criteria MFIs chose to qualify clients should therefore focus on current, rather than future, income.

MFIs currently rely on a wide range of strategies to determine client eligibility for a housing microfinance loan. The objective, however, is always the same: Ensuring that clients will have a reasonable chance of meeting future periodic loan repayments based on their current financial profile. As for any other microfinance lending decision, the more relevant information the MFI has on the income and spending habits of a particular client, the more appropriate the MFI's answer is likely to be.

A key policy decision the MFI must make is determining what portion of a typical client's income should be earmarked for a housing loan payment. In many cases, the home is the most important asset poor people will ever own. Along with food, shelter is the most fundamental human need. It is reasonable to expect that poor families will spend a high percentage of their income toward building, expanding, and maintaining their homes. Many MFIs have already observed that clients use microenterprise loans precisely for these purposes.[3] The question is: If a microfinance loan is designed specifically with housing in mind, is there such a criterion as an acceptable capacity to pay, expressed as a percentage of periodic income?

Most institutions for which information on capacity to pay criteria is available recommend that 20 to 35 percent of either net or gross monthly income can be used to pay for a housing loan.[4] A survey of practice and common sense also suggests that the percentage of disposable income that clients can earmark for housing loans should be inversely related to their poverty level. Everything else being equal, a very poor person will spend a higher proportion of her take-home income on basic necessities, compared with what a middle-income earning person will spend. For instance, a market vendor earning a net income of $50 a month in Port-au-Prince, Haiti, may need a minimum of $42 to feed and clothe herself. A small shop owner working and living in the same neighborhood and earning $250 may only require $175—a larger amount, but a lower percentage of monthly income.

Additional recurrent expenses, such as prior debt, should also affect what percentage of a client's income can apply to a periodic housing microfinance loan repayment. Suppose, for instance, that the market survey suggests most clients will be able to allocate 30 percent of their disposable monthly income toward repayment of a housing loan. Suppose the survey further shows that, on average, potential clients already use 20 percent of their monthly income for existing debt service. The projected monthly debt burden (housing payment plus other payments) for an average potential client would, thus, be 50 percent of monthly income. If the MFI has good reason to believe that future clients will have some form of prior indebtedness, the MFI should establish guidelines on the amount of total debt any client should be able to afford. CHF International, for instance, recommends that clients pay up to 25 percent of their disposable monthly income toward monthly loan repayment. However, CHF also believes that total monthly debt payment should not exceed 40 percent of monthly income (Daphnis and Tilock 2001, 10).

For a specific housing microfinance loan delivered in a specific community and to a specific clientele, MFIs should think of the proportion of a client's income that can go toward loan payment as an acceptable range, rather than a set number. The MFI can assign a particular value within that range to a client, based on what the MFI believes that client will be able to repay. Table 5.1 illustrates housing microfinance capacity to pay criteria for several well-known organizations.

The challenge for the MFI is to determine the percentage of income that maximizes the periodic amount a client can repay, while also maximizing the likelihood that the client will be able to provide for her basic needs. This equilibrium point will vary from client to client and can have multiple determinants, including family size, consumption patterns, and even inflation over the life of the loan. Organizations that offer linked housing microfinance products and that can consult a client's individual repayment history on prior loans could peg the housing payment to the most recent periodic payment they know the client can honor. Organizations that offer stand-alone products and that do not have a prior relationship with the client will have to develop new criteria that correspond to the economic conditions of their target clientele.

Table 5.1 Capacity to Pay Guidelines for Six Housing Microfinance Providers

Institution	Product Type	Eligibility Criteria Towards Loan
CHF/Gaza	Stand-alone	Up to 25% of household income
Calpia	Stand-alone	Up to 25% of household income
FUNHAVI	Stand-alone	Up to 33% of household income
CARD	Linked	2 loan cycles; 1.5 year of savings; Branch Manager recommendation
Grameen	Linked	2 loan cycles and recommendation from group
SEWA	Linked	One year of savings; repayment at around 30% of monthly income

Source: IFC, HIID, Daphnis/CHF MFT Course Survey

Loan security requirements are another important factor that could affect capacity to pay. An MFI that has already collected one year's worth of savings from the client, as a guarantee prior to loan disbursement, does not face the same overall risk as an MFI with no prior relationship with that client. Similarly, a client who is able to secure her loan with two creditworthy cosigners would seem to present a lower overall default risk than a client with no history with the MFI and no guarantors. An MFI could, thus, decide to tighten or relax its capacity to pay criteria based on the perception of default risks it associates with a client.

Current practice suggests that the periodic repayment for economically active poor clients interested in a housing microfinance loan can range from 20 to 35 percent of a client's income during that period. Also based on current practice, the total periodic debt payment (housing loan plus other loan payments) can fluctuate from 30 to 40 percent of disposable income. In addition to the debt burden, the MFIs should consider family size, predictable recurring expenses, and the rate of inflation as factors that can be expected to influence a client's capacity to pay.

REPAYMENT PERIOD

Once an MFI has established a range for clients' estimated capacity to pay, the next step in the affordability analysis consists of deciding on acceptable loan terms, notably repayment period, pricing, and loan security. When the MFI has formulated policies on capacity to pay and on loan terms, it will be in a position to determine the loan amounts its clients are likely to afford.

Current practice indicates that repayment periods for housing microfinance loans range from one year to ten years, with the vast majority in the one- to five-year range. MFIs and traditional housing finance providers attempting to determine the optimal repayment period for a housing microfinance loan all face the same fundamental problem: What amount of time will enable a client to borrow enough funds for her housing needs, given: (1) the client's estimated current capacity to pay; (2) the pricing of the loan; and (3) the MFI's need to minimize the probability that the client will default on the loan? For MFIs, the answer is likely to involve repayment periods that are longer than what they allow for more typical microfinance loans. For traditional housing finance providers, the repayment period will most likely be shorter than what they allow for more traditional (mortgage) housing loans.

In the case of established MFIs, housing microfinance typically involves loan amounts that are higher than what MFIs usually extend to their individual microenterprise clients. Unless the provider has experience with high-value individual loans, fulfilling a demand for housing loans may entail altering the MFI's worldview on what constitutes an allowable repayment period. For instance, MFIs that target poor and very poor clients often develop group-based methods of lending that feature repayment periods of one year or less. The short repayment period is in direct relation to the default risk the MFI associates with its clients. The poorer the client, the more likely the MFI will attempt to manage default risks by reducing the time over which the client must repay the loan. As clients successfully complete lending cycles, loan amounts may increase and repayment periods may expand. MFIs that use a short repayment period to minimize credit risk may have to consider significant increases to the allowable repayment time for housing loans.

For traditional housing finance providers, the problem is reversed. Traditional housing loans typically carry very long repayment periods—sometimes up to thirty years. Until the recent emergence of housing microfinance, housing finance providers, governments, and donors understood the housing microfinance problem as the need to finance a complete dwelling under terms affordable to poor families, attractive to the commercial sector, and on a scale large enough to impact national housing shortages. Unfortunately, in most countries, mortgage lending and a supporting secondary mortgage market never materialized as financially viable options in addressing the housing needs of the poor. Poor people could not afford to borrow enough money at real interest rates to finance a completed home, unless repayments were stretched over long periods of time. This created two problems: (1) few sources of funds existed that could match repayment periods spanning ten to thirty years, creating a severe asset/liability mismatch for commercial institutions interested in housing finance; and (2) when these sources were found (government pension funds, for example) poor borrowers could not sustain repayments over the term of the loans. As a result, investors were not willing to invest in securitized forms of these loans. Housing microfinance shows a way out of this cycle by redefining the *object* of housing finance. The unit financed need not always be a complete home, purchased from a previous owner or a commercial developer. Poor people around the world build incrementally. They finance their construction needs with their savings or with what they can borrow from relatives or informal sources. An incremental approach to financing housing needs significantly reduces the amount to be financed, thus, eliminating the need for ten- to thirty-year repayment periods.[5]

Stand-alone Housing Microfinance

When the provider has no prior relationship with the client, existing practice suggests that MFIs allow poor people to repay a housing loan over periods that range from twelve months to five years. As a result, and given the limited capacity to pay, loans are likely to cover a basic home improvement rather than a substantial addition or a new home. The repayment period is longer than what an MFI engaging in group-based lending usually allows and within the range of (or slightly over) what many MFIs allow for individual loans.

From a strictly financial standpoint, it would make sense that the repayment period for a stand-alone housing microfinance loan would be close to what MFIs allow for individual business loans. Whatever the housing need, MFIs with stand-alone housing microfinance products should not extend a loan to a client if they believe the client would be ineligible for an individual microfinance loan. (An important difference with a microenterprise loan being, of course, that a housing microfinance client can be not only a self-employed entrepreneur but also a salaried worker.) CHF International, CALPIA, ADEMI, and other organizations have demonstrated that poor people with no prior links to the provider can take on such a loan and repay it over periods that extend for up to four years (the CHF maximum is three years). A safe recommendation would be to begin testing the product with an eighteen-month repayment period in cases where the MFI does not have experience with long repayment periods. The period could be expanded for subsequent loans.

Linked Housing Microfinance

Many MFIs link client eligibility for a housing loan to prior participation in a savings or lending program currently offered by the MFI. A survey of current practice shows that many of the MFIs offering linked housing microfinance products tend to work with poor or very poor clients. If they fulfill the eligibility requirement for a housing loan, the clients of these MFIs tend to be offered repayment periods that stretch far beyond what one would expect to see for individual microenterprise loans.

The poorer the clients, the longer the period they will require to afford the sums that housing microfinance requires. Because the expanded repayment periods can bring a higher default risk, MFIs, in effect, institute an internal credit bureau and only offer the service to clients who have demonstrated discipline and a track record such that they can be trusted with the larger amount. For instance the Grameen Bank requires two and a half years of participation in its loan program (in addition to clients' savings) as a precondition for offering a housing loan. CARD and SEWA Bank require clients to make regular savings payments before they are eligible for a housing loan. (See Table 5.2 for further examples.)

PRICING

In principle, pricing a financially viable housing microfinance loan should be no different than pricing any other microfinance product. The effective annual interest rate a provider charges to clients should reflect the competitive costs of providing the service, the financial costs of procuring funds for the housing loans, and the capitalization (including, as appropriate, profit) rate. The rate should also be offset by investment and other income generated outside of lending operations.

Table 5.2 Repayment Periods for Ten Housing Microfinance Providers

Institution	Country	Product Type	Repayment Period
ADEMI	Dominican Republic	Stand-alone	12 to 36 months
Calpia	El Salvador	Stand-alone	Up to 60 months
MiBanco	Peru	Stand-alone	Up to 120 months
FUNHAVI	Mexico	Stand-alone	18 months
CHF/Gaza	Gaza	Stand-alone	36 months
Genesis	Guatemala	Stand-alone	Average of 30 months
BancoSol	Bolivia	Stand-alone	Average of 80 months
CARD	Philippines	Linked	12 months
Grameen (basic)	Bangladesh	Linked	120 months
SEWA	India	Linked	60 months

Source: IFC, HIID, Daphnis/CHF MFT Course Survey

MFIs and NGOs pricing a housing microfinance service should use an advanced financial planning model such as Microfin[6] to estimate the effective interest rate that will lead to financial viability. As Richard Rosenberg demonstrated (CGAP 1996), a simplified pricing formula for microfinance loans can be expressed as follows:

$$R = \frac{AE + LL + CF + K - II}{1 - LL}$$

Where R, the annualized effective interest rate is a function of five elements, each expressed as a percentage of outstanding loan portfolio: administrative expenses (AE), loan losses (LL), the cost of funds (CF), the desired capitalization rate (K, which includes both capitalization and profit), and investment income (II).

The resulting interest rate should allow the MFI to cover all operational and financial costs, capitalize its portfolio at the desired level and, if applicable, provide a return to its investors.

Administrative Expenses

Organizations planning to offer housing microfinance should spend time planning for the expenses to be allocated in support of that service. Assuming the housing loan will seek to be financially viable on its own and will not be subsidized by other products the provider offers, projected administrative expenses should reflect product-specific cost accounting. (All costs should be annualized and expressed as a percentage of the outstanding loan portfolio.)

- *"Line" Staff Costs.* The total cost of paying competitive salaries for program managers, loan supervisors, loan officers, promoters, and for any support staff working to ensure successful delivery of the housing microfinance product. If the provider plans to offer construction assistance to its clients, what will be the costs of paying for staff architects/engineers and construction specialists or for outsourcing these services?
- *Management and Overhead Costs.* If the organization is not built around housing microfinance, what is the estimated value of the senior staff time that will be spent working on the housing service? What is the estimated percentage of indirect costs (rent, accounting, equipment acquisition and depreciation) that is attributable to delivering the service?
- *Other Direct Costs.* Other important costs the provider should consider include staff training on the new methodology; transportation costs (which may be higher than for other products if the provider offers construction assistance involving frequent field visits); communications; supplies; equipment; outside consulting; and "bridge" cost of funds, if the provider is purchasing construction materials in bulk on behalf of clients.[7]

Loan Loss

Setting up a loan loss reserve and provisioning for loan losses should be consistent with best practices in microfinance. At the onset of the program, the provider should set a loan loss reserve as a negative asset on its balance sheet. The amount in the reserve should reflect expectations for long-run losses. Current practice suggests that most successful providers of housing microfinance services have repayment rates of 97 percent or higher. Thus, if the provider has no method for estimating its future long-term losses, the initial loan loss provision should be set at 3 percent of the outstanding loan portfolio. At regular intervals (for instance, every three months) the provider can choose to make loan loss provisions to ensure that its reserve reflects expected long-term losses. The annual total for these provisions should be expressed as an appropriate percentage of the portfolio at risk and incorporated into the pricing formula.

Cost of Funds

When pricing a housing microfinance loan, the cost of funds should reflect a realistic understanding of what the provider would have to pay for the required funds on a nonsubsidized basis. As Rosenberg reminds us, "the figure computed here is not the MFI's actual cost of funds. Rather, it is a projection of the future market cost of funds as the MFI grows past dependence on subsidized donor finance, drawing ever-increasing portions of its funding from commercial sources" (CGAP 1996, 2). Rosenberg goes on to suggest that an appropriate method to estimate cost of funds is to choose a point in the institution's mid-term future and estimate what a weighted average cost of fund will be at that point, taking into account the three most likely sources for these funds: (1) commercial loans; (2) client deposits; and (3) provider equity.

Estimated costs of funds for loans to outside parties should always reflect what the provider would have to pay to borrow funds from commercial sources—even when actual loans on the provider's balance sheet carry a much lower interest rate. This ensures that the provider has incorporated in the interest rate it charges its clients what it will actually cost to raise funds to meet future growth. Rosenberg also recommends that the cost of funds on client deposits mirror what commercial institutions offer their clients, even when the actual rate paid to current clients is lower. If the provider offers clients a higher interest rate than do commercial banks, the higher rate should be used to calculate the weighted cost of funds. Finally, the provider's financial assets net of its financial liabilities should be used to determine the equity to which a cost of funds should be applied.[8] For purpose of calculating a weighted average, a reliable projection of the annual inflation rate should be applied as the cost of funds on this modified net financial equity, as inflation erodes the purchasing power of the organization's equity.

A formula for the weighted cost of funds (CF), calculated to reflect the MFI's market position and to allow for the provider's financial viability at a set point in the future, could be as follows:

$$CF = \left[\frac{i_1 \times L}{P}\right] + \left[\frac{i_2 \times D}{P}\right] + \left[\frac{i_3 \times E}{P}\right]$$

L is the total amount in annual loans that the provider estimates it will have to borrow to finance its total outstanding portfolio and

i_1 is the interest rate it will have to pay to procure these funds com-mercially. D is the value of deposits the provider expects to attract at the time for which the cost of funds is calculated and i_2 is the higher of either the rate commercial institutions pay for client deposits or what the provider thinks it will have to pay at that time. E is the provider's projected modified equity (as calculated above) and i_3 is the annual inflation rate. P, the expected value of the portfolio, is the sum of L, D, and E.

Note that this formula for calculating the cost of funds for a housing microfinance loan only works if the provider assigns the same cost of funds to its entire product line.

Capitalization and Profit

The provider should price its loan in such a way that it can retain some of its yearly earnings after all operational and financial costs have been paid, and after loan losses have been taken into account. The MFI can apply retained earnings to capitalize its portfolio in order to increase the nominal value of the portfolio—real value can also be maintained if the capitalization rate is higher than the rate of inflation. The MFI can also choose to dis-tribute some of its retained earnings as profit to shareholders.

A survey of current practice shows that interest rates charged on housing microfinance loans are either on par with or lower than interest rates charged for other microfinance loans in the same market (see Table 5.3). An important factor in pricing dis-crepancies between housing microfinance and microenterprise lending could reside in the fact that many MFIs view housing loans as less risky (thus, requiring lower loan loss reserve provisions) if the loan is secured by the value of the home. MFIs that offer linked housing microfinance products may also feel that long-term default risk is less than it is for other products.

AFFORDABILITY ANALYSIS

The MFI is ready to look at affordability when it has acquired an understanding of capacity to pay, established a basic range for loan terms (including security requirements, repayment period, and interest rate), and assessed the costs for the hous-ing interventions it believes clients will require. A housing

Table 5.3 Pricing for Ten Housing Microfinance Providers

Institution	Product Type	Microenterprise Loan	Housing Loan
ADEMI	Stand-alone	18% to 24%	Not Applicable
Calpia	Stand-alone	32%	23%
MiBanco	Stand-alone	30% + (Mi Capital)	45% (MiCasa)
FUNHAVI	Stand-alone	Not Applicable	58%
CHF/Gaza*	Stand-alone	11%*	15%
Genesis	Stand-alone	35%	25%
BancoSol	Stand-alone	32%	16% to 22%
CARD	Linked	20%	20%
Grameen (basic)	Linked	20%	8%
SEWA	Linked	17%	14%

Note: *Average interest charged by partner banks
Source: IFC, HIID, Daphnis/CHF MFT Course Survey

microfinance loan is affordable when the MFI projects that clients will be able to finance their housing needs under terms that contribute to overall financial viability.

A successful outcome to the affordability analysis does not guarantee that the loan will be successful in the marketplace—demand is effective only when clients, in large numbers, actually access and then repay housing loans. Still, the affordability test is an important part of the analysis an MFI should go through before it can launch a housing microfinance service.

The affordability framework presented in this chapter assumes the MFI is interested in developing a financial service that matches a perceived demand for an established range of housing needs. As previously discussed, if the MFI's primary objective is to provide its clients with a consumer credit facility that uses housing for marketing purposes or as a touchstone for the loan amount, the affordability test will only be a function of the capacity to pay and of the loan terms—not a function of what types of housing interventions may actually be in demand.

For MFIs interested in assessing whether clients will be able to afford a range of housing interventions perceived to be in demand, the affordability of a loan will be a function of the following variables: (1) the clientele's estimated capacity to pay; (2) the loan repayment terms (including most notably repayment period and financially viable loan pricing); and (3) the costs of the housing solutions clients are likely to demand.

Determining product affordability is not a linear process. Rather, it should take the form of a sensitivity analysis examining the relationships among capacity to pay, loan terms, and housing costs. Client capacity to pay (expressed as a percentage of household income, for instance) should be independent of loan terms and housing need—there is only so much a family can spend on a new loan that does not (necessarily) lead to additional income in the short term. The allowable loan repayment period is a function of the default risks the MFI associates with a particular client and of the MFI's overall worldview on microfinance or housing finance. Loan pricing is a function of variables that are internal (operational costs), external (commercial cost of funds, inflation rate), or a mixture of both (portfolio performance). The affordability analysis brings all these variables together by analyzing various scenarios under which the MFI could deliver the new product to eligible clients.

The process for housing microfinance affordability analysis for can be summarized as follows:[9]

1. In a first phase, the MFI should conduct a sensitivity analysis for each proposed improvement, solving for the monthly loan amount, given a set interest rate. The repayment period will be the variable. Note that this assumes both loan amounts and repayment period can fluctuate within a range the MFI finds acceptable.
2. The MFI can introduce an additional dimension to the analysis by testing affordability for different interest rates. This is useful if the MFI wants to assess impact on affordability of construction assistance or of any other feature that will affect product pricing.
3. The MFI should compare resulting monthly loan payment amounts with the target clients' estimated capacity to repay.
4. From this analysis, the MFI will be able to determine, for each improvement, the percentage of potential clients who will be able to afford a loan, under what repayment period, and at what interest rate.

As an example, assume that an MFI has determined from client surveys and its knowledge of the housing market that strong demand potentially exists for the following housing interventions: roof, $200; latrine, $120; sanitary floor, $150; room addition, $420; new core home, $850. In this example, let's assume the MFI requires that no more than 25 percent of household monthly income should go toward housing loan repayments and that the monthly debt burden should not exceed 40 percent of monthly income. Further assume that the MFI's client survey estimated the average debt burden of potential clients to reach approximately 18 percent of monthly income. The MFI can therefore estimate the allowable average monthly payment to be 22 percent of monthly income (40 percent minus 18 percent).

With respect to pricing, let's assume the MFI estimates that 30 percent (calculated on a declining basis) is the minimum interest rate it will have to charge its clients in order to ensure financial viability over the next three years. Further assume that the MFI estimates an interest rate of 34 percent will be sufficient to pay for the additional cost of pre-loan construction assistance to its clients (budgeting and basic construction design). Finally, assume that the MFI will have to charge 38 percent if it wants to provide a complete construction assistance package to its clients (pre- and post-loan construction supervision.)

Table 5.4 shows the result of a basic affordability analysis, given information available to the MFI.

The affordability analysis can help the MFI estimate income thresholds for each anticipated housing intervention, based on its estimate of clients' capacity to pay and given interest rates that are consistent with its financial planning. From client demand surveys (or based on its prior knowledge of the targeted clientele), the MFI should be in a position to compare the required income for each intervention with income distribution tables for the target population. The results of that analysis (taking into account estimated willingness to borrow for housing finance) should yield a basic estimate of potential demand for various loan sizes.

CONSTRUCTION ASSISTANCE

Many MFIs offer construction advice or supervision as an integral part of housing microfinance. Many more do not. The purpose of this section is not to argue for or against such assistance. Rather, the aim is to provide guidelines to MFIs that are considering developing this type of technical help for their clients.

If the MFI plans to offer no form of construction assistance, the housing microfinance loan is, in effect, a consumer loan whose

Table 5.4 Affordability Analysis

Cost of Improvement		Interest	Monthly Payment 18 months	Minimum Income	Monthly Payment 24 Months	Minimum Income	Monthly Payment 24 Months	Minimum Income
With No Construction Assistance								
Roof	200	30%	$13.93	$63.34	$11.18	$50.83	$8.49	$38.59
Latrine	120	30%	$8.36	$38.00	$6.71	$30.50	$5.09	$23.16
Sanitary Floor	150	30%	$10.45	$47.50	$8.39	$38.12	$6.37	$28.94
Room Addition	400	30%	$27.87	$126.67	$22.37	$101.66	$16.98	$77.18
New Core Home	850	30%	$59.22	$269.18	$47.63	$216.03	$36.08	$164.02
With Some Construction Assistance								
Roof	200	34%	$14.34	$65.17	$11.60	$52.72	$8.93	$40.61
Latrine	120	34%	$8.60	$39.10	$6.96	$31.63	$5.36	$24.37
Sanitary Floor	150	34%	$10.75	$48.88	$8.70	$39.54	$6.70	$30.46
Room Addition	400	34%	$28.68	$130.34	$23.20	$105.44	$17.87	$81.22
New Core Home	850	34%	$60.93	$276.98	$49.29	$224.06	$37.97	$172.60
With Full Construction Assistance								
Roof	200	38%	$14.75	$67.03	$12.02	$54.65	$9.39	$42.68
Latrine	120	38%	$8.85	$40.22	$7.21	$32.79	$5.63	$25.61
Sanitary Floor	150	38%	$11.06	$50.28	$9.02	$40.99	$7.04	$32.01
Room Addition	400	38%	$29.49	$134.07	$24.05	$109.30	$18.78	$85.36
New Core Home	850	38%	$62.68	$284.89	$51.10	$232.25	$39.91	$181.40

Source: IFC, HIID, Daphnis/CHF MFT Course Survey

declared purpose is housing but whose ultimate use is up to the client. The proposed construction project provides a rationale for estimating a required loan amount. In addition, calling the loan a housing loan may help the MFI market the new product to its clients. Ultimately, repayment performance determines the client's future standing with the institution—as opposed to whether the housing work has been completed in accordance with original loan documents.

When an MFI is considering whether to incorporate construction assistance into the design (and pricing) of a proposed loan, it may be useful to consider that MFI's attitude toward the familiar microfinance concepts of due diligence and follow-up. Some MFIs regularly conduct pre-disbursement due diligence on a microenterprise loan in order to determine whether the requested loan amount will match the intended purpose of the loan. In the case of housing microfinance, such pre-disbursement assistance can include the following activities:

- Basic construction design to ensure that the proposed intervention complies with basic safety and legal requirements;
- Budget verification to ensure that the proposed cost estimate for the intervention is appropriate and matches the client's loan request;
- Guidance on materials and labor procurement, tapping into the provider's knowledge of these markets to help clients make cost-effective decisions; and
- Assistance with permits and other legal requirements.

Within the realm of microenterprise lending, some MFIs also follow up, post-disbursement, to ensure that clients fulfill the original purpose of the loan. In the case of housing microfinance, this could be translated into the following activities:

- Construction oversight to ensure that the builder or contractor faithfully executes the work for which he has been hired; and
- Verification that the construction has been completed in accordance with the MFI's agreement with the client or in compliance with applicable law.

From an organizational standpoint, an MFI can provide construction assistance to its clients in one of two ways. The MFI can build the capacity in-house by hiring, training, and fielding the combination of professionals and skilled workers it believes will get the job done. Alternatively, the MFI may decide to out-source the work to a specialized firm, an NGO, or a cadre of individuals.

If the MFI decides to internalize the provision of construction assistance, the qualification and composition of the relevant staff will depend on the extent of the service the MFI plans to provide. CHF International, for instance, recommends that one technical officer should be hired for every two loan officers on staff, if an MFI contemplates a full technical assistance package (pre- and post-disbursements) to clients. CHF also recommends that the MFI retain at least one architect or engineer on staff to supervise the work of the technical officers (Daphnis and Tilock 2001, 16). Genesis and FUNHAVI are among the organizations that currently have or plan to have such a professional as a full-time staff member. MFIs that provide basic construction services to clients should not necessarily plan for housing microfinance loans to generate higher operational costs than other microfinance loans. Current practice shows that housing microfinance loans tend to be priced at the same level or lower than more traditional microfinance loans. One explanation lies in the fact that technical officers can be as much a partial substitute for additional loan officers as they can be an addition to them. Many institutions, including CHF/ Gaza and the Micro Enterprise Bank in Albania, train technical officers to function as loan officers. Ultimately, the full cost of pro-viding the service should be reflected in the administrative costs the MFI uses to price its loan.

MFIs that decide to contract out construction assistance should ensure that their contractors are technically competent, reliable, and honest. The client's relationship is with the MFI, not with a third party. If that client is paying for a nonfinancial service as part of a housing loan, she should expect that the quality of the service provided would add value to her investment. MFIs that are not able to meet this basic expectation may find it difficult to develop a successful product in a competitive marketplace.

Housing microfinance products that include construction assistance will be viable in the long run only if clients determine that the cost/benefit ratio to them—including the added value of technical assistance—is favorable. If the pricing is prohibitively high, clients will look elsewhere for alternative sources of housing financing. They may, as a consequence, choose to access micro-enterprise or other loans for that purpose. If a housing microfinance loan is a flexible consumer loan using housing for marketing appeal or as a gauge for the loan amount, it is possible that the loan will compete with other products the organization offers. Clients will shop around for the loan terms that best suit their various needs. They may access a housing loan for enterprise and other purposes, depending on the level of flexibility the housing loan offers.

Construction assistance in the context of housing micro-finance does not appear to be a predictor of financial perfor-mance. FUNHAVI and ADEMI, for instance, have developed hous-ing microfinance programs that are polar opposites in their attitude toward construction assistance but similar in many other ways. Both report high historic repayment rates. Institutions such as FUNHAVI and CHF see construction services to clients as an important component of housing microfinance. They also believe that the direct and sustained contact with the client leads to better default risk management.[10] ADEMI managers, on the other hand, have stated that construction assistance is contrary to their oper-ating philosophy. Clients, they believe, must decide for themselves how best to use their own money.[11]

There is currently no empirical evidence suggesting that one approach is more correct than the other.

LOAN SECURITY

MFIs use a variety of strategies to secure housing loans. Tradi-tional housing finance providers (including commercial banks), on the other hand, have typically relied on a mortgage (a lien against the actual property) as the main form of security for long-term housing loans. The following is a select list of recommended approaches to securing a housing microfinance loan, as suggested by a survey of current practice.

Cosigners

Many institutions do not believe that formally collateralizing a housing microfinance loan is necessary for the loan's success in the marketplace. CHF International, for instance, makes a strong case for using cosigners instead of actual collateral:

> Cosigners provide the greatest security at the lowest cost [. . .] The
> challenge of using collateral is securing the asset, ensuring the right
> to seize it should the borrower default, and liquidating the asset to
> repay the remaining loan balance. Many countries do not have the
> legal system that supports the use of collateral to secure a loan. The
> lack of legal regulations can make it difficult to secure and seize col-
> lateral offered . . . Placing a lien or deed of trust on a home and, in
> the case of default, foreclosing on the house can be a costly and
> lengthy process. Additionally [. . .] placing a lien on a home for a
> minimal loan amount also would overcollateralize the loan and
> underutilize the borrower's financial asset, thereby putting an
> undue burden on the borrower (Daphnis and Tilock 2001, 14).

Cosigners should be adequate if the loan is small in relation to
the market value of the home. Cosigners must pass the same eligibility tests as the actual borrower, and the MFI should establish a
clear procedure to access the cosigner's resources in case the
client defaults.

Linking Housing Loan to Performance on Other Services

MFIs offering linked housing loans use their credit or savings services as a performance filter, a form of internal credit bureau that
allows good clients to become eligible for the longer-term loan.
From a security standpoint, this represents a more cautious
approach compared to MFIs following the stand-alone approach,
perhaps a function of the typically poorer clientele. Assuming that
microentrepreneurs have financing needs beyond their business
needs, the promise of a housing loan is a powerful incentive to
perform on first-tier loan and savings programs. As a consequence, housing microfinance, when tied to other MFI services,
has the potential to enhance the MFI's overall financial performance and client retention rate.

Mortgage

If the amount of the loan is close to the value of the home, and if
there are no overwhelming legal or cultural barriers to transfer-
ring the home from a client in default to an MFI, the MFI may
consider placing a lien on the house. Some MFIs also choose to
mortgage the home as a psychological deterrent against delinquency, even when they realize that they may not realistically be

able to seize or sell the house in case of default. As previously stated, mortgaging the full value of the house makes financial (as opposed to psychological) sense if the value of the house reflects the value of the loan and if the house can be sold for that value. Table 5.5 illustrates the pricing strategies for various organizations with housing microfinance services.

LAND ISSUES

In many countries in which MFIs operate, poor families cannot reliably produce formal proof of land ownership. Yet for many of these families, that land and the dwelling built on it constitute the most important asset the family will ever own. Governments throughout Latin America, Africa, and Asia have enacted land reform and land regularization programs—but results have not always lived up to expectations. The need for shelter (and, thus, land) is a basic human need. When societies do not develop the legal, organizational, and economic underpinnings to help people acquire land and conclusively document the exclusive right to ownership, people still find ways of procuring, investing in, and holding onto land. Unfortunately, whereas land acquisition can and does take place with varying degrees of legality, the acquired property (including the value of any investment to improve that property) often becomes a locked asset. The asset cannot be transferred to

Table 5.5 Loan Security Approach for Eight Housing Microfinance Providers

Institution	Product Type	Land Ownership Requirement	Guarantee
Calpia	Stand-alone	Yes	Mortgage on 59% of housing loans
FUNHAVI	Stand-alone	No	2 cosigners
CHF/Gaza	Stand-alone	Yes	2 cosigners
Genesis	Stand-alone	Yes (one member of group)	Group guarantee and land title
BancoSol	Stand-alone	Yes	Mortgage and ownership title
CARD	Linked	Yes	5 cosigners; borrower's savings
Grameen	Linked	Yes	5 cosigners; center guarantee; borrower's savings
SEWA	Linked	No	2 cosigners; borrower's savings

Source: IFC, HIID, Daphnis/CHF MFT Course Survey

another party or used to secure a loan from a regulated financial institution because no formal documentation exists to prove ownership. Some economists, including most notably Hernando de Soto (1989, 2000), argue that the lack of documented land tenure and the resulting lock on the asset is a major factor explaining economic underdevelopment.

In an ideal world, housing microfinance clients would live on land that is properly registered, they would pay taxes, and they would be able to enjoy a full range of services resulting from legal ownership. In the real world where housing microfinance thrives, this is usually far from the norm. Land-related issues constitute one of the principal unknowns that microenterprise-lending institutions face when they expand into housing finance. Similarly, the lack of land tenure has long been a source of frustration and a major impediment to scaling up existing services for housing finance institutions that target the poor.

In the specific context of product design, land issues affect housing microfinance from a legal and from a risk standpoint. On the legal side, MFIs must determine whether they are able lend to a client without incontrovertible evidence that the client has a legal right to occupy the land. If relevant regulations stipulate that housing loans may not be extended without formal property titles, MFIs will not be legally able to develop a housing loan.[12] In these cases, interested MFIs can still develop a multipurpose consumer loan and tailor the loan amount and the repayment period to the desired level. ADEMI, for instance, currently offers such a loan— but it is not able to classify it formally as a housing product or track its true impact, as clients are free to use the money for purposes other than housing. If regulations do not explicitly require a link between loan eligibility and evidence of titling, MFIs have greater flexibility in addressing the land tenure issue. In such cases, the financial (repayment) risk MFIs associate with varying levels of land ownership—a function of the MFI's analysis of client land security status, as opposed to their land tenure status— should influence the MFI decision to finance a loan.

For housing microfinance, a client enjoys land security when the following conditions exist: (1) she has the use of a property at the time the loan application is made; (2) the MFI determines that the client will not be forced to vacate the property during the time it takes to repay the loan; and (3) that determination is supported by usual and customary local practices (Daphnis and Tilock 2001,

17). In other words, in the absence of legal proof of ownership, the MFI should satisfy itself that potential clients would not be forcibly evicted while the loan is still active. The underlying assumption is that repayment performance will be enhanced if the client has a vested long-term interest in the property being financed.

Criteria for land security should vary from country to country—and perhaps within a given country, from MFI to MFI, based on the MFI's attitude toward risk. Some of these criteria include:

- A written agreement between the buyer and seller of the land;
- A long-term rental agreement between the home owner and government for use of public lands;
- The number of years during which a family has inhabited a property without paying rent and without due notice from the rightful owner; or
- Payment by the home owner of taxes to the government (Daphnis and Tilock 2001, 17)

In addition to tenure, another important land-related risk factor the MFI should consider is whether the property can serve as collateral for the loan. In many countries, housing loans carry lower interest rates than business loans because the value of the property serves as an actionable guarantee against a potential delinquent loan. The guarantee can be close to the assessed value of the property in the case of a home mortgage loan. It can also be equivalent to the assessed value of the property, clear of existing liens, for home equity loans. For housing microfinance, however, using the property as collateral can be problematic for several reasons. If land tenure is uncertain or foreclosure laws are not well developed, it may be difficult for the MFI to foreclose on the property should a client default on a loan. Even when local laws allow the MFI to take over the property of a delinquent client, other barriers may prevent the MFI from finding a new owner for that property. A formal real estate market may not exist, thus, not allowing for accurate valuation of the property; potential buyers may not have the financial resources (savings or financing) to purchase the property at the agreed-upon value. Assuming all these barriers can be overcome, the MFI must decide whether it wants to be involved in the business of taking over and selling real estate—a new line of business for enterprise-focused MFIs. An equally important issue is that of the relationship between the value of the collateral and the value of the loan itself. In most cases, a housing microfinance loan amount will be far less than the combined value of the home and the land. It is not a given that clients will be willing to mortgage their entire property for a loan that may be worth a fifth (or less) of the value of that property.

In the end, MFIs must decide for themselves whether the property (including the land) is an adequate guarantee for a housing microfinance loan. When the value of the loan approximates the value of the property, or when the relevant laws allow for foreclosure on and resale of that property, or when a real estate market actually exists for the type of property, this may be a viable option. In most other cases, collateral substitutes or nonproperty types of collateral are more realistic options.

OTHER ISSUES IN HOUSING
MICROFINANCE LOAN DESIGN

MFIs offering housing microfinance should understand what impact the new service will have on their institution's capital adequacy. Capital adequacy refers to the credit risk associated with the types of financial assets an institution holds at a given time (for instance, cash, business loans to the private sector, mortgage loans to households, and government securities). In 1988, the Basle Committee on Banking Supervision Commission established guidelines for assessing capital adequacy, specifying that these guidelines were "mainly directed toward assessing capital in relation to credit risk." The Basle Agreement's goal was to standardize supervisory regulation governing the capital adequacy of international banks. The guidelines it set forth have been adopted in more than 100 countries and have become the standard by which formal banks and their regulators determine whether a bank's capital and assets compositions are acceptable from a credit risk standpoint.[13]

The Basle Accord called for a weighted risk ratio "in which capital is related to different categories of asset or off-balance-sheet exposure, weighed according to broad categories of relative riskiness." The Accord established five broad categories of assets and exposures, and assigned risk weights of 0, 10, 20, 50, and 100 percent; a 0 percent risk weigh would indicate the lowest possible level of risk, and 100 percent a very high level of risk. For instance, cash and claims on OECD governments and central banks were assigned a risk weighting of 0 percent. Conversely, claims on the private sector and on companies owned by the private sector were assigned a risk weighting of 100 percent. As a general rule, a Basle risk-weighted capital adequacy ratio of 8 percent is considered the appropriate standard.

The Basle Accord specifically assigns a risk weighting to secured housing loans. Loans fully secured by mortgage on residential property that is or will be occupied or rented by the borrower carry a 50 percent weighting. Thus, the Basle Agreement considers mortgage loans or loans that tap into a residential home's equity as less risky than business loans to the private sector. The assumption is that financial institutions can always recuperate the value of a housing loan by taking over and selling the residence in case of default. In OECD countries and countries with working foreclosure laws and vibrant residential real estate markets, a sizable portfolio of secured housing loans can help the overall capital adequacy of a financial institution. For many countries in which MFIs currently offer housing microfinance loans, however, the situation is more complicated. As discussed previously, housing microfinance loans cannot always be guaranteed by the value of the property. In many cases, loan security comes under the form of collateral substitutes (such as cosigners) or nonproperty types of collateral. Practical problems related to land tenure, foreclosure, or home resale make it unlikely that the 50 percent risk weight would apply, even in cases where the property is attached as collateral. Further, while the Basle Agreement may be suitable for banks and other formally regulated financial institutions, its provisions do not reliably transfer to the typical microfinance institution. As noted by the CGAP, "unlike commercial banking with its Basle standards, the microfinance industry does not have widely agreed performance standards" (CGAP's Financial Transparency: A Glossary of Terms, 3).

In cases where a housing microfinance loan is adequately secured by the value of a property, it is reasonable to assume that the loan should carry a risk that is much lower than that of an unsecured individual business loan. In cases where such a guarantee is not present, a reasonable expectation is that regulators will regard a housing microfinance loan as having an impact on capital adequacy roughly comparable to that of an individual microenterprise loan—that is, regulators will view housing loans as unsecured.

CONCLUSION

Housing microfinance is emerging as an important tool in the struggle to help alleviate the housing needs of poor people around the world. It is also becoming a standard product for many MFIs in Latin America, Asia, the Middle East, and Eastern Europe. At present, its most useful and widespread application consists of a series of incremental loans allowing poor households to build according to established microfinance strategies. MFIs interested in offering housing services to their clients must carefully assess whether they have the administrative and technical capacity to do so. They should also ensure that housing microfinance fits their strategy from an institutional and financial perspective (liquidity, opportunity cost of capital, and interproduct competition).

Housing microfinance is finding its place as an attractive and practical alternative to traditional housing finance and an economically viable complement to more established microfinance services. In most cases, MFIs and housing finance providers should be able to provide housing microfinance services that are affordable to their clients and financially sound from an institutional perspective. Successful strategies from practitioners suggest that such services build on the lessons of the recent microfinance revolution and adapt these lessons to housing lending. Pricing, loan maturity, affordability analyses, pre-loan due diligence, and post-loan financial follow-up closely reflect accepted best practice for microfinance individual lending. Strategies for land security and construction assistance capitalize on decades of work in affordable housing finance. Finally, emerging approaches to land security (as a factor in the overall credit analysis) appear to be uniquely suited to the specifics needs of housing microfinance.

NOTES

1. Including notably the experience of PLAN International. PLAN conducted nine such studies around the world with CHF's help between 1996 and 1999.

2. PLAN International is a nonprofit organization that solicits funds from the general public, most notably in Holland and in America, in order to provide for the needs of very poor children around the world. The housing finance surveys were conducted by PLAN International with technical help from CHF International between 1995 and 1999.

3. As much as 20 percent of MFI business lending goes de facto for housing, according to an estimate by Ferguson and Haider (2000). SEWA Bank estimates that more than 40 percent of its business loans were used for housing before it started offering a specific housing product in the mid-1970s.

4. Genesis in Guatemala, BancoSol in Bolivia, SEWA Bank in India, and FUNHAVI in Mexico, for example, all fall within that range.

5. This paragraph is adapted from Daphnis (see chapter 1) and Daphnis and Tilock 2001.

6. Available from the Consultative Group to Assist the Poorest (CGAP) at www.cgap.org.

7. As FUNHAVI, for example, currently does.

8. In other words, this represents the amount owned by the provider that exceeds what the provider owes to outside parties as loans or client deposits.

9. From notes distributed as part of the Housing Microfinance Course, Microfinance Training Program, July 2000 and 2001. Also based on Daphnis and Tilock 2001.

10. Even though FUNHAVI has phased out parts of its originally extensive construction assistance program starting in 2001.

11. Pedro Gimenez of ADEMI Bank advanced this argument during the June 2000 IADB conference on the microfinance of housing.

12. This is the case in the Dominican Republic, for example.

13. The original Basle Accord has been amended several times since 1988. Currently, the Accord proposes three pillars as a part of its capital adequacy framework: (1) minimum regulatory capital requirements; (2) supervisory review; and (3) market discipline. Also see www.dis.com.

6

Construction Assistance
and Housing Microfinance

Kimberly Tilock

W hether or not to offer a construction assistance service to their clients is one of the key issues many microfinance institutions (MFIs) face when they first develop a housing loan. From a strictly financial perspective, many microenterprise lenders argue that construction assistance is not essential to client eligibility or repayment performance on a loan; they, thus, tend to see such assistance as superfluous and outside their scope and expertise. Other potential reasons for not providing construction assistance include a presumption that MFIs know what is best for the client—a proposition many MFIs dispute—and the possibility that construction assistance subjects the MFI to unnecessary liability (in cases of unsound construction, for instance). As many MFIs subscribe to the industry motto "money is fungible," they tend to perceive any assistance focusing on monitoring loan use to be costly and indeterminate.

At the same time, many MFIs around the world have come to consider construction assistance as an integral component of housing microfinance. Frequently cited benefits include reduced credit risk to the MFI and improved construction quality for the client.

This chapter explores the potential benefits of construction assistance to housing microfinance programs, including why it should be provided, the different forms of assistance, and how construction assistance can be provided.[1] The purpose of the chapter is descriptive rather than prescriptive: it does not argue for or against providing construction assistance nor does it support one type of assistance over another. Rather, it seeks to shed a

useful light on the reasons why some institutions choose to provide construction assistance and to explain the possible forms
such assistance can assume.

RATIONALE FOR
CONSTRUCTION ASSISTANCE

Construction assistance adds to the credit delivery costs. Why then
would MFIs provide such assistance as part of their housing microfinance product? The main reasons tend to include risk management, institutional reputation, client satisfaction, mission, and, to
a lesser degree, donor requirements.

Risk Management

In traditional housing finance, particularly in developed economies, lenders rely on external expertise, including architects,
bonded construction labor, government authorities, and construction codes, to ensure construction quality. MFIs, on the other
hand, tend to work in environments where clients cannot afford
such assistance or, in the case of bonded construction labor and
government oversight, it does not exist.

   Without external assistance and oversight, MFI clients are on
their own in managing their home construction. While clients
know what kind of house they would like to have, they often do
not know how to develop a construction budget that will cover the
full cost of the improvement, particularly for larger projects, or
how to map out a series of improvements that are logical, structurally sound, and affordable. Likewise, they often do not know
how to manage a construction project that calls for contracting
labor, determining types and quantities of materials needed, finding materials suppliers at reasonable costs, and ensuring construction quality. This lack of expertise, along with limited financial
resources, typically leads poor families to focus on the cheapest,
most available fix rather than on improvements that are part of a
long-term housing development plan. It also can increase the
default risk for the MFI financing the improvement. If the construction budget is not enough to cover the cost of the intended
improvement, a client may seek additional funding from other
sources. If a house is not well constructed, the client may be less
willing to pay or return for another loan.

Construction assistance can also help a client map out her desired improvements over several incremental steps, creating a long-term goal with a clear plan of how to achieve it. Once a client has a plan that shows how a series of housing investments will achieve her long-term vision, many MFIs believe that she is likely to have greater incentive to repay her current loan and borrow again. Construction assistance can also help ensure that a loan provides resources sufficient to complete the intended work rather than, for instance, leaving a room partially uncovered or with walls that are not sturdy enough. Construction assistance can provide clients with a basic understanding of the construction process so that they can negotiate with and manage contracted labor and select appropriate materials to help prevent cost over-runs or poor construction quality. It can also help ensure overall structural integrity, such that a new roof is able to support a second story or will not be lifted off during a hurricane.

Institutional Reputation and Client Satisfaction

Housing microfinance produces physical structures that people often identify with the financing institution. Thus, the quality of the improvements financed by the MFI can have marketing and institutional image implications that microenterprise lending does not. While the failure of a client's business may not have an impact on an MFI's reputation, a highly visible, poorly constructed home could have a very negative effect. Likewise—many MFIs[2] believe—a client who is happy with the result of a home improvement is more likely to take another loan and to tell others about the housing loan. According to that logic, the client's neighbors, seeing her improved living conditions, are more likely to take loans to improve their homes. In a competitive environment, construction assistance can be what distinguishes an MFI from other lenders.

Organizational Mission

Some housing microfinance providers (often those with a housing or humanitarian background) emphasize providing affordable quality housing for the poor alongside or over institutional sustainability or loan portfolio quality. These institutions tend to place a strong emphasis on construction quality for reasons other than reputation, and, thus, typically provide extensive construction assistance. Many of these institutions (Habitat for Humanity is one notable example) subsidize construction assistance through resources external to the housing finance component.

TYPES OF TECHNICAL ASSISTANCE

Construction assistance tends to fall within two main categories: pre-loan assistance and post-loan assistance.[3] Pre-loan assistance is a component of the loan assessment process. In other words, it is part of the necessary due diligence to ensure repayment. Post-loan assistance tends to focus on compliance and construction quality.

Pre-Loan Assistance

Construction design. Construction design assistance involves visiting the house to be improved, taking measurements, and sketching out the existing structure and proposed improvements. This can involve developing a simple design for the proposed improvement or working with clients to help determine and map out their needs and aspirations for their home. The design can be used as a basis for the construction budget and should ensure that the proposed improvement is technically sound. The mapping process can help orient clients to what is feasible, given their repayment capacity and existing home, while providing the MFI with an understanding of the needs and aspirations of its clientele. The design can also be used as guide for the builders.

Budget development. This can range from assessing a budget provided by the client to ensure that the proposed cost estimates are reasonable, feasible, and in line with the client's repayment capacity to developing the actual construction budget including pricing the different inputs. Budget development assistance helps verify that loan amounts that are affordable to a client are also sufficient to result in her intended objective, thus, maximizing client satisfaction with the overall outcome of her relationship with the MFI and helping to ensure loan repayment.

Client education. Many MFI clients undertake the actual housing construction themselves but lack construction expertise. As a result they often benefit from specialized assistance to help them with the construction process. This can include guidance on what materials to use and where to purchase them, construction labor including recommended contractors, guidance on how to negotiate contracts and manage the construction process, and training on self-help construction, which can considerably lower the cost of the improvement and in turn the loan amount. FUNHAVI (Foundation for Habitat and Housing) in Ciudad Juarez, Mexico provides its clients with a simple pamphlet that outlines basic construction procedures and costs and that provides a list of recommended masons and other construction workers.

Post-Loan Assistance

Construction follow-up. This assistance is generally used to verify loan use, inspect work quality, and provide advice to the client or contractor. In addition, it can be used to represent the client's interests with contractors and material providers. This type of assistance is typically provided during the construction stage through site visits. In some cases a final visit is conducted to certify completion of the construction project. Generally MFIs make one to two visits during the construction process, but some undertake more. Genesis in Guatemala, for example, conducts four site visits—one preconstruction visit, two visits during the construction period and a postconstruction visit to verify construction completion. As an additional quality control mechanism, some institutions disburse loan proceeds in installments based on predetermined criteria—for instance, if the initial disbursement proves insufficient to purchase all the materials necessary for the construction. A site visit is typically conducted soon after the disbursement to verify the material purchase and, if the loan funds were used as prescribed, authorize the next installment. This level of intervention is used to monitor and control loan use. PLAN International, which uses construction completion as one of the measures of success of its housing microfinance programs, used this method of disbursement and verification in its housing microfinance program in Guayaquil, Ecuador.[4] This level of assistance comes at significant cost for most MFIs yet is one that results in nearly 100 percent compliance with the construction components of the planned investments.

Construction materials. Another form of construction assistance occurs when the MFI either procures the construction materials itself or provides access to such materials at lower cost. This mechanism can help prevent loan diversion and ensure the use of low-cost, quality materials. The Grameen Bank, for example, has developed standard plans for homes with standard material lists and costs to help define loan amounts for housing investments. Loans are disbursed in the form of a materials package to the client according to these lists and in some cases cash is also provided to pay for skilled labor. In this scenario, the MFI has made an investment in technical assistance at the front end and achieves certain economies of scale if one accepts the more standardized solutions it provides. In other cases, the MFI arranges for the client to purchase the necessary materials through vouchers or through prepaid arrangements from a local provider. FUNHAVI purchases certain construction materials wholesale and retails the materials to its clients at both a profit to itself and cost savings to its clients. It is able to do so because of explicit arrangements with material manufacturers in the region. This approach helps ensure that clients use quality materials, guarantees costs for budgeting purposes, and raises funds to help cover program operation costs. Material distribution assistance generally requires administrative systems, procurement expertise, warehousing capacity, even sometimes manufacturing capabilities, which may be beyond the scope and capability of many MFIs. However, examples exist to show that, under certain conditions, these approaches can enhance rather than detract from an institution's sustainability and can help lower a client's construction costs.[5]

These different types of construction assistance can be blended and modified in a number of ways. At one end of the spectrum, some MFIs tend to provide pre- and post-loan assistance including multiple disbursements in the interest of controlling loan use. This approach to construction assistance is expensive and intensive but results in a high degree of construction completion and although not verified, presumably higher quality construction. Many institutions that provide this level of assistance rely on subsidies to cover the associated costs. At the other end of the spectrum some MFIs rely solely on a cursory review of material lists and, in some cases, simple construction drawings to establish loan amounts and purposes. The needed level of involvement of an institution is more consistent with commonly used due diligence approaches such as cash flow analysis of existing businesses to evaluate creditworthiness.

CONSTRUCTION ASSISTANCE
STAFFING CONSIDERATIONS

Construction assistance for housing microfinance, even at minimal levels, may require a potentially different staff profile than what is required for other credit products. While architecture, engineering, and other qualified construction professional expertise is generally needed, this does not necessarily mean a doubling of staff. In the case of most CHF International (CHF) housing microfinance programs there is one technical person for every two loan officers. Many organizations have combined the role of loan officer with the technical knowledge and skills required to evaluate construction plans and budgets. In the case of CHF's housing finance operation in Gaza, engineers and architects have taken on the responsibilities normally associated with a loan officer in terms of evaluating not only the repayment capacity of the potential client but also the technical strength of the proposed construction. FADES in southern Bolivia attempted to implement its construction assistance component by combining the roles of loan officer and technical adviser with adequate results in terms of credit performance but with less than conclusive evidence that construction quality or completion rates were enhanced. Alternatively this assistance can be contracted out to individuals or institutions with greater construction knowledge. FUNHAVI, for example, contracts a certified architect to review the construction budgets and plans developed by its technical staff. While the MFI views this level of review critical to its loan assessment process, the amount of work was not sufficient to maintain this level of expertise in-house.

CONCLUSION

Whether or not MFIs should offer construction assistance to clients has emerged as a somewhat controversial issue in housing microfinance. Many MFIs do not see it as a part of their housing strategy. As discussed in Chapter 5, when MFIs offer no form of construction assistance, the loan is, in effect, a consumer loan. Its declared purpose is housing but the ultimate use is up to the client. The proposed construction project provides a rationale for estimating a required loan amount and calling the loan a housing loan may help the MFI market the new product to its clients. Still, many microfinance providers do incorporate construction assistance in the design of their housing microfinance loans. While perhaps not essential to the delivery of the financial service, construction assistance can help an MFI in mitigating credit risks and improving construction quality. It can also help MFIs build long-term relationships with clients and increase customer satisfaction. Construction assistance may also serve to differentiate the MFI in the marketplace, giving the institution a competitive edge over other products offered.

As currently provided, construction assistance spans a range of pre- and post-loan services, from budget assessment and construction plan design to construction oversight, that can be blended to suit what the provider can offer and what the client demands. Ultimately and in order to justify the added cost, construction assistance should not only help an MFI ensure construction quality and control the use of its loan funds, it should also provide real added value to the client's investment. Many MFIs with housing services currently enjoy a monopoly in the communities where they work and, thus, do not have to pay a price for their failure to include a necessary construction assistance service or for their willingness to provide one that is not particularly valuable to clients. As competition inevitably sets in, however, construction assistance services that fail to meet the value-added criteria are likely to become casualties of the marketplace, as clients seek out the loan products that maximize their value to price ratio.

NOTES

1. This chapter draws on the work of Holsten (Technical Assistance in the Provision of Housing Microfinance, September 2001, unpublished) and Buchenau (Housing Know-How and Housing Microfinance, October 2002, unpublished).

2. Including, for instance, CHF International and FUNHAVI in Mexico.

3. See Franck Daphnis (chapter 5) for an additional discussion of the types of construction assistance.

4. See Holsten 2001 (unpublished).

5. See Holsten 2001.

7

Land and Collateral Issues:
The Asset Dimension of
Housing Microfinance

Irene Vance

Within the microfinance community, the asset dimension of housing finance, land, and collateral is among the least understood constraints in developing financially viable housing microfinance services. The nature of housing microfinance (relatively small loans with a short repayment period marketed to economically active poor people) effectively means that land and collateral strategies associated with mortgage financing do not provide a useful way forward. Conventional mortgage lenders typically will not issue a mortgage loan unless the property being financed is legally registered and can provide adequate collateral in case of default. But clients of housing microfinance institutions often are not able to produce a legally documented title deed for the land on which their property is built. As Daphnis has observed (see chapter 5) even when poor households can produce satisfactory proof of land ownership, inadequate foreclosure laws, contrary social practice, and the absence of a vibrant market for property resale can decrease the value of real estate as collateral in the context of housing microfinance. Further, Daphnis and Tilock also make a client-focused financial argument that is not without merit: "[p]lacing a lien on a property for a minimal loan amount also would over-collateralize the loan and underutilize the borrower's financial asset, thereby putting an undue burden on a borrower" (2001, 14).

The asset dimension of housing microfinance, thus, contributes to an already challenging business environment both for institutions interested in expanding the range of services they provide to existing clientele (in the case of microenterprise lenders interested in housing) as well as for institutions interested in providing an existing service to new clientele (in the case of traditional housing lenders interested in microfinance). The debate surrounding land issues and the effectiveness of land and property as adequate means of securing a loan is mostly foreign to the former, while only aspects of it will be familiar to institutions rooted in the latter tradition.

This chapter describes how microfinance institutions are addressing the challenges and obstacles that face low- and moderate-income families in accessing housing finance when land title cannot serve as part of the collateral for a housing loan. The first section provides an overview of land issues and examines some of the constraints related to land availability, security, and tenure. The second section describes the types of collateral or collateral substitutes microfinance institutions currently require for their housing products when the property itself cannot serve as collateral. Drawing on examples from existing literature and case studies mainly from Latin America,[1] it analyzes and compares these alternative forms. This paper also argues that microfinance can be used for land acquisition and titling. The chapter also addresses two core questions:

1. How are microfinance institutions dealing with the issue of land tenure, given that in many contexts, low-income households do not enjoy full property rights?
2. What other collateral or collateral substitutes are being used and what lessons are to be learned from current practice?

A key finding from the review of country experiences shows that cost recovery rates on unsecured loans with flexible or multiple guarantees are as good as, or even better than, mortgaged loans. More detailed research may be needed to thoroughly substantiate this observation, but preliminary findings suggest that the title deed as collateral for loans may be overstated, a proposition that has important implications for extending housing options to the low-income population.

LAND

More than a billion people around the world live in inadequate shelter without access to piped water, electricity, roads, or long-term security. Up to 60 percent of the world's residents live in illegal settlements and 100 million are homeless.[2]

Latin America is the most urbanized region; three-quarters of its total population now live in cities (UNCHS 2000). One of the features of urban growth is the scale and persistence of illegal, irregular occupancy due to the insufficient supply of serviced land at affordable prices.

In many countries land is generally controlled by the state or concentrated in the hands of large landowners. However, due to the rapid expansion of cities, state ownership of land is dwindling. Furthermore, government's inability to regulate land markets and a reluctance to confront issues of land speculation and concentration has delayed the implementation of coherent urban development plans.

For the majority of the poor, options for shelter are limited to settlement on marginal and environmentally high-risk areas, invasion of private or publicly owned land, or renting in slums often without formal rental contracts. As a result, informal housing is on the increase.[3] In Lima, more than 40 percent of the population now lives in illegal settlements; in Quito this number has reached 50 percent. In Brazil's major cities some 20 to 50 percent of the population lives in favelas or urban slums (UNCHS 2000).

Another major obstacle in accessing land is related to costly and complex land registration procedures (Ward 1998). Virtually all countries that recognize some private rights to land have a complex set of laws, customs, and practices not necessarily written down that govern land transfer (McAuslan 1985). Many of these are based on colonial legal codes. These complicated and unduly cumbersome procedures are often not well understood by the poor, are time consuming, and are prohibitively costly.

In addition, unrealistically high standards required for subdivision, infrastructure, and construction inhibits legal low-income housing construction. The costs incurred in conforming to planning and building regulations, and the time required in following administrative procedures for obtaining official permits, prices the housing units out of the low-income market.

Data from cities in developing economies show that the processes of obtaining construction and occupancy permits underscore this complexity. De Soto, in *The Other Path* (1989), describes the labyrinth of regulations and permits required to build a house in Lima, Peru. The regulations have created one of the largest rates of informality, and families routinely ignore or pay to avoid the regulations. In his subsequent work, *The Mystery of Capital* (2000), de Soto presents additional compelling data on the legal impediments in Egypt, Haiti, Mexico, and the Philippines. Building a legal home in Egypt on agricultural land can take six to eleven years. In Haiti, there are some 176 steps to make a legal purchase. This impenetrable wall of rules means that the poor cannot transform their property into capitalized assets. The untitled land is "dead capital."

Obtaining a building permit in Mexico can take eight to ten months. To buy a low-cost home can involve 117 bureaucratic hurdles. Until recently local authorities charged developers excessively high and fixed fees regardless of the type of housing. Thus, low-income households paid proportionally more to cover the cost of fees. This, together with the down payment requirements, pushed low-income families to the informal market (Shidlo 1994). Since the early 1990s these high regulatory costs, which added as much as 35 percent to the cost of a house, have been recognized as a major bottleneck. Specific targets for lowering and standardizing regulatory charges and permit times were adopted at the state level. These mechanisms included the reduction of direct and indirect local costs, legal fees for social housing, and the creation of *ventanillas unicas* (single offices) for rapid approval of construction permits, and have resulted in a significant reduction in waiting periods for a building permit (Shidlo 1994).

As a result of the complexity of the procedures, and the failure of statutory tenure systems to meet the needs of lower-income groups, research in fifteen countries shows that in most cities urban tenure systems operate under a diverse combination of traditional, statutory, and nonstatutory or customary codes. (Balamir and Payne 2001). Many land tenure systems derive from Western codes. In countries as diverse as India, Cyprus, Vanuatu, and Belize in Central America, the English land tenure system prevails. However in India administrators are reluctant to enforce land use control because of the persistence of traditional beliefs about land use. Customary land tenure persists or coexists with colonial codes and, in some countries, land transfer is of such importance that the rules surrounding it form part of the constitution (McAuslan 1985, 27–31).

Tenure and Land Security

A clarification on terminology is warranted when it comes to a discussion of land tenure and land security. Freehold title secures ultimate control over the land to its owner. It permits the owner to improve, sell, or use it as collateral or mortgage. It may be transferred or bequeathed by the owner. Conventional lenders and banks favor individual freehold title.

Land security, on the other hand, is a de facto arrangement allowing an individual or a group of individuals to use land and residential property in a manner that precludes losing that land or property for a foreseeable period. In the context of microfinance, land security, according to Daphnis and Tilock (2001), is the right to use property, assurance that the user will not be forced to vacate the property, and evidence that usual and customary local practices support this assurance.

Tenure can be effected in a variety of ways, depending on constitutional and legal frameworks, social norms, cultural values and, to some extent, individual preference. A household has secure tenure when it is protected from involuntary removal from the land or residence, except in exceptional circumstances, and then only by means of a known and agreed-upon legal procedure, which must itself be objective, equally applicable, contestable, and independent (UNCHS 1996, 4).

In Latin America within the general trend of democratization and decentralization there is a growing shift toward land reform, the general direction of which has been to revise old systems of state-managed land, confiscation, and redistribution (Smolka and Mullahy 2000). Communal or state-owned land has been redistributed although in some contexts such as Nicaragua, there is a tendency toward reconcentration. Land titling initiatives that seek to encourage land registration and the use of land as collateral in credit transactions are increasing.

Security of tenure, regularization, and urban upgrading programs have become accepted practice by governments. These are supported by bilateral and multilateral donor agencies and NGOs as they recognize the links between property formalization, economic development, and poverty alleviation.[4]

Emerging Approaches to Land Regularization for the Poor

A variety of emerging approaches to land regularization are being adopted. One of the main approaches is juridical regularization, which emphasizes holding of rights and, thus, converting the de facto to de jure land entitlement, such as the land titling programs of Peru and Ecuador. The second approach is physical regularization. This is more concerned with the use of the land and its resources, hence, the formalization package including the provision of infrastructure, such as in the cases of Colombia, Brazil, El Salvador, and Venezuela. A third component encompasses a broader social integration perspective with community management and civic participation as explicit goals fostering citizens' rights and obligations as consumers and taxpayers.

Given the variety of country contexts, assessing the impact and effectiveness of titling programs is difficult; still, despite some successes, a number of political and practical obstacles have emerged. On the whole most programs have been lengthy and expensive. Even when formal titles have been issued and registered, many of the property rights soon revert to informality as subsequent titles and transfers from inheritances are not documented in the registry (Palmer and McLaughlin 2002, 1).

In Mexico, since 1992, national reforms have allowed for the privatization of land held under the *ejido* or communal ownership system. A land-titling program was created to assign certification titles to ejidatarios. In practice only a small proportion of the certification titles have been transformed into private property titles.[5] The low rate of final titling is attributed to multiple factors including fear of increase in taxes, lack of perceived benefits particularly in areas where the land has only marginal economic value, loss of privileges, and the assurances associated with communal ownership (Enterprise Research Institute 1997).

In urban contexts, settlements most likely to be regularized are those on public land where ownership is uncontested. Where land has previous owners, the resolution of disputes and arbitration of assessing the value of title is more complicated. This has been the case in Peru where the greatest success has been titling in the *pueblos jovenes* on the urban fringe. Titling land nearer to the urban centers of Lima has met with resistance.

Peru is, nonetheless, considered to be one of the most interesting and successful examples of granting titles to informal property owners. The efforts made by the Peruvian government in land titling of marginal settlements have undoubtedly overcome some of the critical challenges in land regularization from a number of standpoints. Institutional reform together with the simplification of procedures plus processing supported by community participation have yielded a cost-effective and efficient processing of impressive numbers of titles for the residents of marginal settlements. The provision of title is an important goal per se in formalizing previously irregular settlements and building up the assets of low-income families. As shown below, the Peruvian experience has met with favorable government support, and land title has fostered the flow of mortgage-backed finance for investment in shelter upgrading. Nonetheless given the depth of reforms, the time and cost implications in land titling in the Peruvian case, like other examples, raises the question as to whether titling is a fundamental prerequisite for increasing housing finance.

Beginning in the 1950s, as migration to urban areas increased dramatically, successive Peruvian governments have tolerated squatter settlements on unserviced land on the urban fringe of Lima. Thus, there were favorable conditions since land was already in private hands. The role of the government was simply to formalize ownership. Although the residents lacked formal recognition of their property these *pueblos jovenes* have well-defined planning structures managed by the resident committees with elected local leaders, who were in charge of the community development process, building schools, community centers and roads, and lobbying for the provision of services. The community managed land through a rudimentary register, which recorded property holders (Turner 1963, Lloyd 1980, de Soto 1989).

The first attempts to legalize existing settlements began in the 1960s. The formalization process was costly, complex, and time consuming (Turner 1967, Lloyd 1980, de Soto 1989). Applications could take up to twenty years, and titles were often unregistered. In the 1980s, a comprehensive reform of a wide array of laws and regulations was implemented. Another round of reform took place in the early 1990s, reengineering the Public Registry using simple low-cost technology together with legal reform, particularly in the role of public notaries. Between 1990 and 1991, 400,000 properties were registered, which accounts for 20 percent of informal holdings (Enterprise Research Institute 1997). Community participation enhanced the process of collecting information efficiently, since community members had the opportunity to scrutinize claims made by others, helping to reconcile discrepancies.

Pilot titling began in 1993, however, in 1994 a weakness in the process was that the registry held information only on the size and location of the plots. Omission of the property owners' names was recognized as an obstacle to lending to borrowers. In 1996 the government[6] embarked on an intensive land titling and registration program, supported by private sector institutions, for example, Banco Orion, and the municipality of Lima. It is estimated that more than one million titles have been issued to date.

In addition to titling services, the goal was to create a better system to evaluate credit and ability to pay, which would facilitate mortgage-based credit. The process included more accurate information on potential borrowers, including default information and technical assistance for housing construction. The reforms have reduced the costs of registering formal transactions such as mortgages and property transfers, eliminating the costly requirements of transfer-like certificates from municipalities. The computerized information allows ownership information and transfers to be made swiftly. The registration process has been reduced to a one-step procedure where the household completes one form and a pays a single fee of just over $10. The process can be completed in seven days. In addition to simplifying registration procedures, and reducing their costs, the reforms envisaged an increase in the level of security for lenders providing loans secured by mortgages.

Have titling programs lead to greater access to mortgages? There is evidence, from the Peruvian case and other experiences, that titling does result in more mortgages. According to Palmer and McLaughlin (2002, 9) more than thirty-seven commercial, state, and NGOs have extended credit secured by mortgages registered in the Urban Property Registry. By 1996, Banco Orion had reached more than 20,000 low- to moderate-incomes families who had received new titles, with loans ranging between $650 and $1,000 (Brown and Garcia 2001). The Orion program was one of the first institutions to lend with the new titles as proof of ownership. It is less clear, however, if the titles serve as true collateral or whether the additional information they provide reduces risks and transactions costs. This is an interesting question since the Orion bank also continued to use other types of guarantees, including cosigners and household assets. Credit is often given in small amounts and for short periods, and it would seem that the person's ability to repay the loan is as much a factor as any collateral offered.

However, given that the experience of titling has been lengthy and costly, there is a growing consensus that individual titling is not always the best answer for a more efficient use of the land (Ward 1998). The need to legitimize alternative forms of tenure, enabling the poor to access and establish rights of possession and remain on land in areas that would otherwise not be affordable or available, have been recognized. These often innovative forms, including collective ownership, have increased security without necessarily providing full title.

Some examples will illustrate the variety of and current situation regarding the status of land and land markets. In Colombia legislation entitles all citizens the right to obtain basic services. Local governments are required to invest in social housing and infrastructure in underserviced neighborhoods. A range of tenure rights such as declaration of possession, purchase documents, and communal tenancy provide increased security from evictions and enable them to receive all essential services.

In India, for example, in Hyderabad, government agencies have provided a degree of tenure security to poor households through the Slum Networking Program, which grants residents of unauthorized settlements ten-year licenses to their land, which has provided reasonably good security of tenure, enabling them to improve both their houses and the local environment. Nonetheless, in other Indian cities, the short-term right to occupancy afforded by such policies has been undermined or overturned by court orders, followed by large-scale evictions.

Leasehold conveys the right of occupancy of land or property for an established period of time, often as long as ninety-nine years and under a specified set of legal conditions. The leaseholder retains ultimate control over the property, although for the duration of the lease the occupant does enjoy secure tenure. It also is transferable within the leasehold period.

In Brazil the Concession of the Real Right to Use (CRRU) land has been adopted in several cities, notably Port Alegre and Recife, for the regularization of favelas on public land, and selected private areas (Balamir and Payne 2001). The Concession is a form of leasehold and although it does not confer the full transfer of freehold titles, it does provides legal security of tenure through registration in the public registry. It also gives protection from eviction measures during the period stipulated in the title, which varies between thirty and fifty years. The concession can be renewed, bequeathed, or rented out, and the property can be used as collateral.

Since the early 1990s, community land trusts have been introduced in Kenyan cities. This is a combination of communal tenure and individual ownership that was designed to control transfers and reduce speculation. A group holds ownership and individual members hold leases. Experience has shown that the community land trust model has faced some difficulties, both administrative and operative, and since they are not widely understood, commercial banks have been reluctant to provide loans (Balamir and Payne 2001).

Renting is a form of leasehold agreement, signed by the owner and the user, which confers the right to use of a dwelling for a fixed period of time. For low-income families renting is one of the most common forms of tenure but is seldom formalized or regulated in many countries. Agreements are informal, and renters seldom have any recourse to legal advice: it is not uncommon for agreements to be enforced illegally.

Renters typically use a larger proportion of household income on housing expenditures than borrowers who take out a loan. The major obstacle is that few lending institutions today qualify rented property in their eligibility criteria since ownership is the norm. One noteworthy example of reaching out to renters is a HUD- and OPIC-sponsored program for mortgage bonds that would provide loans to low-income buyers in low-income neighborhoods in the Dominican Republic. Data was collected in the informal settlements on renting prices, and the program was designed to enable people to support a mortgage based on monthly payments that matched the renting costs.

Anticretico is a Bolivian form of rental in which the two parties, the owner and the user, make a legal contract. The user pays the owner a lump sum for the property, which confers the right of use of the property for a period of up to two years and is renewable. What distinguishes anticretico from a normal rental agreement is that at the end of the contract period the owner of the property is obliged to pay back the total amount deposited by the user. There are advantages for owner and user; the owner can leverage capital without recourse to borrowing and the user has security and a return on their initial outlay. The *anticretico*, which developed as a response to the rapid growth of informal settlements around the major cities, is now recognized by national legislation.

Leasehold with option to buy is a variation on leasehold, which can be converted to a freehold when the conditions, including the payment of the lease for a period, are honored. In Brazil and Chile, leasing programs operate along the same principles as a mortgage loan. A portion of the rental payment goes toward the down payment and the lender holds the title to the property until the loan is repaid.

Housing Microfinance—Bridging the Gap

In practice, the large majority of the poor produce their own housing. It is an incremental process that draws on their own resources: interfamily reciprocity and nonconventional financing with the help of semiskilled labor from the informal building market. This process can take from ten to twenty years to complete. Typically the household obtains a plot, either through invasion of public or private land, or purchase in the informal land market where a provisional shelter is built. Once a degree of security is obtained and eviction is deemed unlikely, incremental investment takes place. Financial services enable the poor to leverage their initiative, accelerating the process of building their assets.

Housing and land are key assets for the poor, accounting for 60 percent of the total assets owned by low-income families. In addition to its function as a place of shelter, housing is an important productive resource, providing socioeconomic stability as well as a source of assets creation and savings (Moser 1998). It is estimated that between 30 to 60 percent of housing microfinance clients are engaged in some type of home-based microenterprise (Center for Urban Development Studies 2000, USAID 2000).

Microfinance has developed mechanisms to enhance credit to low-income families in the absence of clear land title through flexible underwriting and alternative collateral. The examples selected illustrate this diversity. Microfinance institutions bridge the gap between conventional lending, and microhousing finance has emerged as a powerful tool since it has found cost-effective ways to judge creditworthiness and to enforce repayment on uncollateralized loans (Ferguson 1999, Baumann 2000, McLeod 2000, Erb 2000).

From the borrower or household standpoint, investment will take place if there is reasonable assurance of security. Information from microlending institutions indicates that even when a separate housing loan is not offered, microloans are still used to finance housing construction and improvement as part of the household strategy for generating income and building assets. For example, FIE in Bolivia estimates that 20 percent of its microenterprise loans were being used for housing improvements (Center for Urban Development Studies 2000, USAID 2000).

Different institutions have adopted different approaches in response to land, collateral, and underwriting requirements, depending on the country context. A gamut of providers exist, and the type of products and conditions vary significantly. The three main categories of finance providers are:

- the formal banking sector, which is subject to banking laws and has been relatively unsuccessful in reaching the low-income segment, largely because of its reliance on real estate as collateral[7]
- public programs, and
- microfinance institutions

Within the microfinance a distinction is made between institutions that provide housing loans for housing improvements; new construction, which relies heavily on microfinance methodologies; and NGO housing institutions, which address land accessibility issues and provide multiple services to their clients (Center for Urban Development Studies 2000). The entry point to the services, both financial and nonfinancial, is related to land: acquisition, legalization, infrastructure, and housing. The services can be divided between a minimalist approach, focused on a credit-only approach or on a credit-plus approach. Recently, the trend has been toward partnerships between the finance institutions and the specialized housing NGOs to address both the land and the finance needs of the low- to moderate-income families, in other words a merging of both approaches. Microlenders that previously limited their services to credit only in some cases are adding technical or advisory services. For example Genesis Empresarial in Guatemala, and BancoSol in Bolivia initially did not provide any technical assistance in housing loans but recently have included architects' services to ensure better quality control of construction.

Collateral and Other Types of Guarantees

Collateral is an asset pledged to a lender until the borrower pays back the debt. It can be real estate or personal goods. In a secured transaction, promises to pay are backed by collateral, and in case of default the lender has the right to seize the assets and sell them to pay off the loan (Balkenhol and Schütte 1995).

Collateral protects the lender by making an assessment of risk management, forming part of the qualifying process of potential borrowers, and acting as an incentive for the borrower to respect the repayment obligation. Not all forms of collateral are accepted by lenders and, due to differences in legal systems and local markets, there are considerable variations within and among countries. This is particularly true where property and removable goods are concerned. One common assumption in housing finance is that the land on which property is built will lower the risk for the borrower, but for housing microfinance land as collateral may not be real collateral. Thus, any discussion of collateral must begin with land, however, given the realities, it also must go beyond land as collateral.

Title deed. Experience to date shows that the use of land title as collateral by MFIs remains limited. A survey of the major microfinance institutions shows that less than 25 percent use it.[8] This trend is changing as the well established MFIs are diversifying and adding a wider range of housing products to meet demand. Title deed is increasingly being required in the credit qualification process for larger loan amounts and for new construction or purchase of completed units. In Bolivia, almost all MFIs require ownership and land title as part of their qualifying process for housing loans, especially if the loan amount is near the value of the property. Banco Ademi in the Dominican Republic, CALPIÁ in El Salvador, La Caja de Ahorro y Préstamo Los Andes and BancoSol in Bolivia have added housing loans for purchases and new construction.

Current practice indicates, therefore, that most institutions accept land title but, due to the high transaction costs, prefer to secure loans with a mix of guarantees to supplement weaker paralegal documents. The CHF International (CHF) in Honduras uses personal guarantees and a contract that enables the lender to seize personal assets and retain wages in cases of default.

LOAN SIZE AND TYPE OF GUARANTEE

There is a close link between loan size and the type and quality of collateralization. The main factors in determining the choice of collateral are the transaction costs involved in verifying ownership of assets and valuating them; the ease of enforcement and foreclosure procedures; and the likely sale price.

Studies in a number of country contexts (Fleisig 1997) illustrate how these three factors can impede the use of moveable assets for collateral. In the United States moveable property is widely used as collateral. In contrast, private lenders in developing countries rarely secure loans with moveable property unless the real estate or the goods are physically under the control of the lender. They may make loans, but these are smaller amounts with higher interest rates and shorter maturities.

The rules governing the creation of security interest may be difficult because laws often require a high degree of identification and description of the property pledged as collateral. Fleisig (1997) illustrates the difficulties regarding moveable assets in the Uruguayan legal context, which requires that property be enumerated very specifically to ensure that designated articles pledged are available to be seized in event of nonpayment. This in turn increases the transaction costs due to additional supervision of loans.

Likewise, verification of ownership and prior claims on the security interest can prove difficult due to weaknesses in the public registers. Fleisig (1997) notes the cases of Bolivia and Uruguay where it is extremely difficult to search records for prior claims against collateral.

La Caja de Ahorro y Préstamo Los Andes in Bolivia uses chattel mortgage, mainly on household items, business goods, or cars to lend up to $7,500 to microentrepreneurs and $5,000 to salaried workers. Above those amounts, registered mortgages are required. The cost of the mortgage is $250–$370 and the time needed to process it depends very much on the legal situation. If the land title is up to date, the average time is twenty days; if not, it can take up to three months.

In the United States, repossession and sale of removable goods can be carried out promptly within one to five days. In emerging countries repossession and sale take longer, from several months up to two years, within which time the removable goods will have depreciated in value. La Caja de Los Andes program has not yet had much experience with repossession of property. Most cases have been resolved in common agreement with the client. It takes up to six months to make the claim. After that it is possible to negotiate with the client so that repossession does not take place. Mutual La Primera and Cooperative Jesus Nazareno, two of the most experienced housing microlenders in Bolivia, do not foreclose on property loans under $1,000, given the legal expenses involved.

Thus, with regard to the transaction cost, the loan size usually determines whether and what form of collateral is taken. The larger the loan, the more likely is the need for some form of collateral that retains its value over time. A review of literature and case studies shows that most institutions accept land title; current microfinance practice indicates that it makes sense to secure a mortgage for a loan of over $5,000. However, due to high transaction costs, there is a preference for securing loans with a mix of guarantees.[9] Given the complexity of foreclosure laws, the title acts more as a psychological pressure to honor the debt.

Case study evidence from PRODEL (The Local Development Program) in Nicaragua underscores that using land title as collateral cannot be an exact science. Even when title is held as guarantee, it is not necessarily realizable—not only because of weaknesses in foreclosure procedures, but also due to vulnerability when economic shocks strike. The data also corroborates findings from elsewhere that there is no significant correlation between delinquency rates and guarantees; loans secured with weaker collateral perform better than mortgaged back loans.

For seven years PRODEL (funded by the Swedish Agency for International Development) has operated microlending for housing improvements in eight major urban centers of Nicaragua. Sixty percent of the borrowers are women. The program funds small infrastructure and community services in selected neighborhoods and offers microloans for microenterprises. The microcredit for housing is accompanied by technical assistance. From 1994 to 1999 a state commercial bank, Banco de Crédito Popular, managed the funds. When the bank closed, the portfolio was transferred to two microfinance institutions; both added housing loan products to their services with PRODEL funds in 1998 after Hurricane Mitch.

Average loans range from $500 to $1,500, and the maximum lending amount is $3,000. Loan-to-income ratio is set at 15 to 20 percent of household income. For loans averaging $700, title deed is preferred. For smaller loans, a variety of guarantees including assets and cosigners are accepted.

Prior to the closure of Banco de Crédito Popular in 1998, the percentage of mortgage loans was 23 percent, but due to the risks associated with the transfer of the portfolio to new intermediaries, PRODEL took specific actions to increase the number of mortgages through inscription of title deeds in the public registry. In the urban centers in Nicaragua typically the documents are private sale documents between two parties, but these are frequently incorrectly registered. To transfer the portfolio, solid guarantees were considered necessary.

Today 42 percent of the portfolio is mortgage loans—a high percentage given that 60 percent of urban properties don't have title deed.[10] Table 7.1 shows the composition of the portfolio. In spite of the stronger guarantees the results in arrears rates were very similar: 8 percent in 1998 and 10 percent in 1999.

The conclusion that can be drawn is that the conservative lending terms adopted are less relevant than effective cost recovery mechanisms. In the period corresponding to bank closure and the transfer, door-to-door collection and pre-judicial procedures were instrumental in maintaining a healthy portfolio.

Only three foreclosures have been carried out in the history of the program. Foreclosure is not really an option given the length of time, the small amounts to be recovered, the depreciation of the goods, and the poor resale prices. The PRODEL data indicates that willingness to pay is not necessarily linked to the type of guarantee but to the vulnerability of income. Even when guarantees are solid—land and buildings for example—shocks to the economy, which directly affect incomes, have enormous and deep effects in the finance sector. The most striking example of recent vulnerability in Nicaragua has been the crisis in the coffee industry.[11]

Finally, it is noteworthy that although PRODEL's lending terms permit loans of up to $3,000, in practice a very low proportion of the borrowers have incomes that will allow larger loan amounts. The average loan today is approximately $900. Poverty and low incomes are the major limiting factors; for those with minimal capacity to pay, the preference both for lender and borrower is to keep loans small and sequential.

Table 7.1 Composition of Guarantees in 1998 and 1999 Portfolio

Type of Guarantee	Number of Loans 1998	Percent of Total	Number of Loans 1999	Percent of Total
Mortgage	773	28%	1417	42%
Coborrower	25	0.9%	877	26%
Lien on Removable Goods	1094	39.66%	842	22%
Cosigner	855	31%	304	9%
Other (signed "I owe you")	11	0.4%	34	1%
Total	2758	100%	3,374	100%

Source: PRODEL database

When loans are kept small, short-term, and frequent the question of security for the loans becomes less important (McAuslan 1985, 46). Thus, much of the microlending for housing is based on the same underwriting criteria, client history, solid credit record, and small loan amounts. Lending is then based more on character and willingness to pay than on collateral. The instruments that housing microfinance currently uses include:

- Land title and buildings
- Chattel mortgage/lien on assets
- Obligatory savings
- Assignment of future income (wages)
- Personal guarantees (cosigners)
- Joint liability and group guarantees (character-based lending)
- Other financial assets (for example, life insurance policies and pension funds)

MOVEABLE ASSETS

Much microlending for housing has strong similarities to microenterprise methodologies. The underwriting and collateral to secure small loan amounts, on short terms, reduces risks. The housing microcredit is treated as just another aspect of lending to the household economy. It is both responsive to the type of assets that low-income households have and is efficient for the lender in terms of cost effectiveness in reaching volume in the portfolio.

The Accion International affiliate MiBanco in Peru is one of the largest microfinance institutions in Latin America with some 70,000 borrowers. Two years ago MiBanco introduced a housing improvement product, MiCasa, which is based on their existing microenterprise methodology with a few adjustments to the loan period, interest rate, and loan size. The eligibility criteria are evidence of residence and good payment record. The guarantees are the same as those of working capital loans. The target group of the MiBanco loans are households with monthly incomes between $110 and $340.[12] The loan process—which is based on simplicity, flexibility, and prompt disbursal—is designed to support progressive upgrading and, as in microenterprise lending, good repayment qualifies the borrower for additional loans. The average housing improvement loan is between $1,000 and $2,000, repayable within two years.

A sworn statement on household assets valued at 30 percent of the loan is all that is required to secure a MiCasa loan. This offers quick access to the loan for the borrowers—the assessment and disbursement are completed in a few days. A maximum loan amount of $800 is used for first-time borrowers or those with unproven or poor credit. In these cases, moveable assets and one or two guarantors are required.

MiBanco's risk management method hinges on two complementary elements: maintaining rigor in the analysis and willingness to pay, and an effective follow-up in collection services. These are the same processes as for microenterprises. Recovery rates are very high with almost no arrears and with no reported losses to date, even though the portfolio is still young. In contrast to other models, MiBanco does not provide any technical assistance.

Only a small proportion of MiBanco's housing loans are backed by mortgage guarantees. Mortgages are only taken on loans over $4,000, particularly given the efforts that have been made by the Peruvian authorities to provide land titles and reforms to the property register. The study by Cities Alliance (Brown and Garcia 2001) suggests there is reluctance among borrowers who have acquired new titles to mortgage the property for small loan amounts that are significantly less than the property value. From the lender's standpoint it avoids high transaction costs and foreclosure procedures in case of default. From the borrower's viewpoint, the time and expense of obtaining a mortgage compared to the time for accessing smaller and repeat loans may be an important factor in explaining why borrowers choose not to take out mortgages.

Collateral Substitutes

Microfinance commonly relies on collateral substitutes to cover the shortfall in solid collateral or where transactions costs are high. The best known examples of collateral substitutes are peer pressure and cosigner arrangements. For example, loan to value shortfall on a property can be covered by a personal guarantee from a cosigner. What distinguishes these is that they are extra-legal or social means that are not enforceable in a court. For some institutions, collateral substitutes have become a major loan-securing instrument. With an unsecured loan the lender relies on the borrower's integrity and trusts that the debt will be honored.

Savings, Group Guarantees, and Joint Liability

In strategies to reach the poorest, mandatory savings is a technique that is common to a broad array of housing lenders. Pioneered by Grameen Bank in Bangladesh, the model has been replicated extensively. Savings mobilization has been the bedrock of much microenterprise lending and has become a widespread practice for MFIs throughout the world.

Within the underwriting alternatives in microlending, savings demonstrates an ability to pay—a key factor especially for the working poor with irregular incomes who have no credit record. It establishes a relationship with the borrower and the obligations and discipline of regular payment. It affects lack of collateral and, for certain groups that cannot afford a housing loan, savings represents the only collateral that can be guaranteed.

Information on current practice shows that potential borrowers will save at a rate equivalent to their future repayment, typically six to twelve months before obtaining a loan. For some MFIs the savings period can be much longer; for example CARD in the Philippines requires up to two years.

In microenterprise lending, savings has gone hand in hand with group solidarity, which has been at the core of much of the success in dealing with the problem of risk management and repayment. Group pressure and sequential lending provide strong repayment motivation and have produced low default rates. However, when it comes to housing loans, the picture is less clear. For housing products, practice varies between continents and within the same institutions. In some contexts, group solidarity is considered less suitable for housing loans, given that it is difficult to hold a group liable for larger sums of money over longer periods.

Increasingly, practitioners tend to agree that housing loans generally should be individual. However, as discussed previously, one school of thought holds that group solidarity among the urban poor may well be more effective loan security than is title to a piece of land, especially where administrative arrangements regarding registration of title, safekeeping of documents, and laws on transfer are not always rigorously observed (McAuslan 1985, 46).

Grameen Bank, which built its classic model of microlending on group solidarity, breaks with this modality in its housing products. Housing loans are made available to its microenterprise borrowers who have a substantial proven credit record over a number of years. And, unlike the vast majority of housing microcredit institutions, Grameen Bank focuses on new build units and not on progressive or incremental upgrading of existing dwellings. The qualifying criteria is strictly linked to being an experienced borrower, savings of 5 percent of the capital borrowed, and a recommendation from a solidarity group. Loans for new construction require land title, although a land purchase product is also offered.

Likewise, SEWA Bank in India offers housing loans with a strong emphasis on savings deposits as collateral, but loans are individual. Experience from Grameen, SEWA, and other cases show that delinquency rates with group loans are higher due to the longer term needed for housing products. In cases where the loan period exceeds one year, higher rates of nonpayment have been recorded.

Yet other institutions, such as SPARC (India) and CARD (the Philippines), use group solidarity for housing and infrastructure loans. Genesis Empresarial in Guatemala is a notable example of group lending for infrastructure. Cooperative Jesus Nazareno in Bolivia provides microloans with a solidarity group guarantee for the purchase of land. The costs incurred in creating a mortgage lien are avoided, and titles are held by the cooperative until repayment is completed.

SPARC is one of the recognized pioneers in mobilizing savings as the entry point for housing loans. To qualify for a loan, women pavement dwellers are first organized into cluster groups for savings. They save the monthly amount equivalent to the loan repayment they will have to make if they get a housing loan. Group organization and training in construction management, together with pooling of resources, is at the core of their approach. SPARC has focused its lending strategy on bridging the gap between informal and formal finance institutions. Its model is also noteworthy in that it has been able to reach the landless poor and provide access to formal housing on a large scale through public/private alliances. SPARC together with the National Slum Dwellers Federation (NSDF), which represents members in thirty-four Indian cities; the Mahila Milan (Women Savings Groups); and housing cooperatives carried out a major slum upgrading program in Mumbai, India's largest commercial city. Citibank is one of the financial partners that have extended loans secured and backed by a guarantee fund arrangement with Homeless International.

Similar savings groups, organized into federations, are increasingly at the forefront of fostering partnerships between NGOS and financial institutions. These alliances recognize that land and housing cannot be tackled exclusively through microcredit. Issues of landlessness or lack of land security require a wide range of services from community organizations as well as counseling, lobbying, and negotiation with local authorities for the right to remain on or acquire land, and the savings mobilization to leverage microcredit. These arrangements demonstrate success in reaching scale in their outreach and coverage.

The Shack Dwellers Federation of Namibia (SDFN), formed in 1998, has a savings scheme that operates nationwide. By the end of 2000 over 180 savings schemes in 42 urban and peri-urban areas had been formed, reaching some 6,000 households. Ninety percent of the members are women and a significant proportion of the members are renters. Land purchase is a prominent feature of the savings groups and, with the support of the Namibia Housing Action Group, an advocacy and support NGO, almost 1,000 households have secured tenure, mainly through communal land ownership (Gold 2002). Households can access loans through their savings schemes; each group approves as well as manages the funds. Loans amounts are up to $2,000, at 12 percent interest, and repayment period is flexible. Loan recovery has been at 92 percent.

In addition to affordability, potential borrowers are qualified based on the degree of active participation in the group activities. The good recovery rates are attributed to the high degree of group solidarity; specifically, the experience of communally negotiating and obtaining secure tenure enhances responsibility.

Casa Melhor in Brazil combines elements of the two methodologies: community-based savings and loans that can qualify for matching funds through loans from NGOs. Individual housing loans are awarded to members of an eligible savings and loans association. The guarantee to the land and collective liability, peer group pressure, and incentives regarding future access to credit— three consecutive loans—ensure timely loan repayment (Serageldin and Driscoll 2000).

Savings has proven to be an effective mechanism for mobilizing resources. One of the best examples is the Bank Rayat Indonesia (BRI) which has mobilized more than $2.7 billion in voluntary savings through 16.1 million savings accounts and provides services to

30 percent of Indonesian households. There is demand for saving services—for every borrower there are five savers.

Although in many countries microfinance institutions are prohibited from taking deposits from the public, nonetheless, there is a shift toward voluntary or client-responsive savings facilities driven by expressed demand from clients and the possibilities to raise long-term finance from deposits. Research shows that there is a marked preference among the poor for voluntary savings. It shows that voluntary and open access savings schemes can generate more net savings per client than mandatory and locked-in savings schemes, while providing a useful and well-used facility for clients (Wright et al. 1997). Savings holds promise for increasing the financial base for MFIs as well as the classical mechanism for reaching the poorest. A new emerging pattern is joint ventures between the formal and informal sector. The banking sector takes advantage of the lower transaction costs and risks so as to reach down to low-income borrowers.

Cosigners

In contexts where foreclosure and titling is bureaucratic, time consuming and costly, cosigners are being used instead of tangible collateral to secure loans.

In Mexico's housing market, less than 10 percent of the housing stock is mortgaged. This market, largely for the higher income groups, is dominated by government institutions (FONHAP, FOVI, INFONAVIT). The majority of housing is informal construction by families who are excluded from the formal finance market due to lack of bank accounts and credit history.

Since 1996, the CHF International has been working with the FUNHAVI program in Ciudad Juarez, Mexico. The area has undergone rapid growth over the last two decades due to the massive influx of migrant workers attracted by the offer of a secure job in the *maquiladoras* industry. Formal employment and informal housing have shaped the city as thousands of inhabitants have settled in precarious locations due to the absence of good land and available housing developments.

The FUNHAVI program offers loans for incremental upgrades, such as the addition of an extra room, replacement of a roof, installation of basic sanitation, and connection to municipal services.

Loans range from $800 to $2,000, with repayment periods of one to three years.

The qualifying requirements are simple: proof of employment in the form of salary stubs; proof of land security in the form of a sales agreement; payment to the municipality for services; or minimum residence of at least one year. Demand is high, and despite the cost and difficulty of obtaining land title, some 43 percent of FUNHAVI's clients have title deed, and 56 percent are in the process of obtaining it.

FUNHAVI also relies on cosigners in order to secure loans, given that in Chihuahua State, as in other parts of Mexico, foreclosure procedures do not operate effectively. The cosigner must have the same repayment capacity standards and eligibility requirements as the borrower, and cannot be a member of the borrower's immediate family. A significant number of the borrowers are well established in the city, some with eight years' residency. There is no difficulty in getting clients who meet all the requirements described above. Seventy-five percent of FUNHAVI's clients work in the *maquiladoras* and the rest are self-employed. For these no additional qualifying criteria are required.

Technical assistance is included not only as an advisory service to ensure that quality standards are met in the construction but also as part of an overall risk management strategy. Establishing a direct and sustained relationship with the client enhances repayment.

The program has had good repayment performance. In case of arrears, a certified delivery service is used to ensure prompt notice to debtors. From its inception to date, only a minimal number of cases required the cosigners to repay the outstanding balance (Cooperative Housing Foundation 2002).

Other Financial Assets

Pension and insurance funds provide a cost-effective way to secure loans for low-income salaried workers. Combined with the facility of payroll deduction it is a highly effective administrative and risk management instrument. Loans can be underwritten with pension funds in such a way to cover the affordability gap between what the household earns and what it needs for a loan repayment schedule.

In South Africa, housing is one of the most acute development challenges, particularly the need to respond to the increase in demand from the townships, which are home to large numbers of working poor. Government subsidies and NGO programs cannot raise the huge amounts of housing finance needed to meet demand. Involvement of the formal financial sector to tap into low-income housing was a need recognized by government.

The development of a mortgage market was met initially by the standard reluctance to deal with low-income earners and the risks associated with the low-income market. Risks associated with high unemployment include poverty, volatile interest rates, and a persistent adverse climate for foreclosure procedures.

Changes in legislation by government provided a favorable climate for public and private partnership. A key change in legislation allowed pension and provident funds to be used as security for home loans—a significant step forward, particularly since providing traditional mortgage-backed loans has been historically problematic. Thus, nonland- or housing-based collateral has greatly increased housing options for low-income employees.

The NGO Group Credit Corp. teamed up with national banks, international investors, and insurance companies and became Cashbank. Cashbank offers housing loans that workers secure with the assets in their pension funds. Borrowers incomes are typically less than $425 per month. The maximum loan is $9,000, but loan-to-income ratios cannot exceed 25 percent of a borrower's gross income or 50 percent of net disposable income. The loans are mostly small amounts over short periods that allow workers to improve their homes incrementally. Repayment is made through irrevocable payroll deductions. Cashbank's excellent loan recovery rates are attributed to this direct deduction, which has kept write-offs to less than 1 percent of the outstanding portfolio.

A boom of financial providers and microlending flourished due to the ease of using pension funds as collateral, but the government had to step in as a result of the severe debt crisis generated by some abuses in the system. Almost half a million state employees had nonstatutory deductions and multiple loans, a result of disproportionately easy access to credit by civil servants. Since June 2001 no nonstatutory deductions on the state payroll have been allowed, and more stringent rules have been introduced to control this underwriting mechanism. Cashbank still relies on pension-backed loans but it is not as yet a widespread methodology elsewhere.

CONCLUSION

Access to land and property rights is a complex issue worldwide. The problems for those without land will remain a major challenge. The legal and administrative barriers for those with land who lack title are also daunting. In some countries progress has been made in tackling the property formalization issue. Lessons are being learned, and the technological advances in property and registry reform are dramatically lowering costs, which should accelerate the titling processes. This should in turn enhance efforts to increase the flow of housing finance to low- and moderate-income groups.

However, increasing flows of housing finance will not only depend upon land titling efforts, but also on simplification of the formal rules to create and enforce guarantees and create a greater transparency in registrars, thus, reducing the overall transaction costs.

The requirement of title for a housing loan varies. Some institutions reviewed in this paper use it; others do not. In general, housing microfinance has found it expedient to design risk-management mechanisms that use land title as a prerequisite. Thus, much of the housing microfinance experience has drawn on the microenterprise methodology that relies on character, cash flow, and savings in the absence of a credit record, or has complemented it with alternative guarantees.

Although there is a gradual increase in the range of housing products offered, much of the lending to date has been for housing improvements. Small and sequential loans over a shorter maturity period have worked well for both lender and borrower. For the lender, the risks are lower. Short-term, small loans match how most low-income households traditionally build their homes and better fit with the financial services they require. Further, for low-income families, incremental improvements help build household assets over time.

Performance has been very good, cost recovery rates are high, and default rates low. The lack of hard collateral—clear title—has historically been cited as a major obstacle in expanding housing finance, particularly by the formal commercial lenders. The review of different examples from housing microfinance institutions nonetheless raises questions to challenge this perceived viewpoint.

Is the lack of collateral in fact a real constraint for the lender? Some of the examples presented in this paper would support the thesis that collateral is overstated, given that current practice suggests that collateral is used to offset weaknesses in other underwriting criteria and is a means to recoup losses if all else fails.

Without question, land title as a qualifying requirement becomes more relevant or essential with greater loan size. Nonetheless, even when title is held for low- and moderate-income housing loans of $7,000 to $10,000, the legal, administrative, and social implications associated with repossession and foreclosure pose the main constraint in many countries.

There is virtually no information on how repossession and resale operate, how common they are, and behavior with regard to foreclosure procedures. A more rigorous understanding of the foreclosure experience is needed. There is general agreement that reforms of foreclosure and legal systems are fundamental but will remain an awesome task for the foreseeable future in many countries. In the meantime, it will be necessary to explore ways to enforce creditors' claims that do not involve the formal judicial process.

However, even if foreclosure were simplified, most banks and financial institutions wish to avoid repossession of homes or goods due to the social impact that this has, especially on vulnerable families. New techniques to enhance better credit and risk management such as credit bureau, credit scoring, and direct debit for loan recovery can greatly assist in making inroads into the underserved markets.

A number of other important issues represent the new frontiers of housing microfinance and finance providers. One major challenge will be to reach larger population segments that have yet to enter the housing market, and particularly to assist households with land purchase.

Partnerships that have begun between the housing specialist or advocacy organizations and the formal financial sector can enhance the efforts to provide financial and nonfinancial services required at different stages of the housing cycle—land purchase, legalization, land titling, and infrastructure provision.

Finally, increasing flows of housing finance to meet demand will continue to be a major future concern. One avenue to be explored is securitization of microfinance, however, this will involve a new angle: the feasibility of introducing nonmortgage portfolios to the secondary market. The high repayment rates that have been achieved to date represent encouraging evidence, but they must be sustained over time and in conjunction with property reforms to allow better-collateralized loans.

A critical factor will be how to reach sufficient scale of operations to make packaging for sale in the secondary market viable. Expansion and scaling up of housing microfinance will, thus, continue to be the immediate goal to mainstream and deepen the housing market.

NOTES

1. Information drawn from Center for Urban Development/Harvard studies (2000) and country case studies by CHF and Cities Alliance.

2. Habitat for Humanity Statistics, 2000. According to UNCHS, Global Campaign for Secure Tenure, 1.3 billion people do not have access to clean water, and these are the poorest, who also live on less than U.S.$1 a day; 2.6 billion people do not have access to basic sanitation, whereas 5 million die from diarrhea diseases caused by water contamination.

3. WHO Commission on Health and Environment. "Our Plant, Our Earth" (1992). These case studies of cities in Africa, Asia, and Latin America show that it is common for at least 30 percent of the population to live in either illegal settlements or in overcrowded tenements and cheap boarding houses.

4. UNCHS-Habitat launched a global campaign for secure tenure rights; the Cities Alliance Programs and Urban Management Program of the World Bank are a few examples of this trend.

5. According to de Janvry, Key, and Sadoulet's research, by July 1996 in the PROCEDE title program only 25 percent of the ejidos had completed the process, but a significant number had not entered into it. This is due to a variety of causes including manipulation, a desire to preserve the communal ownership patterns which acted as a buffer for failure in the markets, and reluctance to relinquish the special privileges enjoyed by the ejido system.

6. The Fujimori government created la Comisión de Formalización de la Propiedad Informal, COFOPRI.

7. The reliance on real estate as collateral means that one quarter of farmers in Argentina that own no land will have no access to formal credit (Fleisig 1997).

8. GHIF's desk study reviewed eighty organizations (forty institutions covered in the CUDS/Harvard study and forty additional institutions) (see Klinkhamer 2000).

9. The complexity of the registry systems and the time and cost especially on small loans makes it unattractive for the borrower and lender. In Peru registration can take about two weeks and cost up to U.S.$200. In Nicaragua

registration and legal fees can represent more than 4 percent additional costs for a loan of U.S.$700.

10. Figures from the 1995 National Census indicate that 49 percent of dwellings have a title deed, 36 percent were owned without deed, 5 percent were rented, and 10 percent *posando,* a Spanish term for "right to abode agreed among friends, or relatives."

11. Since the collapse of international coffee prices a temporary moratorium has been placed on foreclosure for coffee-related loans.

12. The families are classified as poor and improving poor with a smaller percentage of extremely poor (see Brown and Garcia 2001). The information in this section was drawn from this report.

8

The Context for Housing Microfinance in the United States

Kenneth Temkin with Bruce Ferguson

Housing microfinance is used in the developing world to allow poor and low-income families to improve their housing. In general, housing microfinance loans are similar to other types of microfinance efforts: they are for relatively small amounts, have short repayment periods, have interest rates that reflect higher costs associated with servicing and financing the loan, have little collateral, and are typically originated to borrowers so that they can make incremental improvements to their housing (Daphnis and Tilock 2001). Such loans allow low-income residents access to capital without being served by a county's mainstream housing finance system.

The housing microfinance model just described has few analogs in the United States. That is not to say the U.S. housing finance system does not serve low-income families. On the contrary, numerous institutions and policies in the United States support and encourage mortgage lending to low- and moderate-income borrowers. Moreover, these efforts address income and credit issues that are the basis of housing microfinance programs around the world.

There are, however, crucial differences between the context of housing markets and housing finance in the United States and emerging countries that bear on the potential of housing microfinance. A group of laws, regulations, and programs joined with the great depth of the U.S. financial system have encouraged mainstream housing finance institutions to move downmarket, rather than use microfinance providers.

Of all these factors, the most important have to do with the context—particularly the great depth of the U.S. financial system and the country's macroeconomic stability (although secure property rights and a legal framework facilitate securitization, and secondary markets also play important roles). The U.S. financial system and the housing finance system, in particular, are recognized as highly efficient capital markets. Immense pools of long-term sources of funding (liabilities) from pension funds, insurance companies, and other sources seek long-term investment opportunities, with mortgages and mortgage-backed securities as one of the main outlets. The competition for attractive investment opportunities helps drive lenders into new niches. This pressure has lead steadily to the democratization of capital in the United States. As the best investment opportunities diminish, lenders have gone downmarket in many sectors. In the housing finance sector over the last forty years, mortgage lenders have moved from offering only one product (the fixed-rate, thirty-year mortgage) largely to prime investment risks—typically, a salaried worker with excellent credit and long-term employment in a single company—to a rich tapestry of financial instruments not only to prime but also to subprime borrowers such as families with little or flawed credit or with a checkered employment and income history.

Real interest rates in the United States are correspondingly modest. Joined with inflation at less than 2 percent, the resulting mortgage rates have greatly enhanced affordability of mortgage payments. Relatively low, long-term interest rates have made manageable the "tilt" problem—the concentration of real payments in the first years of a loan that amortizes conventionally—and, thus, greatly increased affordability. Finally, although the ratio of median house price to median family income has risen from two in the 1950s to three today (see chapter 10 for a discussion), this is still moderate in international terms. The great U.S. financial depth and stable macroeconomy—as in other rich countries—has formed a solid platform on which to build a housing finance industry and democratized access to capital.

Emerging countries suffer from the reverse situation. Few emerging countries have significant pools of long-term funding (from pension funds and insurance companies). There is limited competition in the financial sector, and financial institutions are often very conservative in their lending practices. Hence, only short-term funds, if any, are available for housing finance. Financial institutions create substantial term risk if they extend long-term (twenty to thirty year) mortgage loans in substantial amounts, and they limit these loans to their best customers. Real interest rates are frequently over 10 percent, particularly in countries with a history of monetary instability such as inflation and government deficits (leading to foreign exchange risk), and incomes typically fluctuate greatly in developing economies. Lack of capital and risk of all sorts contribute to high real interest rates—often over 10 percent. When joined with inflation, the resulting high interest rates (14 to 30 percent depending on the country) create an enormous tilt of real interest payments toward the beginning years of the loan and greatly limit affordability. Distortions in housing markets lead to much higher costs of a median-priced house relative to income. The ratio of the price of a median complete house to family income is typically 5 to 10 to 1 in developing countries, compared to 3 to 1 in the United States.

Thus, the financial and economic context of developing countries places many barriers in the way of conventional mortgage lending moving downmarket to reach the bulk of the population. Not surprisingly, mortgage lenders serve only the top 30 percent of the income distribution for a very limited range of transactions. Lenders in many developing countries offer financing only to purchase a newly built, single-family unit. Even for this purpose, mortgage lending has gone downmarket substantially in only a few developing countries and its reach is limited even in these countries. The remaining 70 percent of households who cannot afford to pay the debt service to purchase such a home usually build their housing incrementally. Housing microcredits are a finance method that best fits the effective demand of these households.

In the United States, in contrast, it has made sense to leverage the resources of the existing system to make conventional housing finance more accessible to underserved markets. And, as discussed in more detail below, this is exactly what has happened. Incentives for large lenders to move downmarket has led to an increase in the number of specially tailored mortgage products and underwriting standards that make it easier for traditionally underserved borrowers to qualify for mortgage credit (Listokin and Wyly 2000).

Table 8.1 demonstrates the differences between the U.S. approach to serve borrowers who rely on housing microfinance in other countries. Microfinance loans allow borrowers to overcome income and wealth constraints as well as a lack of a formal credit history. The difference is that affordable lending, unlike housing microfinance, results in loans with terms similar to traditional mortgages.

Table 8.1 Comparison of Affordable Lending and Housing Microfinance Approaches

	Affordable Lending	Microfinance
Income constraint	Allows for higher debt-to-income ratios so that lower-income borrowers can qualify for mortgages	Provides relatively small mortgages that are afford-
Wealth constraint	Allows for higher loan-to-value ratios that require little or no cash to close	able to lower-income families
No formal credit history	Underwriters consider rent payments and other forms of periodic financial obligations	Borrowers may participate
Relatively poor credit history	Credit counseling that provides assistance in improving credit, risk-based pricing	in peer group or other less formal support groups
Lack of knowledge about mortgage process	Home buyers counseling and other forms of formal education	

It is important to note that the affordable lending strategies presented in Table 8.1 resulted, in part, from federal legislation. In particular, the Community Reinvestment Act (CRA) and the Federal Housing Enterprises Financial Safety and Soundness Act (FHEFSSA) created pressure on lenders and the Government Sponsored Enterprises (GSEs) to take more aggressive steps in their service of low- and moderate-income and minority families.

The CRA, adopted in 1977, requires federally-regulated lenders to help meet the credit needs of local communities in which they are chartered. CRA examination procedures create strong incentives for lenders to originate as many loans as possible to creditworthy low- and moderate-income borrowers and in low- and moderate-income neighborhoods. Therefore, lenders subject to CRA offer low- and moderate-income borrowers a range of mortgage choices, including FHA, conventional, and targeted affordable products in order to maximize origination volumes in areas that count in a CRA examination (Williams 1999).

Congress enacted FHEFSSA in 1992. Its purpose is to place more pressure on Fannie Mae and Freddie Mac to serve lower-income families and lower-income and minority neighborhoods. As a result, the Act contained three provisions: quantitative targets for purchases of loans made to low-income borrowers and in low-income and minority neighborhoods; a mandate that the GSEs "lead the industry in affordable lending"; and language that prohibits the GSEs from discriminating based on prohibited factors, such as a borrower's race, ethnicity, or gender, in their loan purchase activities. Rather than just provide liquidity, the GSEs under FHEFSSA are expected to take a leading role in serving lower-income and minority families by purchasing more loans originated to such borrowers and initiating demonstrations and partnerships that facilitate affordable lending.

Lenders and the GSEs adapted their business practices by changing underwriting guidelines, initiating new lending programs, and forming partnerships with organizations and groups connected with underserved markets. In most cases, these efforts initially began as experiments: lenders originated loans to borrowers with little or no equity, less than perfect credit, and relatively high debt-to-income ratios. Many lenders, at the time these products were introduced, were skeptical that loans originated with such flexible guidelines would perform. The existing guidelines in the early 1990s reflected the industry's common wisdom on acceptable underwriting standards: any changes, some lenders believed, would represent intolerable risks.

This perception has changed. The lending industry has undergone a quiet revolution by offering credit to borrowers who previously would have been categorized as prohibitive risks (Office of the Controller of the Currency 1997). Now many lenders believe that originating loans in previously underserved markets is sustainable and profitable. Moreover, lenders are aware that future mortgage market demand will be driven by increased lending to minority and immigrant households: groups that have been traditionally underserved. There is every reason to believe that lenders will continue in their efforts to increase their service of these borrowers.

This chapter provides an overview of the current methods used in the United States to serve families that, in other countries, benefit from housing microfinance programs. In general, such families have one or both of the following characteristics: they are wealth- and/or income-constrained, and they lack a satisfactory or formal credit history. U.S. home ownership rates increased without a large housing microfinance component; rather, lower-income home buyers benefited from affordable mortgage products introduced in the 1990s that allowed home buyers to qualify for thirty-year loans despite having little or no equity for a down payment and imperfect or nonexistent formal credit histories. Such products obviated the need for microfinance loans, which typically do not allow for high loan-to-value ratios and have shorter terms.

Nonetheless, the U.S. housing finance system is still not serving all potential creditworthy families. There are gaps, and housing microfinance products may help in meeting them. The innovations introduced into the mainstream housing finance system in the 1990s may be approaching their limits in increasing service to lower-income families. Therefore other techniques, such as housing microfinance, may be able to assist certain lenders in reaching segments of underserved markets that are beyond the reach of current affordable lending products. This paper will also describe some markets, such as home equity, that may be amenable to a larger housing microfinance role.

AFFORDABLE LENDING FOR HOME OWNERSHIP: A 1990s SUCCESS STORY

The U.S. home ownership rate increased dramatically during the 1990s. As of the fourth quarter of 2000, 67.5 percent of American families owned their own home—up from 64 percent in 1993 (U.S. Bureau of the Census 2000). Most of this gain resulted from large increases in home ownership rates for traditionally underserved markets: members of minority groups and low- and moderate-income families. These gains resulted from increased lending activities in such traditionally underserved markets. Between 1993 and 1997, the number of conventional home purchase loans originated to African-American borrowers increased by 72 percent; the increase for Hispanics was 45 percent. These gains are impressive, especially compared to the 22 percent gain of such loans originated to non-Hispanic whites during the same period (Scheessele 1999).

Lending in minority neighborhoods also increased during the 1990s: mortgage loan originations in predominantly minority census tracts increased by 40 percent between 1993 and 1997, twice the growth rate for overall lending volume in Metropolitan Statistical Areas (MSAs). The pattern is similar for lower-income borrowers. Between 1993 and 1997, loans to buyers with an income less than 80 percent of local median increased by 38 percent, compared with 25 percent for higher-income home buyers. Similarly, lending volume in lower-income census tracts increased by 31 percent, more than ten percentage points higher than the increase in overall MSA lending volume (Scheessele 1999).

Some of the home ownership gains in underserved markets result from favorable economic conditions in the 1990s. During this period, the median family income for all families increased, especially for African-Americans and Hispanics. In real terms, the median income for African-American families grew almost 50 percent, from $21,423 in 1990 to $31,778 in 1999. The increase was slightly less for Hispanic families, from $23,341 in 1990 to $31,663 in 1999. Moreover, the median income for families with earnings in the lowest 20 percent of the total distribution increased, in real terms from $9,833 in 1990 to $13,320 in 1999 (U.S. Bureau of the Census 2000). These increases made it easier for lower-income and minority families to consider home ownership, increasing the demand for owner-occupied housing. While incomes increased during the past decade, interest rates fell. The contract interest rate for a thirty-year, fixed-rate mortgage declined from more than 10 percent at the start of the decade to as low as 7 percent in 1999.

That higher incomes and lower interest rates explain some of the increase in U.S. home ownership during the 1990s is beyond dispute. But these trends do not fully explain the increase in home ownership rates during the past decade. The U.S. mortgage finance system changed substantially in the 1990s as industry participants—lenders, mortgage insurance companies, secondary market conduits, and government agencies—made concerted efforts to improve their service to lower income and minority families (Bostic and Surette 2000, Martinez 2000). As a result of these innovations, low- and moderate-income home buyers, in contrast to the 1980s, now have a wide variety of products and programs to choose from when applying for a mortgage. The U.S. mortgage finance currently offers low- and moderate-income home buyers a "rich tapestry" of programs that make home ownership possible for many more American families (Stegman 1999).

The mortgage industry did not change in a legislative vacuum: federal legislation had a large impact on the appetite among industry participants to serve lower-income and minority borrowers. In particular, the CRA and the FHEFSSA put pressure on lenders and the GSEs to take more aggressive steps in their service of low- and moderate-income and minority families.

Lenders and the GSEs adapted their business practices by changing underwriting guidelines, initiating new lending programs,

and forming partnerships with organizations and groups connected with underserved markets. In most cases, these efforts initially began as experiments: lenders originated loans to borrowers
with little or no equity, less than perfect credit, and relatively high
debt-to-income ratios. Many lenders, at the time these products
were introduced, were skeptical that loans originated with such
flexible guidelines would perform.[1] The existing guidelines in the
early 1990s reflected the industry's common wisdom regarding
acceptable underwriting standards; any changes, some lenders
believed, would represent intolerable risks.

This perception has changed. Many lenders now believe that
originating loans in previously underserved markets is sustainable
and profitable. Moreover, lenders are aware that future mortgage
market demand will be driven by increased lending to minority
and immigrant households. There is every reason to believe that
lenders will continue in their efforts to increase their service of
such traditionally underserved borrowers.

While lenders and other mortgage market participants use a
variety of techniques to increase home ownership opportunities
for underserved markets, two elements are particularly important:

- More flexible standard conventional lending guidelines
  introduced by Fannie Mae and Freddie Mac in the 1990s
  that allow lenders to serve borrowers with little equity, less
  than perfect credit, and relatively high levels of debt.
- Affordable lending programs that allow even more underwriting flexibility for eligible borrowers than do standard
  conventional loans. Some of these mortgages are sold to the
  GSEs, others are retained in lenders' portfolios.

Since Fannie Mae and Freddie Mac purchase so many loans,
their underwriting guidelines, summarized in Table 8.2, have
become industry standards (MacDonald 1995). Since 1992, both
Fannie Mae and Freddie Mac have made significant changes to
their standard underwriting guidelines (Temkin et al. 2001.) In
contrast to GSE standards of the late 1980s, the current standard
guidelines allow borrowers to qualify for a 95 percent LTV mortgage (down from a maximum LTV of 90 percent). Allowable
house payment-to-income (28 percent) and total debt-to-income
(36 percent) ratios are higher as well (36), up from 25 and 28 percent, respectively. Moreover, the GSEs will now purchase loans

Table 8.2 Underwriting Guidelines for Portfolio Lending Product

Guideline	Standard GSE	GSE Affordable Loan Product	Sample Targeted Affordable Portfolio Mortgage
Maximum Loan-to-Value Ratio	95%	100%	97%
Maximum CLTV	95%		103%
Down Payment	5%. Must come from borrower's funds.	Minimum of 3% equity. Fannie Mae's Flex100 and Freddie Mac's Affordable Gold 100.	3% down payment. Greater of 1% or $500 from borrowers' funds for down payment or closing costs. Balance of down payment & closing costs can be made from gift, grant, down payment assistance program, seller second.
Subordinate Financing	Secondary financing from all sources is allowed if first mortgage is less than 75% and combined LTV < 90%	Some products allow borrower to use unsecured credit for down payment.	Up to 103% CLTV
Ratios	28/36	33/38	33/42
Mortgage Insurance	Required if LTV > 80%	Required if LTV > 80%	None required.
Reserves	2 months required	None required	None required.
Credit History	No minimum FICO, though FICO scores lower than 660, if manually underwritten, trigger a more comprehensive review.	Same as standard	Minimum 580 x FICO. Nontraditional credit reports accepted.
Closing Costs	Must come from borrower. Seller can pay up to 6% toward nonrecurring closing costs when the LTV is 90% or less: 3% when the LTV exceeds 90%.	Can come from grants and gifts.	Can be from gift, grant, down payment assistance program, seller second. 3% seller concessions.

Source: Listokin and Wyly 1998.

from borrowers who do not have a formal or perfect credit history. Borrowers may still qualify for a GSE standard mortgage despite some lapsed payments, so long as they provide compensatory factors (Listokin and Wyly 2000).

These underwriting changes make it easier for income and wealth constrained borrowers to qualify for standard conventional loans. During the 1990s the GSEs made other changes to make home ownership more obtainable: emphasizing a borrower's income stability, allowing appraisers more flexibility in choosing comparable sales, and allowing collateralized loans as a source of borrower funds.

In addition to increasing the flexibility of their standard underwriting guidelines, the GSEs have promoted the use of credit scoring and automation to try to make the underwriting process faster, fairer, and less expensive to borrowers. Each innovation, according to the GSEs, makes underwriting more objective and reduces the potential for differential treatment of minority and lower-income applicants. Moreover, both Fannie Mae and Freddie Mac claim that credit scores and automated underwriting systems make it possible for underwriters to identify creditworthy applicants more easily, reducing the costs associated with evaluating mortgage applications. These innovations are discussed below.

Credit Scoring

A credit bureau score is a statistical measure that estimates how likely a borrower is to pay back a loan. The score measures the relative degree of risk a potential borrower represents to a creditor and is based on the credit information contained within the files of the three national credit bureaus. Each credit bureau reports a separate credit score, which is not based on prohibited factors, such as a borrower's race, color, national origin, sex, and marital status, nor on occupation or length of time a person has resided at his or her current address (Fair Isaac and Company). Instead, a credit score is calculated by a system of scorecards that have been generated using actual credit information from millions of consumer payment records. Credit scores, which range from about 400 to 900, are based on the following factors: past payment history; amount of credit already owed by the borrower; search for and acquisition of new credit; and types of credit established (Fair Isaac and Company).

Fannie Mae and Freddie Mac standard underwriting guidelines do not set minimum FICO scores. Indeed, their guidelines stress the fact that credit underwriting should not be based solely on a borrower's credit score, and underwriters may use compensating factors, such as higher down payments or extenuating circumstances, that created a prior credit problem (Fannie Mae 1997). Nonetheless, the vast majority of borrowers served by the conventional mortgage market have excellent credit: about 80 percent of loans originated since the first quarter of 1997 were issued to borrowers with a FICO score greater than 660 (Feshbach and Schwinn 1999).

Analysts have found a strong statistical relationship between credit scores and mortgage performance. Using information on mortgages that were current as of March 1997, Fesbach and Schwinn found that about 20 percent of mortgages originated with FICO scores of less than 580 had at least one missed payment during a six-month period; only 0.45 percent of loans with a FICO score over 720 had a late payment during the same period. Avery, Bostic, Cale, and Canner, using data from 1994, found that FICO scores predict loan performance. The authors conclude, "For each type of loan, regardless of seasoning period, borrowers with lower scores have substantially higher delinquency rates than those with medium and high scores" (Avery, Bostic, Calem, and Canner 1996, 632).

Although the GSEs encourage mortgage underwriters to use FICO scores when evaluating loan applications, some applicants have low FICO scores, or no formal credit histories. In these cases, lenders must use other methods to evaluate an applicant's creditworthiness. Both GSEs recommend originators assess a borrower's payment history with a variety of forms of credit, including rental payments and various types of consumer debt. By using this methodology, lenders can originate loans to borrowers who do not use credit or who do not have the type of credit history that will appear on a traditional credit report and sell the mortgages to the GSEs.

Automated Underwriting

Credit scores are based on a borrower's past use of debt, including consumer loans, credit cards, and other types of financial obligations. While they are indicative of a borrower's creditworthiness, they do not take into account all of the items used by a mortgage underwriter when assessing an application. To fill this gap, lenders are increasingly using automated underwriting systems. These applications are based on statistical models and assess an applicant's creditworthiness based on observed relationships between loan performance and underwriting standards (Avery, Bostic, Calem, and Canner, 1996). Automated systems evaluate loans much more quickly than manual underwriters, and so are promoted by the GSEs as an aid in making home ownership more affordable.

The mortgage credit score generated by an automated underwriting system is calculated with information that a manual underwriter would use. Fannie Mae's Desktop Underwriter® analyzes debt-to-income ratios; whether the borrower is salaried versus self-employed; loan amortization period; adjustable or balloon mortgage; number of units in the mortgage property; co-op, condo, or attached; funds from other parties; loan purpose; number of borrowers; prior bankruptcies and foreclosures; and prior mortgage delinquencies (Fannie Mae 2000). Freddie Mac's Loan Prospector® system uses similar variables (Freddie Mac 2000).

The major difference between manual and automated underwriting is that an automated system can estimate a borrower's risk in a matter of minutes, as compared to a period of days or weeks needed for a manual underwriter. In addition, an automated system can simultaneously balance various risk-contributing factors in assessing an application (Pachura and Zorn 1996). This is an important point, as many mortgage applicants, especially those with lower incomes and wealth, do not meet more than one underwriting guideline. Consequently, some analysts believe that automated underwriting systems can help standardize the underwriting decisions and in doing so improve the overall fairness of the underwriting process. Expediting the underwriting process can also help reduce origination costs by as much as $400 for each borrower (Mahoney and Zorn 1996).

The benefits of automated underwriting, discussed above, have led to an increase in the number of mortgage applications analyzed with such a system. About 60 percent of lenders use an automated underwriting system, and about 75 percent of all lenders use some type of automated system. In 1999, 50 percent of newly originated loans purchased by Freddie Mac were scored through the company's automated underwriting system; 39 percent of such loans purchased by Fannie Mae were scored through Desktop Underwriter® (OFHEO 2000).

But some housing market analysts are concerned that automated systems may not make it easier to serve low- and moderate-income lending. First, these systems may not be flexible enough to assess applications from previously underserved borrowers accurately. Moreover, it is not clear how lenders underwrite applications that have been referred by the system to a manual underwriter. Fannie Mae and Freddie Mac argue that lenders will spend less time on loans that are approved, thereby freeing up resources for more problem loan applications. This may happen, but there is little evidence about how these systems are being used in practice (Madison 1999). In addition, minority mortgage applicants, on average, have lower credit scores, fewer funds available for closing, and less equity available for a down payment. Fannie Mae, in analyzing loans evaluated by its automated underwriting system, found that almost 25 percent of loans originated to African-American borrowers had a loan-to-value (LTV) ratio over 90 percent; the same data indicated that the percentage of white borrowers who received a loan with a LTV of over 90 percent was less than 10 percent. Similarly, Fannie Mae found that about 16 percent of African-American and Hispanic borrowers had less than one month reserves at closing, compared to 11 percent of whites. Minorities also had lower credit scores: only 20 percent of loans originated to African-Americans and purchased by Fannie Mae in 1999 had a borrower credit score over 740. This percentage is about one-half of the proportion of such loans originated to white borrowers (Fannie Mae 2000).

In addition to making changes to standard guidelines, lenders offer targeted affordable loans to borrowers who are eligible, as defined by their income or the location of the mortgaged property. There are two major categories of such loans: those available for sale to Fannie Mae and Freddie Mac, and loan products (summarized in the second column of Table 8.1) offered by lenders that contain features that make them more likely to be held in a lender's portfolio.

Fannie Mae has developed and introduced affordable loan products under its Community Home Buyers Program (CHBP). Typically, CHBP products have more flexible guidelines relating to down payment requirements, debt-to-income ratios, and a borrower's credit history. Some lenders have introduced targeted affordable mortgage products with underwriting guidelines even more flexible than those allowed by Fannie Mae and Freddie Mac under their affordable product lines. In many cases, lenders use these programs in their effort to comply with the Community Reinvestment Act (Federal Reserve Board 2000). These programs generally are targeted to borrowers who have an income below 80 percent of area median, or purchase a home in a census tract with a median income below 80 percent of area median. Lenders use these eligibility criteria because CRA examiners base a large part of their evaluation on the extent to which lenders originate mortgages to lower-income borrowers or in lower-income neighborhoods (FFIEC 1997).

While many different types of products are offered, in general targeted portfolio affordable loans have several features—higher allowable loan-to-value and payment-to-income ratios, more flexible sources of borrower contribution, and more liberal credit underwriting standards—that make them affordable to lower-income borrowers. Column 3 in Table 8.2 details the underwriting guidelines for a sample portfolio affordable loan product offered by a U.S. lender. Moreover, some portfolio loan products do not require borrowers to have mortgage insurance and provide mortgage finance at below-market interest rates. These two features are not available from any GSE product. The GSE charters require them to purchase loans with credit enhancements. As a result, they may only buy loans with recourse back to the seller, mortgage insurance, or in a sale in which the seller retains 10 percent participation.

Primary lenders are not under similar constraints: they can waive the mortgage insurance premium. Since mortgage insurance, on average, costs 50 basis points per year ($500 on a $100,000 mortgage), targeted loans that waive the requirement are more affordable to lower-income borrowers. Lenders originating such loans are exposed to a higher level of risk, and they use home buyer counseling and more aggressive servicing to help lower the probability of borrower default. In a recent survey of lenders, the Federal Reserve Board (2000) found that about one-third of lenders required borrowers receiving an affordable loan to take some sort of prepurchase home buyer counseling.

While it is difficult to sell these loans to the secondary market immediately after origination, they may be sold to investors under certain market conditions. Securitizers use affordable loans as collateral for mortgage-backed securities that use the Real Estate Mortgage Investment Conduit (REMIC) structure. In such a transaction, the underlying cash flow generated from the mortgages used as collateral is structured in order to create certificates that differ by expected maturity and risk grade. The REMIC structure mitigates some of the credit risks associated with the underlying mortgages to certain investors, while allowing those investors with a higher-risk tolerance to earn above-market returns. Certificates or bonds that represent the lowest credit risk to investors are included in the senior tranche, while other certificates that are more risky, are issued as part of the subordinate tranche (DeLiban and Lancaster 1995).

This structure allows originators to sell portfolio affordable loans for their full value, since investors in the subordinate tranches are exposed to the risks associated with higher defaults for loans that do not conform to standard underwriting guidelines. While these transactions provide additional liquidity for portfolio affordable lending, they are not feasible in all types of interest rate environments. Indeed, these transactions became feasible: (1) when prevailing interest rates dropped below coupon rates of affordable portfolio loans, and (2) after the loans had seasoned and demonstrated satisfactory performance that allowed rating agencies and potential investors to analyze the risks and returns associated with mortgage-backed securities issued with targeted affordable loans as underlying collateral (Temkin and Johnson 2000).

The New Landscape in Mortgage Lending

The U.S. mortgage finance system has made great strides in meeting the needs of more low- and moderate-income families. Through experimentation, lenders have come to realize that new mortgage products can be used to qualify borrowers without sacrificing profits. As a result, low- and moderate-income and minority home ownership rates increased in the 1990s, in part because mainstream lending institutions adopted new business models and offered more flexible loan products that were unimaginable even ten years ago. Target borrowers may now apply for mortgages that finance the entire purchase price of the home, and in some cases receive below-market interest rates. Moreover, many of these programs do not require borrowers to purchase mortgage insurance. Borrowers also benefit from more flexible conventional mortgage underwriting standards; Fannie Mae and Freddie Mac now purchase mortgages originated with lower down payments and higher debt-to-income ratios than in the past.

This "quiet revolution" in the lending industry has been driven by legislative requirements of CRA and FHEFSSA, but these changes are sustainable because many lenders perceive low- and moderate-income lending as a profitable and essential aspect of their day-to-day operations. Indeed, lenders recognize that the mortgage industry's growth can only be sustained by serving more minority, low- and moderate-income, and immigrant families, since these groups are overrepresented among renters. As a result, lenders and the GSEs now require more borrowers to attend formal home buyer counseling classes in order to reduce the probability that these new home owners will fall behind in their mortgage payments.

These changes suggest that lenders are now better able to serve lower-income and minority home buyers. They have more experience in underwriting nontraditional borrowers, build better relationships with community organizations in underserved communities, and originate loans to borrowers who are more familiar with the home buying process. Given these trends, it is no surprise that more lower-income and minority families own their home.

REMAINING PROBLEMS: UNDERSERVED MARKETS AND SUBPRIME LENDING

The above discussion highlights changes in the U.S. housing finance system in the 1990s that have helped increase the home ownership rate for members of traditionally underserved markets. But problems still exist with the housing finance system, and some of those problems may represent opportunities for a larger housing microfinance market. In particular, existing home owners with blemished credit are likely to rely on subprime lenders as a source of refinance mortgages.

However, the subprime market may not be the most beneficial source of funds for home improvements. Subprime loans carry relatively high interest rates, which are supposed to reflect the higher risks associated with lending to credit-impaired borrowers, and may have less favorable terms such as balloon payments, negative amortization, or excessive fees. Indeed, many analysts believe that a large share of the subprime market consists of loans that are not in the best interests of the borrower and that are originated by using deceptive and illegal practices. Of course, the subprime lending industry vehemently disputes such claims and argues that subprime lending provides needed mortgage credit to borrowers who do not meet standard credit underwriting guidelines.

Borrowers use subprime loans for a variety of purposes, including home improvements, debt consolidation, and as an alternative source of consumer credit. Relatively few (16 percent) subprime mortgages are used for home purchase. According to a joint HUD-Treasury report, "by 1999 more than three out of every four loans in the subprime mortgage market were first liens . . . the vast majority of these subprime first lien mortgages—82 percent—were used for refinancing as opposed to purchasing a home. Of these refinance loans, a majority (59 percent) were 'cash out,' indicating that borrowers used these loans for home improvement, for making other consumer purchases or consolidating other forms of debt" (U.S. Department of Housing and Urban Development 2000).

Borrowers Served in the Subprime Market

Subprime lenders serve a much higher proportion of minority and lower-income borrowers than prime lenders (Canner and Passmore 1999). In 1998, African-Americans (3.4 percent) and Hispanics (4.2 percent) accounted for less than 8 percent of conventional home purchase mortgages in the prime market. In the 1998 subprime market, however, African-American (11.7 percent) and Hispanic (7.6 percent) borrowers accounted for nearly 20 percent of subprime home purchase mortgages originated. This pattern is also evident for refinance mortgages. In 1998, African-American (2.7 percent) and Hispanic (3.1 percent) borrowers accounted for about 6 percent of all prime conventional refinance mortgages. Yet in that same year African American (12.6 percent) and Hispanic (4.1 percent) borrowers received nearly 17 percent of subprime refinance mortgages (Scheessele 1999).

These racial differences, according to analysts, are evidence that residential finance markets are hypersegmented. African-American home owners, similar to African-American home buyers, are more likely to receive both home purchase and refinance mortgage credit from a subprime lender than are whites. Using HMDA data, Immergluck and Wiles (1999) found that more than 50 percent of refinance loans in predominantly black census tracts were originated by subprime lenders, while less than 10 percent of refinance mortgages in predominantly white tracts were originated by subprime lenders. In fact, subprime lenders accounted for nine out of the top ten companies receiving refinance mortgage applications in predominantly black Chicago neighborhoods. In predominantly white Chicago neighborhoods, only two subprime lenders were among the top ten companies that received refinance mortgages from area residents. These racial disparities are not solely due to income; in a multivariate analysis of subprime lending activity, Immergluck and Wiles found that the proportion of loans originated by subprime lenders in a given census tract was most affected by the tract's racial composition, irrespective of income.

Other reports also find similar racial patterns. Analyzing 1998 HMDA data, HUD found that subprime loans accounted for 51 percent of the dollar amount of all refinance loans in predominantly black census tracts, compared with only nine percent of the dollar amount of refinance loans in mostly white neighborhoods.[2] In a recent study, Pennington-Cross, Yezer, and Nichols (2000) found that minority home buyers are more likely to use subprime financing, even after controlling for credit-risk factors.

Low- and moderate-income families are also overrepresented in the subprime refinance market. In 1998, subprime loans accounted for a little more than one-half of refinance loans originated to low- and moderate-income borrowers, about 16 percentage points more than the proportion of low- and moderate-income borrowers receiving refinance mortgages in the prime, conventional market (Scheessele 1999). Not surprisingly, subprime borrowers are also more likely to live in poorer census tracts: a little more than two-thirds of subprime loans originated in 1998 were in lower- and moderate-income census tracts, compared to only 58 percent of prime loans.

Under the Microscope:
The Subprime Market and Predatory Lending

As the subprime market continues to develop, it is attracting more scrutiny from consumer groups and government regulators. These organizations are concerned that some lenders in the subprime market take advantage of borrowers by engaging in questionable marketing techniques and borderline or outright fraudulent business practices. Companies that employ these techniques have been accused of practicing predatory lending. While there is no common definition of predatory lending, government agencies and consumer groups are working to develop an applicable definition. According to a recent HUD report (2000), predatory lending refers to a wide range of abuses. Typically, predatory lending involves practices in which lenders, brokers, or home improvement contractors "engag[e] in deception or fraud, manipulating the borrower through aggressive sales tactics, or taking unfair advantage of a borrower's lack of understanding about loan terms. These practices are often combined with loan terms that, alone or in combination, are abusive or make the borrower more vulnerable to abusive practices." In conducting public forums on predatory lending, HUD identified four frequent predatory practices: loan flipping, charging borrowers excessive fees and packing them into the loan amount, lending without taking into account a borrower's ability to repay, and outright fraud and abuse.

The federal government and state legislatures are taking steps to assess the extent to which predatory lending exists in the subprime market, and they are considering legislative measures that will make it more difficult for lenders to practice predatory lending. The Federal Reserve Board, HUD, and the Treasury Department convened meetings with industry stakeholders in response to a perceived increase in predatory lending. HUD issued a series of reports in 2000 that analyzed the extent to which subprime loans are originated to minority borrowers or in minority neighborhoods. Moreover, the House of Representatives' Committee on Banking and Financial Services held hearings in May 2000 on predatory home equity lending.

Regulatory agencies are also increasing their oversight of the subprime lending market. Subprime companies purchased by depository prime lenders are subject to federal banking regulations. As a result, the Federal Reserve, Federal Deposit Insurance Corporation, Office of the Comptroller of the Currency, and Office of Thrift Supervision are starting to set policies, such as capital standards, that will affect more subprime lenders. As an example, the four banking industry regulatory agencies issued an interagency guideline on subprime lending in spring 1999, cautioning that the subprime market is highly volatile and the assets have higher risk than prime mortgages. These guidelines provide recommendations for the banks, from managing the risks of subprime lending to selling the mortgages.

A number of states and localities are considering, or have passed, legislation to curb predatory lending practices. Two states whose actions have garnered considerable attention are North Carolina and New York. In 1999, the North Carolina legislature passed Senate Bill 1149, which went into effect on July 1, 2000. This bill identifies and prohibits certain loan terms and lending practices associated with high-cost mortgages and places limits on discount points and fees that can be charged on all first lien loans. The New York legislature is also considering a bill, the "Home Equity Fraud Act," that would prohibit specified terms and practices associated with predatory lending. Other states are considering legislative proposals. Moreover, the Mortgage Bankers Association of America developed and published a set of best practices for subprime lending, in an attempt to provide guidelines for member lenders.

Loan Prices and Terms in the Subprime Market

That subprime borrowers pay higher prices (in terms of interest rates, fees, and points) than those in the prime market is beyond dispute. What is not clear, however, is that the higher prices paid by individual borrowers accurately reflect their underlying risk. The subprime market may be inefficient because borrowers are paying interest rates that are in excess of the risks associated with the mortgage.

While subprime lenders do not adhere to rigid underwriting guidelines, there is evidence that, on average, more risky borrowers are categorized into higher-risk categories. In a study of subprime loans, the Office of Thrift Supervision found that the median FICO score for A– loans was 630, 60 points higher than the median FICO score for B loans. The median FICO score was 550 for loans categorized as C and D loans. This seems to indicate that subprime lenders categorize borrowers with lower FICO scores into higher-risk grades, even though they do not rely on a common set of underwriting criteria.

There is some published information about average subprime rates. Weicher, in his study of home equity lending, found that average rates charged to subprime borrowers by four large lenders in the mid-1990s ranged from around 11 percent to 14 percent. In general, A– mortgages have a rate that is 200 basis points higher than an agency rate; B grade loans are 300 basis points; C grade mortgages 450, and D grade 600 basis points over agency con-forming rates. In its study of subprime loans, the Office of Thrift Supervision found that A– loans, in 1999, had an average coupon interest rate of 9.9 percent; the rate for B, C, and D loans was 10.6, 11.5, and 12.6 respectively. In the same year, coupon interest rates for conforming loans ranged between 7 and 8 percent. One sub-prime lender interviewed for this study confirmed this pricing scheme. The company charges A– borrowers a rate between 100 and 150 basis points above A borrowers; C and D borrowers receive a rate 350 basis points more than A borrowers.

Lenders argue that the higher interest rates charged to bor-rowers in the subprime market reflect the risks commensurate with lending to borrowers with poorer credit histories, higher loan-to-value, and/or front- and back-end ratios. Loan perfor-mance data may support such a view: 3.36 percent of subprime mortgages in the A– range were seriously delinquent as of Sep-tember 30, 2000; and 21 percent of mortgages originated to bor-rowers in the D range were seriously delinquent as of that date. These delinquencies are substantially higher than those in the prime market, only 0.54 percent of loans in the prime market were seriously delinquent as of that date.

Higher rates and fees charged to borrowers are also necessary, according to industry participants, because of the higher servicing costs associated with these mortgages. Advanta reports that their annual servicing cost per loan is $170 for a B/C loan, slightly higher than the A loan servicing costs of approximately $126 per year. This difference is due to higher delinquency and default rates for subprime loans, and the subsequent need for more serv-icing staff.

Yet some subprime loans are originated to borrowers with terms and conditions that are highly unfavorable: loans may have negative amortization, balloon payments, and high prepayment penalties. In addition, subprime refinance lending volumes have increased in all types of interest rate environments. This is a dif-ferent pattern from prime market refinance volumes, which in-crease as home owners take advantage of lower interest rates.

Despite these findings, industry participants argue that their prices reflect the costs in serving higher-risk borrowers, and the loan terms reflect the unique needs of subprime borrowers. We are aware of only one study (Freddie Mac 2000) that addresses the question: "Is the subprime market efficient?" This study suggests that many prime borrowers are served by subprime lenders, and so pay higher costs for mortgages. In addition, some borrowers may pay prices that are in excess of the true costs associated with borrowers with more problematic credit. Therefore, there is reason to believe that a housing microfinance market, targeted to borrowers who would otherwise use subprime credit, would make it easier for home owners to have access to capital required for home improvements.

Counseling

There is an alternative to subprime credit. Underwriting changes, innovative lending consortia, and partnerships make it easier for lenders to serve low- and moderate-income and minority home buyers. Yet many of these new borrowers are unfamiliar with the home buying process: they may be first-time home buyers or may have relatively little knowledge about household finance and budgeting techniques. In response, many organizations now offer home ownership and education services through formal classes and other methods, such as videos.

The content of individual home ownership classes varies, but most teach participants about the steps needed to become a home owner. As a result, these programs instruct a potential home owner about (1) searching for a property that is suitable for his or her income, (2) different types of mortgage programs and products that meet his or her particular financial situation, and (3) other forms of financial planning and home maintenance that will reduce the probability that the home owner will default on the mortgage (McCarthy and Quercia 2000).

The GSEs and many lenders require home ownership counseling for borrowers who receive a mortgage through special affordable programs in order to offset the higher risks associated with lending to borrowers with little equity, high debt, and relatively poor credit. While sparse, there is some evidence that home buyer counseling works. In their study, Hirad and Zorn (2001) find that prepurchase counseling can reduce borrower delinquency rates.

Based on the success of home buyer counseling, the GSEs and other market participants are promoting financial literacy and education programs as a means to inform potential subprime borrowers about the potential hazards associated with such loans. Such initiatives may reduce the demand for subprime refinance loans and provide an opportunity for potential beneficiaries to learn about housing microfinance loan programs.

NOTES

1. GE Capital offered the first affordable lending product in 1989 under its Community Home Buyer Program, which allowed borrowers to place less than five percent down and have higher debt-to-income ratios. It became the model for Fannie Mae's products offered under its Community Home Buying Program, and Freddie Mac's affordable products offered to borrowers under its Affordable Gold initiative.

2. See, for example, U.S. Department of Housing and Urban Development 2000. *Unequal Burden: Income and Racial Disparities in Subprime Lending.*

9

The Market for Housing Microfinance in the United States

Kil Huh and Lopa Purohit Kolluri

W hy should the United States consider housing microfinance for a housing market context that differs so greatly from that of developing countries?

The United States has the largest, most vibrant, and efficient housing finance system in the world. In the past decade, the U.S. housing finance system has made tremendous progress in reaching out to low-income households with innovative and affordable mortgage products, and it continues to develop new approaches to serve these mortgage needs. Indeed, when we think about how progressive housing financing solutions can be applied to the U.S. housing context, a significant number of legal, financial, and construction-related barriers immediately come to mind that rule out housing microfinance—as we have come to understand it—as an required option for the majority of U.S. households.

This chapter makes the case, however, that characteristics of the practice make it interesting and potentially attractive for three select segments of the U.S. housing market:

1. The rehab market;
2. Progressive housing; and (to a lesser extent)
3. Rental housing

Housing microfinance is not a subsidy-driven model but a market-based, demand-driven solution that has made housing an affordable and economically viable option for low-income households in developing countries. It addresses a failure of established capital markets to extend traditional means of housing finance to low- and moderate-income households.

Housing microfinance builds on informal approaches to improving habitat based on a community's needs and interests while providing links to the mainstream financial market, thus, creating great potential for broad-based replicability and scalability. Housing microfinance not only represents another appropriate and affordable financing option for low-income individuals to improve housing, it also increases a household's potential for creating sustainable wealth.

Despite the success of the U.S. housing finance market model and the major strides made to move downmarket to low-income families, a significant number of U.S. households still face considerable barriers to accessing home ownership and realizing the full asset-building potential that comes with owning a home. A significant number of low-income working families are not considered bankable by conventional market standards, and consequently are unable to access the mainstream financial market.

While many of these barriers differ from those that low-income households in developing countries confront, there are similarities in the reasons for why low-income households are not able to access the mainstream housing finance market. These similarities warrant an examination of whether housing microfinance may help break down some of the barriers to accessing home ownership.

This chapter explores the potential demand for housing microfinance in the United States and examines the extent to which housing microfinance may help address the challenges that many low-income households encounter in achieving and sustaining home ownership over the course of a lifetime.

HOUSING FINANCE AND HOME OWNERSHIP IN THE UNITED STATES

The Harvard Joint Center for Housing Studies (2002) reports that the number of U.S. home owners hit a record 72.6 million in 2001, 67.8 percent of the households. Since 1994, minorities have accounted for 40 percent of the gain in home ownership. Overall, minorities make up 25 percent of the nation's households and 17 percent of the home owners.

Home ownership rates in the United States are at historic levels, particularly for minority groups. Higher incomes and a low-interest rate environment have contributed to the gains in home ownership, but this does not capture the entire story. Many of the gains in home ownership can also be explained by efforts of the housing finance industry to adopt more flexible underwriting standards, efforts by Government Sponsored Enterprises (GSEs) such as Fannie Mae and Freddie Mac to create more affordable loan products and underwriting experiments to encourage greater home ownership, partnerships with community-based organizations to penetrate markets and assist with transactions, and loan guarantees and credit enhancements to sell to the secondary market to increase liquidity for affordable lending. Further, the Community Reinvestment Act (CRA) of 1977 has increased the lending commitments of banks to underserved communities, although it is difficult to explicitly attribute increased home ownership rates to CRA since 50 percent of all mortgages are originated by mortgage banks not subject to CRA (Temkin 2001).

However, while home ownership rates are at historical highs for most groups in the United States, the gap between whites and minority groups remains significant, particularly for low-income minority groups.[1]

Housing as a Financial Asset

Past research has documented that housing represents the main capital asset of most low- and moderate-income families. Housing remains the primary vehicle for building and accumulating wealth for the majority of the world's population. Households leverage this asset in many ways—for example by renting out spare rooms and conducting home-based businesses—and use it to mitigate the impacts of job change and illness. Further, "[t]here is the growing recognition that housing plays a prominent role in many other policy areas. For example, housing stability is now seen as key to both the well-being of the lowest-income elderly and working families, and to the ability of welfare recipients to find and keep jobs. Public health officials are also focusing on reducing the many hazards present in structurally inadequate housing, and public safety officials have attested to the success of housing choice vouchers in enabling families to move to safer communities (Harvard Joint Center for Housing Studies, 28)."

In addition, the Joint Center for Housing Studies clearly outlines the importance of housing as a vehicle for building assets. As
the study points out, for most American home owners (nearly two-
thirds of the population), home equity is by far their single most
important asset. "In fact, in 1998 half of all home owners held at
least 50 percent of their net wealth in home equity. In comparison, less than half of U.S. households hold stocks; of those, the top
one percent own more than one-third of the total value" (2002, 7).

Housing, particularly home ownership, is inexorably linked to
how individual households build wealth and is a primary driver of
the U.S. economy; thus, it is important to examine the existing
barriers to and opportunities for home ownership and ways to
maximize and protect this important asset.

A CLOSER LOOK AT THE
U.S. HOUSING FINANCE MARKET

The U.S. housing finance system has successfully addressed a number of the existing barriers to home ownership by tailoring its
methodologies to serve low- and moderate-income (LMI) populations, and great strides have been made to increase programs to
help LMI and minority households access financial services and
home ownership. The rapid expansion of lending to lower-income
households represents one of the most significant accomplish-
ments of the 1990s.

However, a closer examination of the U.S. housing finance sector shows that, despite the rapid expansion in mortgage finance
products for low-income households from the conventional
finance market, borrowers are not able to take full advantage of
the products available through the system. Low-income working
families that are not considered bankable by conventional market
standards are unable to access the mainstream financial market.

Financial Services in LMI Communities

An estimated 10 million households (over 9.5 percent of households) in the United States have no relationship with a traditional
financial institution (Kennickell 2000). These unbanked households are disproportionately low-income and minority; 30 percent
earn less than $15,000 annually and another 10 percent earn

between $15,000 and $30,000 (D'Amours 2000, Kim 2001). Further, fewer than half the households with income below 80 percent of the area median have a credit card. This failure to access mainstream financial service products prevents many families from efficiently and effectively managing the income they have, building savings, and becoming home owners, "because having a well-documented credit history (including capacity to manage checking accounts and credit cards) increasingly influences mortgage terms and lending standards" (Harvard Joint Center for Housing Studies 2002, 27).

As many low- and moderate-income households lack access to traditional financial markets, these families turn to high-cost fringe financial services to meet their immediate and long-term financial needs. Fringe financial services commission $5.5 billion annually in fees charged to low-income and minority residents. This amount is roughly equal to the entire asset base of all Community Development Financial Institutions operating in the United States—and it is an annual funding stream (Carr and Schuetz 2001). Add the above sum to the hundreds of millions of dollars unnecessarily paid each year in excessive subprime lending costs, and it is clear that the U.S. financial markets do not optimally serve the needs of all low- and moderate-income populations.

A whole host of barriers prevents unbanked households from accessing mainstream financial services. On the supply side, the financial provider may perceive the clients as high risk and unprofitable for the institution. The financial institution's underwriting standards may be too stringent or inflexible for low-income households. From the consumer's perspective, distrust of financial institutions and lack of experience with banking have also been cited as barriers. Further, within the unbanked segment, historically marginalized and newly emerging segments of the U.S. population face a host of barriers specific to their own circumstances that deny them full access to the mainstream housing finance sector.

Although finding affordable financial services is a major challenge for low-income families, a surprising 48 percent own their own homes. Pointing to the fact that 61 percent of lowest-income home owners are elderly, the State of the Nation's Housing report indicates that this group is vulnerable to losing their home as they are subjected to high housing-related costs, unexpected emergencies, and predatory lenders (Harvard Joint Center for Housing Studies 2002).

Housing Challenges for LMI Owners

A number of disadvantaged households reside in aging housing stock in the center of U.S. metropolitan areas. As employment and housing construction move outward, those left in the core areas must live in older, often deteriorating, housing. Unfortunately the number of lenders willing to fund construction or rehabilitation of affordable housing in older neighborhoods is few.

In addition, according to Louie et al. (1998), lower-income home owners are overrepresented in the South and Midwest. More than 8 million lower-income home owners live in southern states, comprising 37 percent of all owners with lower incomes, and another 5.8 million live in the Midwest. As with other lower-income owners around the country, this segment of the population faces challenges related to housing maintenance and repairs as their families grow, special needs arise, or incomes decrease.

Closing the home ownership gap not only requires more financial options to access home ownership, but also to ensure that recent first-time home buyers are able to remain home owners. According to the State of the Nation's Housing Report, a growing number of low-income borrowers with thin equity cushions may undo recent home ownership gains and introduce new risks into the overall housing market (Harvard Joint Center for Housing Studies 2002).

Furthermore, home owners need to invest in the upkeep of their property to allow for increases in the value of the home. This is especially important for those low-income households residing in distressed areas that are subject to declining property values. "The cardinal axiom of home ownership is simple and inexorable: Homes require maintenance. Maintenance—the yearly checkups, the minor repairs, the troubleshooting—is essential" (Louie et al. 1998, 3). However, many home owners are not spending the necessary funds to maintain their homes. For 1998 and 1999, 42 percent of home owners reported spending less than $500 on upkeep of their homes (Belsky 2002, 5).

Louie et al. (1998) continue, "The housing challenges that lower-income home owners face stem largely from the high costs of owning and maintaining a home relative to their incomes. As a result, many lower-income home owners spend large shares of their incomes for housing, often diverting funds from other necessary expenses. Many can only afford homes of lower quality, and, thus, experience high levels of housing deficiencies ranging from damaged roofs to peeling paint. Millions do not have sufficient funds to maintain their units, leading to further housing deterioration and a range of negative consequences for individual occupants and surrounding communities" (10).

Growth of the home ownership rate is itself a hollow goal if these gains are easily erased or if the homes deteriorate over time and lower-income owners are trapped in a cycle of disrepair and high costs. As federal housing policies focus on supporting low-income households to become first-time home owners, a close examination of the post-purchase experience of lower-income owners is essential for meeting the goals of increased home ownership, while helping these families realize the benefits of building equity, putting down roots, and helping to build a community.

According to David Dangler of Neighborhood Reinvestment Corporation,[2] while significant resources have been focused to date on expanding first-time home buyer programs for low-income individuals, there is a real need to focus national efforts on post-purchase support for families and other programs to ensure that low-income home owners are able to sustain these gains in home ownership.

A number of nonprofit organizations, with support from foundations, and government programs have focused their efforts on rehab and post-purchase programs for low-income home owners residing in distressed communities. These programs focus on helping low-income individuals sustain gains in home ownership and also play a vital role in the neighborhood revitalization process. However, these programs are stifled by limited funding sources. Many of these programs are unable to draw on conventional financing, and they typically operate outside the realm of the traditional financial sector. More innovative market-driven solutions are needed that leverage scarce subsidy funding to attract private sector capital to support the needs of low-income home owners residing in distressed communities.

EXPLORING A NEW APPROACH TO FINANCING HOUSING: HOUSING MICROFINANCE

While the housing finance system has allowed many low-income families to access home ownership, the system has been less successful in

offering nonmortgage-based products to help low-income households sustain home ownership. With regard to existing low-income
home owners, there are currently a number of mostly government-
based financing options for maintaining and rehabilitating their
homes. While many of these programs have been effective, funds
are often limited and many households remain on waiting lists for
years before they are able to access these funds. Housing microfinance offers an innovative alternative to households in need of
products and services to maintain and rehabilitate their homes.
Housing microfinance also has the potential to attract resources
from the conventional financial sector, making it different from
current approaches that aim to address the needs of low-income
home owners. As Daphnis notes (see chapter 1): Housing microfinance includes financial services that allow low-income households to finance their housing needs with methods adapted from
microfinance. The major features of this type of financing include:

- Loans for relatively small amounts based on the clients'
  capacity to repay;
- Relatively short repayment periods (especially compared to
  mortgage lending) on par with mid- to high-end microfinance individual loans;
- Loan pricing expected to cover real, long-term operational
  and financial costs of providing the service;
- Loans not heavily collateralized, if at all, and often use of
  collateral substitutes;
- Loans tending to finance housing needs incrementally, a
  function of loans with short repayment periods and relatively low monthly payments.

THE POTENTIAL U.S. MARKET
FOR HOUSING MICROFINANCE

The potential demand for housing microfinance products is likely
to arise from those low- to moderate-income households that need
short-term, affordable home rehabilitation loans and that—for a
number of reasons—do not have access to the formal financial sector. Specifically, the demand for the product is likely to arise from
existing home owners and households that need nonmortgage-
based loans to finance their homes. One major segment of this

demand includes existing home owners, which consists of new home owners, long-time home owners such as elderly individuals, second generation home owners (those whose ownership came via inheritance), households residing in aging housing, and small property owners.

In addition to this segment, households engaged in nontraditional approaches to financing their homes also represent a market for housing microfinance products. These include emerging populations such as immigrants residing in distressed areas along the U.S.-Mexico border, and low-income households residing in isolated rural areas and on Native American reservations. These segments of the U.S. population, given access to appropriate and affordable housing-related finance products, could improve their housing situation and move into the financial mainstream. Another small but important segment is the small rental property owners market (ten units or less). Nearly one-third of the total rental stock in the United States was built before 1950. This deteriorating rental stock is an increasing problem for communities facing an affordability crunch in rental markets, particularly when it is easier for small property owners to abandon their properties than to maintain them properly.

The following sections broadly survey the state of these various market segments and assess whether housing microfinance can play a role in helping address some of the housing challenges that exist in these markets.

Existing Home Owners: Market for Rehab Loans

State of the market. A significant share (14 percent) of lower-income households also live in units that are overcrowded or structurally inadequate. This percentage is based on the Department of Housing and Urban Development's (HUD) procedure for identifying structurally inadequate units, which has not been updated for many years. Recent research by the National Association of Home Builders in fact suggests that the incidence of structural inadequacy is nearly twice that level (Harvard Joint Center for Housing Studies 2002).

Moreover, a look at the American Housing Survey data (see Table 9.1) further illuminates the structural deficiencies of housing units that many households, including low-income households, confront. In 1999, more than 6.8 million housing units (6.1

percent of all housing units) were found by HUD's methodology
to be structurally inadequate; of those housing units nearly 3 million (or 42.5 percent of all inadequate housing units) were owner-
occupied units. Further, that same year, more than 6.2 million
households (44 percent of all households living below the poverty
level) living in owner-occupied housing were living below the
poverty level. Indeed, the total number and percentage of households living below the poverty level (both renter and owner-
occupied) increased significantly from 1991 to 1999. The number
of owner-occupied households living below the poverty level
increased by more than 1.2 million households and 5 percentage
points (see Table 9.1).

Moreover, the majority of households living below the poverty
level are located inside the metropolitan statistical area, in central
cities and older suburbs (see Table 9.2). As the Harvard study
(2002) underscored, "[w]ith departure of higher-income household from central cities, disadvantaged households have become
increasingly isolated in deteriorating core areas. In the nation's
largest metropolitan areas, a quarter of all home owner families
and more than a half of all renter families reside in the central
city. The central-city share of lower-income renter families—especially minorities or families with children—is larger still" (11).

The concentration of lower-income households in central
cities poses difficult housing challenges. As jobs and new housing
developments continue to be located outside urban areas, those
left behind in these core areas (central cities and older suburbs)
must live in older, often deteriorating, housing. Further com-
pounding the difficulties that many low-income households in
central cities face are the dearth of lenders willing to fund the
construction or rehabilitation of housing in older neighborhoods.
The number of individuals willing to invest in these areas is few,
even among existing residents, including home owners.[3]

Further, even if lower-income residents are willing to invest
back into their neighborhoods, many are not able to afford it.
Many lower-income home owners cannot afford even basic upkeep,
let alone extensive renovations. Many of these households barely
have enough money for their mortgages, taxes, and insurance payments. The U.S. housing finance model is debt-heavy and does not
account for drops in income, changes in family size, or increases in
housing expenses over time. Given that nearly 10 million owners
spend more than 30 percent of their income on housing—and of

Table 9.1 National Outlook: Owner-Occupied Units with Physical Problems and Household Poverty Characteristics

Year	Total Occupied Units	Total Owner-Occupied Units	Total Number and Percentage of Housing with Severe or Moderate Physical Problems	Number and Percentage of Total Owner-Occupied Units with Severe or Moderate Physical Problems	Number of Households Below Poverty Level	Number and Percentage of Owner-Occupied Households Below Poverty Level (relative to all households below poverty level)
1991	93,147	59,796	7,405 (7.9%)	3,683 (6.2%)	12,836	4,994 (38.9%)
1993	94,724	61,252	6,126 (6.5%)	2,963 (4.8%)	13,787	5,386 (39.1%)
1995*	97,693	63,544	6,370 (6.5%)	3,244 (5.1%)	14,695	6,034 (41.1%)
1997**	99,487	65,487	6,987 (7.0%)	2,895 (4.4%)	15,728	6,619 (42.1%)
1999	112,292	68,796	6,878 (6.1%)	2,925 (4.3%)	14,264	6,275 (44.0%)

Note: U.S. Department of Housing and Urban Development, American Housing Survey (in thousands).
*Revised version of the 1995 American Housing Survey was used.
**This data is being revised. No firm conclusions should be formulated based on this data, though it can be used to get a general picture.

Table 9.2 National Outlook: Location of Household Below Poverty Level

Year	Households Below Poverty Level	Inside Metropolitan Statistical Areas		Households Below Poverty Level Outside Statistical Area
		Households Below Poverty Level in Central Cities	Households Below Poverty Level in Suburbs	
1991	12,836	5,182	3,877	3,777
1993	13,787	5,736	4,486	3,565
1995*	14,695	5,925	5,004	3,767
1997**	15,728	6,202	5,245	4,280
1999	14,264	5,596	4,893	3,775

Note: U.S. Department of Housing and Urban Development, American Housing Survey (in thousands).
*Revised version of the 1995 American Housing Survey was used.
**This data is being revised. No firm conclusions should be formulated based on this data, though it can be used to get a general picture.

these half spend more than 50 percent—for many there is little surplus cash for maintenance and repairs.

Indeed, in addition to the financing barriers and environmental challenges identified above, according to Belsky, 45 percent of the nation's seven million extremely low-income home owners have difficulty properly maintaining their homes because they spend more than half their income on other housing costs. Further, about one-fifth of the nation's nearly 25 million low-income home owners have a tough time accessing credit for home repairs and improvements, because they spend more than half their income on other housing costs (Belsky 2002, 4–5).

Yet despite these burdens on lower-income home owners very few of these owners receive government assistance to mitigate cost burdens or repair serious physical problems. Two programs, HOME and Community Development Block Grants (CDBG), help existing home owners repair and rehabilitate their homes. However, the bulk of these two programs is directed at other needs such as rental housing. The federal government also has the Rural Housing Service Section 502 direct loans that assist with some housing rehabilitation, but the direct loans are overwhelmingly used to assist first-time home buyers. Finally, the federal government offers the Federal Housing Administration (FHA) mortgage insurance on home improvement loans regardless of owner income, but customers pay a premium that is intended to cover the cost of the insurance.

These programs may be able to address some of the housing maintenance and rehabilitation needs of lower-income home owners, the HOME and CDBG programs in particular, but the scope and scale is ultimately limited due to insufficient funds. The severely cost burdened, elderly, or disabled home owners are the subset of lower-income home owners who most need assistance and subsidy. And while home owners with extremely low incomes or high housing costs cannot afford needed home maintenance and rehabilitation, many lower-income households are able to undertake such work (Louie et al. 1998). However, while a significant portion of lower-income home owners can afford housing maintenance and structural replacements, many households defer such work. According to Louie et al. (1998, 24), "over the ten year period from 1984 to 1993, nearly 1 million lower-income owners spent an annual average of less than $100 on home maintenance and/or replacements." In addition, about 765,000 home owners live in small properties that the federal government deems severely inadequate, and 1.6 million are exposed to unhealthy or unsafe homes with moderate problems (Belsky 2002, 5).

Due to their limited incomes, many lower-income individuals already tend to live in older housing that needs improvement, and deferment of maintenance and repairs may result in deleterious impacts for the household itself and the surrounding neighborhood. Inadequate housing conditions have health consequences, result in greater energy consumption, and decrease property value. Further, deteriorating housing may negatively impact the overall neighborhood and diminish the value of nearby units. Given that homes are the primary asset for many U.S. families, disregarding maintenance and replacement can result in a devaluation of that asset and adversely impact the transfer of wealth to the next generation.

Housing maintenance and rehabilitation is an important part of protecting housing as an asset for U.S. households in the post-purchase phase. "Most wealth among lower-income owners is held in the form of home equity. It accounts for 52 percent of the aggregate net wealth of lower-income households with an elderly member and 50 percent of the net wealth of households without an elderly person. Half of lower-income elderly owners have 69 percent or more of their net wealth in home equity" (Louie et al. 1998, 33).

Tapping into home equity for repairs and modifications is a solution for many elderly individuals via the reverse mortgage, but many low-income elderly are perhaps unaware of the Home Equity Conversion Mortgage program or unwilling to use their equity for these purposes. Instead, these elderly defer using their equity for home improvements to hedge against other emergencies, or they simply wish to pass the housing onto the next generation (Louie et al. 1998). More lenders are offering reverse mortgages, and community-based organizations are beginning to market this program to their lower-income elderly constituents. As outreach and marketing for reverse mortgages increases, many more lower-income elderly owners may opt for this opportunity to tap into their equity to modify and improve their homes. However, this program targets one particular segment, albeit an important one, of the lower-income owners. A number of nonprofit organizations manage home rehabilitation and owner-occupied rehab programs to support the needs of a broader cross-section of low-income home owners. The following section looks at one specific program that is meeting the needs of low-income home owners in a few neighborhoods in Baltimore, Maryland.

Demand for Housing Microfinance in Baltimore Neighborhoods

One urban market that represents potential strong demand for rehabilitation loans among low-income home owners is Baltimore. Like a number of major U.S. cities, many of Baltimore's distressed neighborhoods are home to a significant number of low-income home owners. According to the 1998 American Housing Survey for the Baltimore PMSA, approximately 69 percent of the total occupied units are owner-occupied. Of the total owner-occupied households, approximately 18.4 percent have severe or moderate physical problems. While a number of these units are in areas of relatively higher levels of distress, low-income home owners also reside in borderline neighborhoods. According to Cheryl Casiani, Program Director of the Baltimore Foundation, some Baltimore neighborhoods have a high percentage of low-income home owners, and because of the lack of investment, they have high potential to fall into severe distress. These are often referred to as "at risk" or borderline neighborhoods because of their fragile state. According to Casiani, a number of programs in Baltimore focus on first-time home buyer programs but not in invested property upkeep, which has led to the sagging value of houses and deterioration of neighborhoods. Modest investments, public and private, in the form of loans and technical assistance could prevent these neighborhoods from declining further into serious disinvestment and abandonment.

Over the last two years, the Baltimore Community Foundation has responded to the needs of low-income home owners through a program that seeks to stabilize and increase housing value in these fragile communities. The systems and loan products include user-friendly loans aimed at home owner rehab and customer service rehab estimating services, complex processes to meet requirements for lead safety and historic district rehab, and other technical assistance to support broader revitalization strategies for the neighborhood.[4]

For these types of neighborhoods, housing microfinance offers a potential solution that couples the provision of credit with technical assistance to help low-income home owners support much needed rehabilitation for their homes. Housing microfinance offers affordable short-term credit, which low-income households often find difficult to access in the mainstream financial market. Housing microfinance also offers technical assistance consisting of pre- and post-loan counseling, which home owners often find invaluable. The housing rehabilitation or repair process can be complex and intimidating for many home owners. The process of finding a contractor at a competitive price, conferring with an architect to ensure that the rehabilitation or repair complies with local zoning laws and housing codes in addition to obtaining financing for the rehabilitation or repairs can be daunting. Moreover, as the effort increases to move more minorities and immigrants to home ownership, their unfamiliarity with the housing finance system, contractors and local laws, ordinances and codes could have profound negative repercussions for their ability to maintain and repair their homes.

Currently, the low-income population needing assistance to rehabilitate homes depends largely on existing government programs to fulfill their rehab needs. These funds are often insufficient, limiting the number of households that can access these programs to meet their rehab needs. Despite the innovative efforts underway by nonprofits to implement housing rehabilitation programs, government sponsored rehabilitation efforts are limited in scope and scale. Housing microfinance as a market-based approach has potential for allowing rehabilitation efforts to reach a scale that can meet the demand.

The Baltimore Community Foundation program represents an innovative solution to target the rehab needs of households in at-risk neighborhoods in Baltimore, as housing microfinance loan amounts are tied to a customer's ability to pay back that loan, and the pre- and post-loan technical assistance that accompanies each loan. Housing microfinance also helps instill a discipline that allows the provider to respond to effective demand for the product. Furthermore, it responds to a significant need in the community for investment needed to keep a community from falling further in distress. However, it is important to note that any form of housing microfinance program will initially rely heavily on foundation and government funding for operational viability. Further study is needed to explore whether there is role for traditional financial institutions to play in the program and whether housing microfinance can help the program become more efficient, market-driven, and sustainable in the long run.

Progressive Housing: Market for Housing Microfinance

A significant number of legal, financial, and construction-related barriers come to mind when one thinks about the application of progressive housing to the U.S. market. For most of the U.S. market, progressive housing or the incremental approach to building a house does not apply. Neither starter housing (that does not meet code) nor an incremental approach (to meeting standards) are options. Self construction is the exception rather than the rule (Merrill and Temkin 2002). The exceptions, however, are worth further exploration. One of the closest examples of progressive housing in the United States is the self-help method, an approach typically used in rural areas, where the geography may lend itself to this type of construction. Specifically, distressed rural areas and Native American reservations are areas where this type of building is taking place. However, even in these isolated rural areas, a focus is on developing housing using conventional methods and accessing mortgages, even though it means the support of deep subsidies. One specific niche market in which households practice nonmortgage housing development (due to a number of reasons discussed in the following section) is the colonias, housing settlements along the south Texas border. The following section takes a look at the state of the market, reviews the challenges, and discusses potential opportunity for applying the principles of housing microfinance to improve housing conditions.

Market for Housing Microfinance in Rural Areas:
The U.S.-Mexico Border

An estimated 400,000 people reside in the *colonias,* unincorporated settlements that flourish along the U.S.-Mexico Border. Housing, generally constructed piecemeal by owners, often lacks electricity, plumbing, and basic amenities. A limited supply of adequate affordable housing in the cities and rural areas along the Texas-U.S. border has contributed to the development of new colonias and the expansion of existing ones. A report by the University of Texas estimates that if current trends continue, by 2010 more than 700,000 additional people will need affordable housing on the Texas border (Federal Reserve Bank of Dallas 2001).

In the early 1950s, colonias became a way of life for thousands of people when developers began creating subdivisions in unincorporated, isolated, rural areas on land that had no agricultural value or that was located in a floodplain. The developers divided the properties into small lots with little or no infrastructure, and then sold them on contract for deed to low-income people. The residents often built their homes piecemeal with whatever materials they could find or afford.

The colonias have three major problems: contract for deed, inadequate infrastructure, and substandard quality. A contract for deed is a financing arrangement in which land ownership remains with the seller until the total purchase price is paid. Many colonia inhabitants bought land on contract for deed because they had neither the credit history nor the resources to qualify for traditional financing. According to the executive director of Projecto Azteca, a nonprofit organization developing housing in the colonias, contract for deed sales continue but the properties now have infrastructure. The contracts generally carry about 14 percent interest. The sales continue because the buyers can get a half acre tract in a colonia versus a smaller lot in a city, and they aren't required to follow city building codes and restrictions. The buyers can also build and get financing as their incomes allow (Federal Reserve Bank of Dallas 2001).

The infrastructure in these border communities is lacking. Many of today's colonias' residents still use septic tanks and cesspools. They buy water by the bucket and drum and use potentially contaminated wells. According to a report by the Federal Reserve Bank of Dallas (2001) as recently as June 2000, only 54 percent of Texas colonia residents surveyed had sewer service and more than 50 percent drank water from sources other than taps. Even with water and sewer systems in place, many colonia residents do not have hook-ups because their houses can't pass inspections to qualify and the owners can't afford repairs or improvements to meet codes. State legislation passed over the last decade has led to some infrastructure improvements in the colonias.

In terms of housing itself, colonia houses are primarily built incrementally by the residents, using available, often indigenous, materials. The houses often begin as tents or makeshift structures of wood, cardboard, or other materials. As their sparse finances allow, the owners add improvements but rarely use professional builders. Housing in the older colonias tends to be better developed because residents have had more time to improve it.

As a result of the incremental housing development practices, substandard housing flourishes throughout the colonias. A variety of new initiatives have been developed to address the housing situation. Colonias residents, nonprofit organizations, financial institutions, foundations, and local, state, and federal governments are involved in improving colonia living conditions and providing alternative housing options. Unique partnerships between nonprofits, government, and financial institutions have helped bring a variety of resources and expertise to the housing problem, resulting in some innovative solutions to improve the living conditions of colonias residents. As a way of providing alternatives to colonias, one nonprofit organization is tearing down homes in colonias and rebuilding homes in the same areas.

In Hidalgo county the colonias, where more than 4,000 colonia families are on a housing waiting list with Projecto Azteca, the nonprofit plans to develop as an alternative $6,000 houses with limited interior finish. The owners would put 30 percent down, get five-year loans at zero interest, and make monthly payments of $75 to $100. They can finish the interiors as their finances allow. This type of housing development seems to mirror the progressive housing solutions used in developing countries and, therefore, may lend itself to housing microfinance solutions.

A wide variety of organizations including Fannie Mae, lenders, and nonprofits have joined the efforts to address the housing situation in the colonias. Despite the resources and great effort put forth by various parties challenges remain, and additional solutions are needed to address the housing problems that persist in this market. For most colonia residents, their only option is living in the colonias. Complex mortgage-based products are not a viable option for these residents. According to Ninfa Moncada, Director of Fannie Mae's Border Partnership Office, bank participation is nonexistent because of lack of infrastructure and the lack of standards in the colonias. Even in the older, more developed colonias, lenders are still nonexistent; microloans for housing could help lead the way for lenders to come into these areas.[5]

Colonias residents differ from other would-be home owners in three important aspects. First the colonias housing market is characterized by buyers with extremely low incomes. Many colonia residents are farmworkers or service industry workers with household incomes close to minimum wage. Typically their earnings will support monthly payments of $200 or less. Yet monthly payments for new housing within border cities commonly exceed two or three times that amount. Second, the lack of affordable credit turns residents to expensive subprime credit sources such as contract-for-deed offered by colonia developers. Many buyers become entangled in payment schedules that they cannot afford, which ultimately makes them unattractive to lenders with more favorable rates. Third, many people with a housing need already own a home. Although the home or its location may be considered substandard, to the owner it is a work in progress, representing considerable financial sacrifice and physical effort. Colonia residents desire financing so they can accelerate their efforts to complete their homes. Yet the substandard nature of the existing construction or location generally will not meet lending standards (Henneberger 2000).

The need for more affordable short-term financing to rehabilitate colonia homes is also confirmed by Homero Cabello, Director of Colonia Initiatives at the Texas Department of State.[6] Cabello refers to the potential need for financing to be the greatest in the older colonias as these tend to be better developed, have access to water and wastewater services, and residents have invested time and money in improving their homes.

Several nonprofit organizations on the border have developed programs tailored to the housing needs of low-income families and colonia residents. Building on the residents' willingness to construct their own homes, these programs provide materials, instruction, and a team approach to construction. This combination has proven to be an effective means of making decent, affordable housing available to hundreds of border residents.

Given the potential need for rehabilitation loans to meet the housing needs of the colonias residents, housing microfinance represents one solution that may be applied to the colonia housing market. While a few large nonprofit organizations have successfully provided a similar product, a number of smaller organizations are providing rehab loans to support housing development. According to Homero Cabello, one issue for these organizations is the limited capacity to carry out this type of work. If housing microfinance presents a viable strategy to improve housing in the colonias, smaller nonprofit institutions may benefit from partnering with microlending institutions such as Accion to provide effective housing microfinance products to families.

Rental Housing

Another area to explore the possibility of an intersection between housing microfinance and the U.S. housing market is the rental housing market, particularly the significant number of small properties (less than 10 units) that house most of this country's renters.

According to The State of the Nation's Housing 2002, even the most recent construction and substantial rehabilitation projects have done little to expand the supply of affordable rental units. Rental housing continues to serve the housing needs of 34 million households, especially for lower-income minority and immigrant families unable to buy homes. Of all the households that rent, 41.2 percent spend more than 30 percent of their incomes for housing, while 20.6 percent spend 50 percent or more.

The success of the Low-Income Housing Tax Credit in increasing the supply of affordable rental housing is well-known and widely documented in the literature on affordable housing, but rising costs and the diminishing supply of low-cost rental units continue the considerable stress on renters, particularly lower-income minorities and immigrants. The rental stock in the United States is also aging, and the Harvard Joint Center for Housing Studies (2002) finds that nearly one-third of all rental units were built before 1950. Further, the "American Housing Survey estimates indicate that 4 million (11.6 percent) have moderate or severe structural deficiencies. Indeed, renters are more than twice as likely as owners to reside in structurally inadequate housing" (2002, 22). This fact is amplified in the central city neighborhoods where structural deficiencies are most prevalent, where one in two properties built before 1950 are inadequate.

The Joint Center for Housing Studies (2002) found that 65.4 percent (17 of 26 million) of the unsubsidized rental units are owned by an individual or married couple. Ownership of these properties is at best a part-time commitment, as most of these properties are small properties (less than 10 units) controlled by absentee owners. Further, many of these owners are ill-equipped to manage and maintain their units. In addition, the "lack of suitable financing vehicles is . . . a major obstacle. During the 1990s, options for permanent financing or large properties expanded rapidly as secondary markets developed and other new forms of financing came on line. Loans for the acquisition or refinancing of smaller apartment buildings, in contrast, are poor candidates for securitization because of their lack of standardization. As a result, the small rental property market has yet to benefit from the expansion of financing options" (23). The study goes on to state that "the limited availability and higher cost of financing prevents owners from either investing in capital improvements or selling their properties to more capable owners. In addition, subsidizing smaller multifamily property owners is often difficult because the administrative complexity and costs may be just as great for a property owner with a 100-unit building. In consequence, today's major supply-side housing assistance programs—including the Low-Income Housing Tax Credit—typically provide subsidies to larger properties, even though most renters needing assistance live in smaller properties" (23).

With financing as a major barrier along with the dearth of experienced landlords, housing microfinance provides an opportunity for small property owners to take advantage of the financing and technical assistance that housing microfinance has to offer, to make small but marked improvements to their rental properties.

NEXT STEPS: HOUSING MICROFINANCE IN THE UNITED STATES

One may argue that housing microfinance is an international practice, with limited applicability to the U.S. housing market. However, the examination of potential demand within specific market segments indicates the need for further study on applying housing microfinance to the U.S. housing context. Given the enhanced emphasis on efforts and programs to help home owners sustain gains in home ownership, housing microfinance represents one product among many that aim to address the needs of low-income home owners. While the traditional housing finance sector has made significant strides in providing affordable mortgage products to low-income individuals, little has been done to support the needs of low-income home owners. There are a number of nonprofit organizations managing programs for this purpose, but these programs rely heavily on limited sources of government and foundation funding to operate their programs. Whether in the colonias or in Baltimore, there is a demand for the products and services offered by housing microfinance. Community development corporations, faith-based groups, and some private-sector development companies are already playing a central role in providing home repair and improvements to lower-income home owners who receive government subsidies. Can housing microfinance bring scale, efficiency, and discipline to support the needs of low-income home owners?

Given the potential of these markets, a next step may be to consider developing a housing microfinance pilot program. To develop such a program, a number of complex issues and planning activities must be considered. The initiation and implementation of a pilot program would not be easy however, it would allow one to determine whether housing microfinance has a broader role to play in the U.S. housing context, and whether the practice has viability for replication on a wider scale.

Scoping Out a Housing Microfinance Initiative

The purpose of developing a housing microfinance initiative is to test the assumption that housing microfinance can play a role in serving the financial and technical assistance needs of low-income home owners, which in turn will help preserve household wealth and strengthen distressed neighborhoods. The goal is to demonstrate that such a program ultimately can be self-sustaining for the financial institutions and its partners, while also being cost effective and affordable for the clients who are served by it.

Before a new program can be implemented, a number of research and design activities will need to be in place to help inform the pilot phase of the initiative. One of the first steps is the development and framing of a broad-based site selection criteria to identify sites for the initiative at both the city and neighborhood level. This initial step is important when addressing critical issues such as the potential for the program to be replicable and scalable. Selection of diverse sites is important in applying the findings and lessons from the pilot program to a larger scale. Factors in selecting the urban and rural settings may include some overlapping variables such as home ownership rate, income, and other demographic characteristics such as age. However, for a housing microfinance program to be successful, local considerations will play a central role in the program design. Nonetheless it is essential to articulate some general design guidelines to create a U.S. housing microfinance initiative. Some salient characteristics to consider when developing such a housing microfinance pilot are:

- The existing level of investment made by government and/ or private funding sources (i.e., foundations, banks, etc.) in owner-occupied rehabilitation strategies for the purpose of revitalizing city neighborhoods and/or the presence of active community-based organizations engaged in facilitating this activity.
- An examination of the supply and demand conditions needed to drive a successful program will need to be in place. A closer look at HUD's American Housing Survey is an appropriate place to begin, supplemented by an examination of housing and income data on the local level, preferably by census tract. On the demand side, one would need to gauge potential demand for housing microfinance loans and assess willingness to pay for these products and services. While there may be a need for such products, this need may not necessarily translate into effective demand— that is, clients' ability or willingness to pay. On the supply side is the need to examine the existing conditions and the sources of funding and programs for housing microfinance services. A supply-side assessment may uncover information on the nature, extent, and terms of various funding sources. While subsidized funding may serve as a challenge to the introduction of new programs, such programs may also present a unique opportunity to leverage resources in favor of a housing microfinance initiative. This on-the-ground research will help guide the development of the program

components and potential models that may be tested in the pilot phase.

- Another integral component of the program is an analysis of the costs and profitability. Such a program can be successful only if it is affordable to clients and sustainable for the institutions that are delivering the program. Any successful housing microfinance model must be able to create market-driven financial services for low-income consumers. It will be important to develop the financial projections for the program to ensure that, at some point, some level of sustainability can be achieved.
- A well-articulated funding strategy is central to ensuring strong institutional relationships and program sustainability. An optimal mix of grants and loans will need to flow into the program, with likely partnerships being created by foundations, banks, governments, CDFIs, and nonprofit organizations.

The planning phase and implementation process for such an initiative should involve forming a core group of national and local partners to provide initial funding. The next steps are to initiate local market surveys, select sites for the initiative, and recruit outside technical expertise to tailor the program design to meet specific requirements of the local communities and develop local business plans for implementing the program. Finally, as housing microfinance programs are rolled out, formal mechanisms of tracking, monitoring, and evaluating program outcomes will be needed to measure the overall effectiveness of the initiative.

NOTES

1. There are several reasons this gap persists, including credit redlining, racial discrimination, and lack of familiarity among low-income and minority households within the mainstream financial sector.

2. David Dangler, Rural Initiative, Neighborhood Reinvestment Corporation, telephone interview, September 10, 2002.

3. Economists speak of a prisoner's dilemma, in which property owners do little to maintain their homes if others nearby are not maintaining theirs. This simply means that what your neighbor does affects you. If his or her actions, for instance, have the effect of driving down the value of your home, it might be foolish for you to spend money on a sinking ship.

4. Cheryl Casiani, Director of Programs, Baltimore Community Foundation, telephone interview, August 26, 2002.

5. Ninfa Moncada, Director, Fannie Mae Border Partnership Office, San Antonio, Texas, telephone interview, May 23, 2002.

6. Homero Cabello, Jr., Director of Colonias Initiatives, Texas Department of Community Affairs, telephone interview, August 16, 2002.

10

Expand Entry-Level Housing: A Key Lesson from Developing Countries for the United States

Bruce Ferguson and Michael Marez

The U.S. housing system has worked splendidly in some respects over the last fifty years. The single-family detached house is still the American dream attainable by many families. Home ownership has risen recently to a high of 66.2 percent. Beneath this shining exterior, however, lies rot. Most fundamental household income has steadily fallen behind increases in housing costs over the last five decades, particularly in high-cost metropolitan areas. Even many middle-class families now have little hope of affording a new home in such high-cost metropolitan areas as Los Angeles, New York, and San Francisco—which all have home ownership rates below 50 percent. The increase in home ownership in the U.S. as a whole has come largely from two temporary factors that are now played out: (1) favorable mortgage finance, which has reduced the down payment and the monthly payment below the level otherwise required; and (2) the added family income from women going into the workplace.

Housing problems are, of course, worse for U.S. low- and moderate-income households. An increasing inequitable income distribution and declining real income and wealth for the bottom 60 percent of the population over the last three decades underlie the difficulties faced by this group. In contrast to the 1950s—when massive home production occurred for the working class—U.S. developers now increasingly build large houses for the most prosperous households. Only token production of lower-cost units occurs, mainly due to the heroic efforts of a highly subsidized but small-scale affordable housing industry that is dependent on underfunded government programs. In poor areas such as the U.S. border with Mexico, where low-income households represent 30 to 40 percent of the total population, housing problems have reached crisis proportions. Over half a million people have settled in unplatted ("informal") subdivisions without basic infrastructure (water, paved roads, sanitation) near the border in the U.S. Southwest—a pattern formerly seen only in developing countries. Overall, a steady reduction in home ownership rates seems likely if the U.S. housing system continues on the same track.

Concurrently, U.S. population growth and, hence, the need for massive new entry-level housing, is accelerating. Demographers project that the U.S. population will expand much faster than those of other advanced industrialized countries—from 281,000,000 in 2000 to as much as 550,000,000 by 2050, at the present rates of immigration and native-born fertility.[1] If the current income distribution prevails, the bulk of this increase will come in low- and moderate-income households. In this respect, the United States will resemble developing countries much more than most of Europe and Japan, which are experiencing a population bust. Where and how will all these new Americans live?

New approaches to housing offer the potential to face these challenges. Emerging countries have had far less to work with in terms of resources and institutions dealing with far more serious problems in housing and urban development and much worse distributions of income. Partly as a result, they have had to innovate in ways that now offer lessons for advanced industrialized countries, particularly the United States. They have also had many decades of experience dealing with housing problems that have begun to afflict parts of the United States—such as large-scale informal settlements along much of the U.S. border with Mexico.

The previous chapters have shown how microfinance can play a key role in the process of progressive housing used by the low- to moderate-income majority in developing countries to afford home ownership. Simply put, can the principles of microfinance or progressive housing apply to the radically different U.S. context? The answer is a qualified yes. Housing microfinance and progressive housing have utility for some niche markets such as the U.S. border with Mexico. The principles that make these practices work in developing countries, however, have much broader relevance for helping U.S. housing exit its current cul-de-sac. The main principle from developing countries can be summarized: greatly increase the production of and choice among a wide range of entry-level housing products. This chapter explores this principle and applies it to housing in the United States, with a focus on the U.S.-Mexico border.

HOUSING IN DEVELOPING COUNTRIES AND THE UNITED STATES

The twin practices of microfinance and progressive housing work well in developing countries because of the context. Most households (typically, 60 percent to 80 percent of the income distribution)[2] earn too little to purchase the least expensive commercially built unit. Thus, they resort to progressive housing to afford shelter. The progressive housing process usually starts with securing land through purchase or invasion. Households then build a makeshift unit on this land and gradually improve it with permanent materials and expand it over five to twenty years. Gradual improvement in the rights that families hold to their property usually accompanies this physical improvement. Families start with few or no legal rights, achieve security of tenure (i.e., no threat of eviction) and, finally, full legal (freehold) title if it is useful to them. Even with freehold title, however, they typically have little access to and interest in standard mortgage finance, and stay with the security of tenure short of freehold title.

Thus, housing in developing countries spans a wide range of types of physical housing solutions (as international housing professionals call them) and legal rights to property. This wide spectrum allows households to get on the home ownership ladder near the bottom at low cost and move up as their income improves and families grow. However, most of low- and moderate-income people in developing countries could never have started the progressive housing process and become home owners if they faced the prevailing U.S. system, which is characterized by: only complete, relatively large, fully legally, and high-cost units available to purchase; and only full freehold tenancy—again with relatively high cost—available for property tenure. Smart developers of low- to moderate-income housing and well-designed government programs in developing countries mimic, support, and accommodate the process of progressive housing already used, for example by financing or helping to build a wide range of low-cost housing including a serviced lot, a sanitary core, improvement, expansion of an existing unit, replacement of a deteriorated unit on the lot owned by the family, and purchase of a core expandable unit.

The wide variety of housing solutions and tenancy spectrum offers a niche for most of the population of developing countries. Largely as a result, owner occupancy rates[3] in developing countries usually substantially exceed those in industrialized countries (83 percent in Mexico, 86 percent in Nicaragua, and 85 percent in Bangladesh, compared to about 66 percent in the U.S. and Canada). The average home ownership rate of sixteen Western European countries of 59 percent (Finnish Ministry of the Environment 2001) compares to that of over 70 percent for Latin American countries.

On the face of it, the housing system and conditions in the United States appear dramatically different. While mortgage finance is typically scarce or absent in developing countries, the United States enjoys the deepest capital markets and most efficient and sophisticated housing finance system in the world. Instead of starting small and building their homes over a long period as most families do in developing countries, the great bulk of U.S. home owners buy a complete unit up-front.

In contrast to the continuum in types of housing unit and tenure found in developing countries, the United States has a binary housing system in important respects. Nine out of ten U.S. home owners have bought a detached single-family home. If they cannot afford such home ownership, households rent. About one-third of U.S. households rent rather than own. Renters and rental housing, however, have second-class status. In comparison, freehold ownership of a detached single-family home is by far the best housing asset for many reasons. However, very little is available between renting and freehold ownership of a detached single family home. The economic and cultural dominance of freehold ownership by the owner-occupant household has largely eclipsed other types of tenure and housing. As a result, households that lack the means to purchase a detached single-family house are unable to acquire a low-cost housing solution to get a foot on the housing ownership ladder and build home equity. Many types of tenure and housing exist, but on a very small scale (see Box 10.1).

The limited diversity of U.S. housing types and tenure has caused modest concern until now because the bulk of households have had enough income to purchase freehold ownership of a

Box 10.1 Range of Unit Types and
Tenure in the United States and Developing Countries

Alternatives to U.S. freehold tenure include cooperative housing, housing for special populations with use restrictions (such as senior communities that only permit residents over age 55), and community land trusts. These other forms of tenure place limits on the use of the property beyond the restrictions normally associated with freehold (such as zoning and land use). These restrictions lower the property's market value in order to preserve access to this housing solution, often by low- and moderate-income households or other special populations (e.g., the elderly).

However, these forms of alternative tenure are miniscule in size and variety in the United States relative to the developing countries. In most developing countries, 30 to 70 percent of owner-occupants hold rights short of full legal tenure (60 percent in Mexico, 47 percent in Nicaragua). Payne (2002) identifies seven forms of tenure that convey ten different levels of property rights in most developing countries. Some developing countries and cities have created types of tenure specifically to maintain housing affordable to low- and moderate-income families on an ongoing basis. In contrast, a small share of U.S. owner-occupants hold rights in some form other than freehold title.

The situation is similar with the unit type. The main physical alternatives to a detached single-family house in the United States are condominiums, townhomes, mobile homes, and manufactured homes. The share of these alternatives, however, represents less than one-fifth of the housing stock. In some areas—affluent suburbs, for example—zoning and subdivision standards prohibit these alternatives outright or eliminate their economic viability.

Similar to the scarcity of alternatives to freehold title, this modest diversity of lower-cost housing solutions suitable to U.S. low- and moderate-income households is far less than that of developing countries. The limited diversity that does exist in U.S. housing also achieves comparatively little in cost savings to reach families and bring them onto the ladder of home ownership. In comparison, in Mexico the cost of a serviced lot ($2,500 to $4,000)—the ownership starting point of many low-income families—is only 6 to 20 percent that of a complete basic unit ($20,000 to $35,000).

In summary, the lack of choice in tenure and unit type restrict access of U.S. households to home ownership. Expanded choice has a critical role to play in well-functioning markets, in general, and in housing markets, in particular. Households require different types of housing solutions for different stages of the life cycle, and households with widely different incomes find their housing in different niche markets. Hence, it is quite a paradox that developing countries offer a wider choice in housing types and tenure compared to the United States.

detached single-family home over much of the last half-century. However, when 30 to 40 percent of the population becomes poor or low income—the situation in most counties on the U.S. border with Mexico—this rigidity starts causing severe problems. Basic data on home ownership, income, and housing costs strongly suggest that serious difficulties now afflict the U.S. housing system. The relation of housing price to household income is the crux of the problem. The ratio of median house price to median family income is the most robust measure of this relation. In 1970, the median priced house cost 2.33 times the median family income. According to the U.S. National Association of Realtors, by 2002, this ratio had risen to 2.94. This ratio and, hence, the fundamental housing cost-to-income problem varies significantly among U.S. regions. While the Midwest still has relatively affordable housing (2.33), the West has the least affordable (4.11) while the Northeast (2.77) and the South (3.07) are in between.

Looking a bit further back, the deterioration of income relative to house cost is even more stark. During the 1950s, the cost of the median family home was only twice that of one median salary. Thus, the G.I.s returning from World War II could purchase a new home in one of the many tract home subdivisions that sprang up in the suburbs of U.S. cities and support their family with only one income! Although this actually happened to many of the parents of the baby boomer generation now in middle age, it seems incredibly remote from present realities.

The deterioration of U.S. income distribution and the stagnation of real income of the bottom three quintiles over the last two decades underlies the housing problems of low- and moderate-income households. Average after-tax real household income declined for the bottom three quintiles of the income distribution from 1977 to 1999: by 12 percent for the lowest income quintile, 9.5 percent for the second quintile, and 3.1 percent for the third quintile. The net worth of the median household also declined in real terms from 1983 to 1997, according to the Congressional Budget Office (1999). In comparison, the top two quintiles gained in real income from 1977 to 1999: 5.8 percent for the fourth quintile and 38.3 percent for the fifth (and highest) quintile. The top 1 percent gained 119.7 percent income during this period, while the concentration of wealth in the hands of the top 1 percent of the U.S. population increased from 19.9 percent in 1976 to about 40 percent by the end of the 1990s (Phillips 2002, 129). Thus, low- and moderate-income households have less real income to qualify for a mortgage and less real wealth for down payments.

As the income distribution gap has widened, the types of housing produced have also tended to bifurcate. The last three decades have shown a steady increase in the size of houses built, especially in the share of very large houses on small lots popularly called "tract mansions" as builders have responded to the enhanced purchasing power of the well off.[4] Interestingly, some data indicate an expansion in the production of smaller rental units, despite the straightjacket imposed by land-use planning and lack of low-cost housing finance.[5]

The rising housing cost-to-income ratio has hit high-cost urban areas the hardest. Overall, home ownership rates in 2000 averaged 56 percent in the ten largest U.S. metropolitan areas compared to 66.2 percent nationwide.[6] Home ownership declined in the largest and most costly metropolitan areas from 1970 to 2000—from 49.2 to 47.9 percent in Los Angeles, 36.3 to 34.7 percent in New York, and 51.4 to 49.0 percent in San Francisco. The low level of home ownership in these cities is striking. Only about half the households in Los Angeles and San Francisco, and about a third of households in New York, own their own homes compared to two-thirds nationwide. Home ownership rates are also below the national average in many low-income areas. The twenty-three counties along the U.S. border with Mexico (from Texas to California), for example, have an average home ownership rate of 61.4 percent.[7]

Nationwide, however, U.S. home ownership has risen from 61.5 percent in 1970 to an all-time high of 66.2 percent in 2000. How is a rise in home ownership possible while the cost of housing is outstripping household income and, especially, per-capita income? Essentially, innovations in mortgage finance and wholesale entry of women into the workforce have compensated for this deterioration in per-capita income relative to housing cost.

Better terms for and innovations in mortgage finance have helped households make up for the deterioration in their income relative to home prices. Examination of housing affordability indices of the U.S. National Associations of Realtors—which show how well median household incomes can support the debt service on the median priced home by taking into account the terms of credit finance—largely explains this result. These indices of housing affordability were higher (indicating greater housing affordability) during the first half of the 1970s, then declined substantially during the 1980s, and recovered to close to the 1970s rates from the last half of the 1990s to the present (2002). In addition to more favorable terms (produced by a combination of lower interest rates and the expansion in alternatives to the thirty-year, fixed-interest-rate mortgage), programs of the GSE secondary market institutions (Fannie Mae, Freddie Mac, Federal Home Loans Banks) featuring low down payments and more flexible underwriting have contributed to expanding home ownership. Thus, while housing costs have risen relative to household income, more favorable mortgage finance in the last thirty years has allowed families to compensate.

The wholesale entry of women into the workforce over the last half century is the second major factor that has allowed U.S. households to afford higher-cost housing, by raising household income. The share of women above the age of twenty in the workforce increased from 31.6 percent in 1950 to 58.7 percent in 2000, whereas in 1960 only 19 percent of married women with children under age six worked outside the home (U.S. Bureau of the Census 2000, Phillips 2002).

These mitigating factors, however, are likely to be nearing their limit. Mortgage interest rates in mid-2002 were lower than they had been in forty years, comparable to those of the 1960s. Short of radical (and unlikely) change such as the double indexed mortgage common in Mexico, further innovations in credit finance offer modest potential for making housing more affordable. In addition, with both adult partners in a typical U.S. household already employed, there is no one else left to send to work to increase family income.

THE UNRAVELING OF THE U.S. HOUSING SYSTEM ALONG THE BORDER WITH MEXICO

The rising ratio of housing costs to household income increasingly strains U.S. housing. A worsening distribution of income exacerbates this problem for the bottom 60 percent of the population. The U.S. border with Mexico offers an interesting case study that presages the housing problems and solutions likely to apply increasingly throughout the United States. This section profiles housing problems along the border with a focus on the city and county of El Paso, Texas.

Colonias: A Symptom of Housing System Malfunction

The poverty rate along the U.S.-Mexico border is more than 30 percent compared to about 20 percent in Texas as a whole. From 1995 to 2020, the Texas border population is expected to increase by about 60 percent, from 4 million to 6.3 million. Incomes are also lower along the border. For example, the average 1995 wage in El Paso was only 80 percent of the state of Texas and 77 percent of the U.S., although forty years ago it was 100 percent of the national average (City of El Paso 2000, 110).

Although the border area is poorer than elsewhere, housing construction costs are the same. It is difficult to find a new entry-level home for less than $65,000. However, a household receiving the minimum wage—which is above the amount that many unskilled workers actually receive along much of the border—can only afford a unit costing about $40,000. As a result, nearly one in three workers in the U.S. counties along the border earn less than the amount necessary to afford a house or apartment, compared to one in seven nonborder workers in Texas (Sharp 1998). In El Paso, more than 40 percent of the population cannot afford the median priced home of $75,000. In addition, a substantial share of households along the border that do have sufficient income to qualify for a loan are unable to meet the underwriting standards to qualify for a mortgage loan.

As a result, 12 percent of border Texans have opted to live in informal subdivisions called colonias, which have many similarities to those on the other side of the border in Mexico and throughout the developing world. Texas colonias start when a landowner in an unincorporated area of a county sells raw land to low-income families. These landowners are frequently the original farmers of the area. Increasingly, however, domestic and international investors buy land from the original owner with the intent of developing colonias. The landowner typically requires a modest down payment, and takes back the remainder of the purchase price with monthly payments. The landowner uses a contract for deed to sell this unserviced lot, and does not convey title until the family makes the final monthly payment. Fraud and failure to convey title on payment of the last installment are common, as is repossession of the property when families miss payments. At most, the landowner lays out streets and lots, but provides no services or infrastructure. These basic characteristics of colonias in Texas and other U.S. border states are identical to those of unplatted (informal) subdivisions in many developing countries.

Texas alone has 1,450 colonias—up from 1,193 in 1992 (Texas Department of Human Services n.d.). These settlements house about 350,000 residents (280,000 in 1992). Approximately half lack adequate water supplies, and virtually none have approved wastewater service. Most have dirt roads. Median annual household incomes in Texas colonias range from $7,000 to $11,000, and the average household numbers five to six residents. The population of existing colonias appears to be growing as they densify at rates of 7 to 10 percent per year. Household interviews of a sample of 1,200 colonia households by the Texas Department of Human Services showed that 65 percent have no health insurance, 67 percent of residents over age eighteen had not completed high school, and 15 percent reported they usually lack enough to eat. About 10 percent of residents had had either tuberculosis or hepatitis. Unemployment ran at 41 percent for those over age sixteen not in school. Of those working, 37 percent earned the minimum wage or less. In another sample drawn from the Lower Rio Grande Valley and El Paso County, the average age of colonia residents was twenty-one (compared to about thirty-five for the U.S. population as a whole). This sample also showed that two-thirds of colonia residents were born in the United States, although two-thirds speak mainly Spanish at home. Although colonias are heavily concentrated in the U.S. counties along the Mexican border, such unplatted subdivisions are spreading northward to other semirural areas in the Southwest.

Colonias along the U.S. border generate large public as well as private costs, as do the informal subdivisions in developing countries. Most fundamentally, the reordering of informal settlements, which are typically settled in chaotic fashion and extend basic road-related infrastructure (roads, water, sanitation), typically costs two to three times more than providing these services in a new subdivision. The extension of water lines alone costs $1 million per mile. In other words, it is much more expensive to fix a broken settlement pattern than to lay out a new subdivision properly in the first place.

Worse, U.S. colonias cost even more to fix than informal subdivisions in developing countries because U.S. colonias are typically located in rural or semirural areas, whereas those in developing countries are urban and much closer to existing infrastructure lines. Not surprisingly, Mexican planning and municipal officials familiar with U.S. colonias expressed amazement that their U.S. counterparts would allow such costly informal settlement to occur.[8]

It has been argued that government has made no commitment to extend infrastructure to colonia residents who have knowingly bought lots without water. Nevertheless, the moral and political pressure of colonia residents and their advocates creates a de facto government obligation to extend water and other services in the U.S. Southwest, as it does in developing countries. Whether in the U.S. or developing countries, government cannot ignore informal settlements, which rarely disappear. If a program provides funding for the colonia to be resettled elsewhere in more adequate quarters, the large backlog of unsatisfied housing demand ensures that a new group will replace them. Colonia settlement, thus, creates huge unfunded infrastructure and development liabilities that government (mainly local government) will sooner or later be forced to assume.

The private costs of colonias are also significant. The lack of basic infrastructure, low incomes, and poverty in colonias combine to produce rates of serious disease (AIDS, meningitis, pneumonia) many times the nationwide rates as well as other socioeconomic problems that burden both colonia households and society as a whole. Finally, building a unit in a colonia is no bargain. The cost of the land—$25,000 plus that of a trailer or manufactured home ($30,000–$50,000) that families often bring onto the land totals close to the amount needed ($75,000) to buy a new formally-developed home elsewhere. For a significant portion of colonia residents, then, the problem is one of qualifying for credit finance.

Some have laid the blame for the colonias problems on Texas state government, which curtails the ability of counties to control land use, and on Texas counties, for allowing politically powerful farmers to divide raw land without providing services. Recent Texas legislation has made the formation of new colonias legally impossible, although it is in practice merely more difficult.[9] Others have blamed the individual families and say that they (not government) must take responsibility for their lifestyle choice.

The formation of colonias, however, is more the result of the housing system's inability to create low-cost, entry-level products. The high cost of regularizing U.S. colonias (and informal settlements in developing countries) underscores the importance of getting ahead of demand through producing new entry-level housing, rather than trying to fix a broken settlement pattern after the fact. A comparison of the experience of El Paso, Texas, with its Mexican twin city, Juárez, sheds light on the potential for commercially viable, entry-level products.

Entry-Level Housing in El Paso, Texas vs. Juárez, Mexico

El Paso forms part of a broader urban conurbation with the city of Juárez on the other side of the border in Mexico. Juárez has drawn many *maquiladora* assembly plants under the North American Free Trade Agreement, which generate a large number of jobs. Twenty-five percent of U.S.-Mexico trade passes through Juárez-El Paso (city of El Paso 1998). As a result, Juárez had a 2001 population of 1.21 million, expanding at the rapid rate of more than 4 percent per year and new household formation of 11,000. Roughly 45 percent of the city has been settled and built informally, starting mainly as illegal subdivisions and invaded land with no infrastructure. Similarly, 12 percent of El Paso county residents live in unplatted subdivisions that the county officially designates as colonias, while a substantially larger share of the county's population lives in similar settlements without infrastructure. Thus, both El Paso County and Juárez suffer from informal subdivisions of low-income people lacking water, sanitation, and other basic infrastructure. However, Juárez has applied a strategy used by many cities in developing countries that has largely solved this problem, whereas El Paso lacks such an approach.

In essence, Juárez's successful strategy consists of producing enough formal-sector housing solutions to cover its annual population growth. This production comes in the form of a wide variety of different types of housing solutions. The municipality of Juárez and the state government housing institute have, over the years, subdivided about half the total number of lots in the city and sold these lots to families either as partly serviced (progressive) or fully serviced. The private sector accounts for the other half of production, largely in the form of core expandable units costing $16,000 to $20,000 that are affordable to the median-income Mexican worker.[10] As a result new informal settlements have largely halted in Juárez. The municipality is now focusing on upgrading the existing squatter settlements gradually, through providing bus service to these areas, schools, electricity, water, and drainage. In Mexico as a whole, the formal housing sector produced 330,000 units in 2001. The bulk of these homes sold for $16,000 to $25,000 per unit, many of them basic core units that could later be expanded.

The overall strategy of Juárez resembles that of other developing countries (such as Costa Rica, Chile, and El Salvador), states, and cities that successfully address the low- to moderate-income housing problem and thereby reduce the huge public and private costs of informal settlement. Essentially, this strategy is to increase the rate of formal-sector production of low-cost, entry-level, affordable products to near that of new household formation. And as the rate of informal settlement slows and stops, the next step is to upgrade the existing informal settlements systematically and gradually, starting with the least problematic and expensive and progressing to the more difficult cases.

In contrast, a small number of affordable units are produced in El Paso area relative to the demand—the one-third of the population unable to afford the least costly housing unit. The main source of low- to moderate-income housing production is the city of El Paso,[11] which supports the production of 50 to 100 affordable units per year under the two federal programs that fund most affordable U.S. housing, the Community Development Block Grant and HOME programs. In comparison, the city of El Paso estimates its housing deficit at 30,000 units (city of El Paso 2000). This assistance flows mainly in the form of low-interest loans and grants to community development corporations (CDCs) for rental and first-time buyer housing. As a result, only a token production of units affordable to the bottom third of the population occurs on the U.S. side of the border in El Paso. This scant production, supported mainly by relatively large per-unit subsidies from federal programs, characterizes affordable housing in most of the United States. The lowest priced commercially built unit in much of the U.S. border area sells for about $60,000 and is far beyond the means of the 30 to 40 percent of the population that is low income.

The comparison of Juárez with El Paso raises some key questions. Could a low-cost, entry-level unit be produced in United States border areas similar to that used in Mexico to cover a substantial part of the unsatisfied demand? What is the nature of a commercially viable housing product and the accompanying finance that could go downmarket en masse in the United States, to greatly expand home ownership? The next section answers these questions.

COMMERCIAL VIABILITY OF CORE AND EXPANDABLE UNITS

The Mexican home-building industry has noticed the lack of entry-level products in the U.S. market. In 1996, the largest Mexican home builder, GEO, sought to fill this gap by bringing its expertise in building homes in Mexico to a joint venture with the sixth-largest U.S. home builder, Beazer Homes. In essence, this joint venture attempted to apply the formula that has worked so well for GEO in Mexico—very large-scale production of basic core units affordable to working-class families. The characteristics that create these lower costs are:

- Smaller living space;
- Greater density (smaller lots);
- Lower level of finish;
- Fewer amenities (e.g., garage, finishing).

In Mexico, an important aspect of the acceptability of such a house to the home buyer is that it is designed to be progressively expanded and improved as the owner's financial circumstances permit. Table 10.1 compares costs of the end product in Juárez to El Paso.

Experience of a Core-Unit Developer in El Paso, Texas

In 1997, GEO and Beazer Homes joined forces to apply this formula on a massive scale to build low-cost housing projects along the U.S.-Mexico border and in Florida. While the homes in the project were not designed to be built out progressively, they did incorporate features, including some of those listed above, that are associated with progressive housing. The experience of the El Paso joint venture exposed some of the barriers to delivery of low-cost housing in the United States. They also suggest that the development of core and possibly progressive housing may be

Table 10.1 Development Costs of Core Expandable Unit in Juárez vs. Lowest-Cost Home in El Paso

	Ciudad Juárez (A)		El Paso (B)		(B-A)
	Percent of Total		Percent of Total		
Cost	100%	$18,000	100%	$57,000	$39,000
Lot	23%	$4,140	24%	$13,680	$9,540
Labor	21%	$3,780	28%	$15,675	$11,895
Materials	31%	$5,580	28%	$15,675	$10,095
Other	25%	$4,500	21%	$11,970	$7,470
Square Feet		450		1000	550
Cost/Square Foot	100%	$40	100%	$57	$17
Lot	23%	$9	24%	$14	$4
Labor	21%	$8	28%	$16	$7
Materials	31%	$12	28%	$16	$3
Other	25%	$10	21%	$12	$2

commercially viable for some niche markets if a number of key problems are resolved.

The idea behind the venture was simple: achieve low price through mass production of core units. The homes were to be smaller and built on smaller lots. Some of the homes would be duplexes. These characteristics mimicked those of the homes sold in Mexico. The venture expected these to be embraced by, or at least familiar to, the El Paso home buying public, many of whom were expected to be recently arrived immigrants from Mexico.

GEO and Beazer invested $13 million in the joint venture (60 percent Beazer, 40 percent GEO) and broke ground in El Paso in 1999. Their short-term goal was to build 1,000 homes for the El Paso market by the end of the year. Their long-term goal was to build 3,000 homes a year across the United States. The vice chairman of the joint venture commented that the U.S. market was tremendous because no one was building affordable homes.

The Oasis Ranch project, the El Paso development, was to consist of 430 single-family attached homes ranging in size from 727 to 1,227 square feet in a planned community with landscaping, recreational facilities, and a community center. As GEO does in Mexico, the joint venture constructed a facility in El Paso to manufacture the basic blocks and special construction components for

Box 10.2
A Core Unit in Mexico vs. the Least Expensive
Commercially Produced House Along the U.S. Border

Las Palomas (not its real name) is situated on the edge of Juárez. Like many social interest housing projects in Mexico, it is built on a large scale: 6,000 units built and sold, with an additional 5,000 in progress. Las Palomas is laid out in a grid, with paved streets defined by curbs and gutters. The lot for each home is small—1,300 square feet compared to 4,500 square feet standard lot in El Paso. The design of the unit integrates some purely aesthetic architectural features, such as arches over the windows, which soften and add variety to the otherwise angular lines of the units. The 660 square foot (f^2) interior of the model home accommodates two bedrooms, each with its own closet, a kitchen, bathroom, living room, and dining area. However, prospective buyers are also taken through the "dream" unit, which is the basic model expanded into 1,100 square feet in two stories and containing three bedrooms and two baths. At the time of closing the homebuilder will provide buyers with the Progressive Housing Manual, which contains the floor plans, instructions, and a list of the tools and materials that the home buyer will need to complete the expansion. What is most notable about the homes for sale in this development is their price. The lowest priced home (450 square ft.) sells for US$18,000. Across the border in El Paso, the lowest priced new home (excluding the core-unit Oasis Ranch project discussed below) sells for around $57,000. A number of key factors account for this cost difference:

Smaller Size. The $18,000 Juárez home has 450 square feet of living area—meant to be expanded—while its El Paso counterpart is over twice as large at 1,000 square feet. Size is not the only factor affecting the price differential between the El Paso and the Juárez homes. The El Paso house sells for $57 per f^2 while the Las Palomas home sells for $40 per f^2. The factors that contribute to the price difference between El Paso and Juárez entry-level housing are described below.

Land. Undeveloped land costs in El Paso and Juárez are similar, about US$1 per f^2. However the El Paso home is on 5,000 square feet vs. the 1,300 in Las Palomas. Juárez allows higher density construction than El Paso, and homebuilders in El Paso build on larger lots in response to the preferences of consumers with the credit and income stability to qualify for a loan (which leaves out a large share of potential buyers). The impact of land cost on the price differential is greater when the relative costs of the finished lots are compared—that is, lots to which water, sewer, and electrical service have been extended: $13,000 for the El Paso home vs. $4,100 for the Juárez home. The higher cost of finishing a lot in El Paso is due to the higher cost of permits and impact fees as well as the higher price of labor.

(continues)

Box 10.2 Continued

Labor. Labor is significantly more expensive in the United States. Construction workers in El Paso earn $50–60 per day, while in Juárez they earn $10–15. The $18,000 units in Las Palomas include $3,780 in labor costs (21 percent of total) as opposed to the El Paso entry level home, which incorporates $15,672 in labor costs (28 percent of total).

Materials. The cost of materials is $15,675 for the El Paso home vs. $5,580 for the Juárez house. The Mexican cement or cement block wall construction method is actually more expensive than the frame and dry wall technique employed in El Paso. The lower materials cost of the Juárez home is due, not to lower unit materials costs (approximately the same in Juárez and El Paso), but to the lengthy list of standard amenities and finish items for the El Paso home that are absent from the Juárez home: an attached garage, a central heating system, flooring (tile or carpet vs. cement), counters, counter tops and trim, lighting fixtures, and appliances.

these homes, and brought in machinery from as far away as Italy for this purpose. Based partly on the support of local affordable housing developers and advocates,[12] Fannie Mae extended a $3 million credit line for the construction through its Housing Impact Fund, and the Texas Department of Housing and Community Affairs used HUD Home funds to help 430 families with annual incomes below 80 percent of the median come up with the necessary down payment (in effect, requiring only 2 percent from the family).

From the start, however, the subdivision ran into a series of problems. Two loomed largest: the inability of most would-be home buyers—including many with sufficient income to make monthly payments—to qualify for a loan, and resistance of a significant share of the interested families who did qualify for loans to the features that made this entry-level product affordable.[13]

The single most important reason for the lack of commercial success of the Oasis Ranch project was the difficulty for potential buyers to qualify for mortgage finance. The builder and his sales agents reported great interest in the product from a large number of families who visited the development. Unfortunately, nine of every ten potential buyers' loan applications were reportedly rejected. This rejection rate caused major financial problems for the developer.[14]

Although the evidence suggests that many of these potential home buyers had sufficient income to afford the monthly payments on these low-cost homes, they lacked the ability to demonstrate credit and income stability necessary to be considered acceptable credit risks. Typically, these potential home buyers failed to score above the cut-off point on automatic underwriting programs—the method now used to screen home buyer loan applications against the criteria of secondary market institutions by most U.S. loan originators.

A number of other features of traditional mortgage loans also made access difficult for these lower-income, non-English speaking buyers, including the fee structure for loans, the rules relating to down-payment source, and a lack of understanding regarding immigration status. Mortgage lenders have little financial incentive to originate the small-balance loans sought by lower-income borrowers buying entry-level homes. The fees earned by a lender are calculated as a percentage of loan amount at a rate capped by the Federal Housing Administration (FHA), the guarantor for most smaller loans. Underwriting standards often fail to suit creditworthy low-income borrowers. Many loans programs, for example, do not allow the use of "mattress money"—funds outside of bank accounts for more than three months that many lower-income borrowers use for their down payment. Immigration status, nontraditional credit, and seasonal income also often create underwriting problems. Borrowers with difficulty speaking English face problems interacting with financial institutions, particularly in cases where explanation of late credit card payments, multiple sources of income, immigration status, and other such factors make a difference.

As a result, the overwhelming majority of lower-income, non-English speaking borrowers who sought to qualify to buy units in Oasis Ranch failed, although the evidence suggests that many would have been good borrowers. Interestingly, most such families in Mexico also lack credit and income stability, but nevertheless many qualify for a mortgage loan.

In addition, most of the would-be buyers with credit and income stability that did qualify them for a home loan resisted the house features that made this development low cost. This group disliked the cement block construction, attached units, and smaller yards. Sales agents reported that these characteristics made the units appear more Mexican, while these families—although primarily of Mexican origin—wanted an American-looking home.[15]

By 2000, the GEO/Beazer joint venture was running into serious financial trouble, which was compounded by GEO's cash flow problems elsewhere. Frustrated by its inability to build and sell very large numbers of homes quickly as it did in Mexico, GEO backed out and the partnership dissolved after only half of the total homes planned had been constructed. GEO sold the project to an employee who continued to build out and sell the development slowly over the next two years (2000 to 2002).

Informed observers such as the head of the local Fannie Mae office and the president of the nonprofit affordable housing development corporation that had vouched for the joint venture with local leaders and lenders believe Oasis Ranch was a success. The local Fannie Mae manager sums it up: "They built very affordable homes, but GEO's expectations were too high."

So what is a reasonable plan for housing along the U.S. border with Mexico?

ACTION PLAN FOR ENTRY-LEVEL HOUSING ALONG THE U.S.-MEXICO BORDER

A strategy for entry-level housing along the U.S. border with Mexico best reflects a basic principle from experience with similar conditions in developing countries: balance large-scale production of entry-level housing to get ahead of demand with upgrading of existing colonias, which are politically impossible to eliminate.

The production of new entry-level housing represents the most important part of this two-pronged strategy. Colonias are, most fundamentally, a symptom of a severe shortage in the amount, unit type, tenure type of low-cost housing. When a substantial share of the population consists of low- to moderate-income people unable to afford the lowest-cost commercially produced unit, many will look outside formal channels. In parts of the U.S. Southwest as well as developing countries, one of the main alternatives consists of unplatted subdivisions—colonias.

Production of New Entry-Level Housing

The Oasis Ranch experience helps demonstrate that the production of commercially viable, new entry-level housing costing $40,000 to

$55,000 can serve a sizeable niche market along the U.S border with Mexico. The bottom rung of this range—$40,000—allows reaching a household with one full-time worker and one half-time worker earning the minimum wage (i.e., as little as $15,000 per year).

However, successful commercial production of such a product requires two innovations. First, builders must assess the preferences of this market and gear the characteristics of the house accordingly. Second, selling this product requires new methods of qualifying creditworthy low-income families. Experience in Mexico shows that many such families can be good borrowers, but lack the credit and income stability necessary to meet the cut-off on the automated underwriting programs of U.S. secondary market institutions (see Box 10.3). Despite the notable efforts of Fannie Mae, in particular, to reach households on the border with mortgage finance,[16] the experience of the Oasis Ranch project and data on mortgage denial rates along the border (see below) indicate that many creditworthy families remain left out. Taking each requirement in turn:

Gear product carefully to client preferences. The experience of Oasis Ranch suggests that at least two distinct submarkets with the effective demand for an entry-level product characterize the overall category of low- to moderate-income families along the border. The lowest-income group capable of purchasing such a product—households earning around U.S.$15,000—find acceptable an entry-level product similar to that widespread in Mexico: attached units (duplexes, for example), cement block (rather than wood), a small yard, and a modest level of amenities and finishing in relatively large projects (over 500+ home subdivisions). Many households earning somewhat more—$20,000 to $25,000 per year—prefer the American standard: detached single-family home with a larger yard, wood-frame construction, and full finishing in somewhat smaller projects (150 to 400 homes).

A number of other low-cost housing solutions may have potential in addition to the purchase of a new, complete entry-level unit—the type provided by Oasis Ranch:

1. Niche markets may exist for progressive homes—core houses specifically designed to be easily expanded in pre-programmed steps. Along the border, these units would sell at prices starting around $40,000. The original builder could provide home owners with a manual of how to undertake expansion. The finance and construction of these

additions represents good business for remodeling and other sorts of contractors.

2. Developing lots and providing appropriate financing, so that buyers can build their own homes. may also have potential as a means of providing entry-level U.S. housing. Provision of building lots in the United States has some currency, but this has been mainly for vacation, retirement, and move-up homes of the middle and upper-middle class. In much of the rest of the world, however, serviced lots are the first step of low-income families on the housing ladder.

3. The creation of accessory units in existing single-family detached neighborhoods offers enormous potential for increasing the affordable housing stock in existing urban areas, albeit mainly for rental units. Accessory units typically cost a fraction of the production of new stand-alone units. They also blend into the existing urban fabric. In comparison, neighborhoods fight the introduction of new multifamily, low-income, multistory buildings—the current main mode of affordable housing production. Many U.S. jurisdictions—particularly affluent suburbs—hinder or prohibit outright the creation of accessory units that could have more impact than all the existing affordable housing production efforts combined. Financial institutions sometimes refuse to take into account the income from an accessory unit in financing or refinancing a home, although FHA mortgage-insured loans do.

Despite these efforts to discourage accessory units, some evidence suggests that their production is growing rapidly in high-cost metropolitan areas with escalating housing costs. Some jurisdictions suffering from plummeting housing affordability and experiencing heavy immigration of ethnicities accustomed to creating accessory units have largely stopped enforcing their rules against this superb low-cost housing option in appropriate circumstances.

Regardless of the particular type of entry-level housing product chosen, allowing ample room for small-scale business, particularly retail, is critical for creating attractive low- to moderate-income neighborhoods. These neighborhoods typically contain large numbers of small stores and family businesses in developing countries and in the older urban neighborhoods of advanced industrialized countries. This neighborhood retail base serves many functions including quick access to basic consumer goods (particularly food) without a car (which many of these families cannot afford), an important source of income particularly for homemakers raising children, and a focus of community. In developing countries (Mexico, for example), formal-sector social housing subdivision projects often allow and set aside corner lots and other suitable places for such small businesses. The great bulk of new U.S. residential development, however, leaves out the small-scale retail and other mixed uses that allow neighborhoods to function fluidly, that add vibrancy, and that allow residents to conduct basic daily business quickly within the community rather than spending large portions of their day in automobiles.

At first, the stakeholders in the U.S. housing production process are likely to underestimate the market for and potential of these alternative entry-level housing products. These cultural tastes, however, are hardly immutable and are beginning to change. Builders, city planners, financial institutions, and others can affect these tastes through persuasion (advertising, public announcements), favorable regulation, and injecting resources into the alternatives. In some higher-cost U.S. metropolitan areas, a substantial share of new production consists of townhomes (over 30 percent in the Washington, D.C. metropolitan area in the 1990s, for example). The New Urbanism movement has adopted much denser housing development that attempts to mimic traditional urban neighborhoods. The exploration of new housing types and tenure accompanied by new urban development patterns, however, has just begun.

Introduce new underwriting methods of qualifying low- and moderate-income households. Mexico's mortgage banks (SOFOLES) and the secondary market institution to which they sell loans (the Sociedad Hipotecaria Federal or SHF) have successfully extended credit on a substantial scale to low- and moderate-income households with no credit and fluctuating incomes. Essentially, these lenders apply a method that dates from the origins of mortgage finance in building societies in western Europe and the United Kingdom in the nineteenth century: a mandatory savings requirement to demonstrate creditworthiness prior to qualifying for the loan.

The mandatory savings program of the second largest of these Mexican mortgage banks, Su Casita, serves as an example. To qualify for a loan would-be borrowers agree to save at rates sufficient to cover their proposed mortgage for six months to a year (see Box 10.3). The program has worked well at substantial scale, and

**Box 10.3 Mandatory Savings Program
of Mexico's Second-Largest Mortgage Bank**

The majority of home buyers in Mexico lack the credit normally expected of U.S. borrowers. One indicator is that only 30 percent of the population has any relationship (checking or savings account, for example) with a financial institution. Large-scale mortgage lending has therefore required the development of underwriting methods that can work with such potential borrowers. One example is the mandatory savings program of Su Casita, Mexico's second largest mortgage bank.

Home buyers who do not immediately qualify for a mortgage loan may elect to participate in the Su Casita savings program known as Su Meta (Your Goal). Participants agree to save a specified amount of money monthly for a period of six months to a year, depending on the borrower's circumstances. The required monthly savings is an amount which, when added to the borrower's current housing costs, is at least equal to the mortgage payment on the home the borrower would like to purchase. If the borrower successfully completes the program by making the monthly savings deposits as scheduled, Su Casita will approve the mortgage loan. By making timely monthly deposits into the savings account, the borrower establishes that he has both the income sufficient to make a mortgage payment and the financial discipline necessary to do so. In addition, the goals for each participant are set to ensure that by the end of the program they will have enough total savings to meet the down-payment requirement and pay the closing costs.

Su Casita relies on Mexico's secondary mortgage finance institution, the Sociedad Hipotecaria Federal (SHF), to provide the funding for the mortgage loans it grants. Like major secondary U.S. market housing institutions such as Fannie Mae and Freddie Mac, SHF establishes the standards that borrowers must satisfy to qualify for a SHF-funded loan from Su Casita. SHF has agreed to consider the successful completion of the Su Casita savings program as an acceptable substitute for a borrower's otherwise inadequate credit history and the lack of verifiable income that occurs when the borrower works in the informal sector.

Su Casita markets the Su Meta program as a "factory that creates borrowers," and the results support this slogan. The program—begun in 1995—currently has 8,000 enrollees. More than 70 percent of those who have completed the program have done so successfully and received a loan. Most importantly, a recent study shows that Su Casita borrowers who participated in Su Meta were four times as likely as nonparticipants to remain current on their mortgage loan payments.

Source: Marez, Michael. "Case Study: Adapting Risk Management Practices to the Realities of the Mexican Mortgage Market" in *International Journal of Real Estate Finance*, Vol. 1, No. 2, November/December 2000.

Su Casita borrowers who participated were four times as likely as nonparticipants to remain current on their mortgage loan payments.

A contract savings program such as Su Meta is key to helping lower-income U.S. borrowers qualify for a loan, just as it has been in Mexico. The United States has the advantage of numerous non-profit organizations whose mission is to promote home ownership among lower-income families. These organizations would be natural candidates to establish and operate "factories that create borrowers." The creation of such programs would require the participation of mortgage loan funding sources such as Fannie Mae and Freddie Mac, mortgage insurers such as FHA, and private mortgage insurance companies by allowing successful participation in a savings program to satisfy their requirements regarding credit history and proof of income. Either Fannie Mae or Freddie Mac could test this approach on a pilot basis (as they do other innovations) by allowing a few lenders in different border areas to introduce this method to qualify low- to moderate-income households.

A contract savings program to qualify these households for mortgage credit would have tremendous impact on housing along the border. The denial rate for home purchase mortgage applications nationwide was 24 percent in 2000. However, the twenty-three U.S. counties along the border with Mexico (in Texas, Arizona, New Mexico, and California) had an average denial rate of nearly 39 percent while a third of the counties had denial rates above 45 percent (HMDA 2000). These denial rates understate the extent of the problem as many low- to moderate-income households have no hope for qualifying for a mortgage and, hence, do not even apply for a home loan.

Upgrading Existing Colonias

Although large-scale production of entry-level housing products holds the key to halting the formation of new colonias in the U.S. Southwest, existing U.S. colonias will not disappear. Indeed, the population of existing colonias will increase substantially as these settlements densify. The households and landowners of new, thinly settled colonias typically subdivide their properties and sell off pieces until these settlements fill up. Most of the colonias in the U.S. Southwest are thinly settled and have ample room to grow within their current boundaries. Thus, even if the formation of new colonias were to stop today—an unlikely prospect—the population of existing colonias would increase substantially.

Existing colonias must be upgraded for many reasons. Partly because the problem is relatively unfamiliar, U.S. governments have taken a haphazard approach to this task. A plethora of small programs exist at the federal, state, and local (mainly county) level that, collectively, have had modest overall impact, largely because of the lack of a strategic framework. The upgrading of colonias consists of two overall tasks: extending and improving collective services (particularly water and sewer lines); and improving and expanding individual houses. Experience in Mexico and other developing countries suggests how to proceed with both.

Extending and improving collective infrastructure. The high costs of basic services requires phasing these investments, perhaps over five to ten years for U.S. colonias. Such predictability in service provision helps generate the virtuous cycle of public and private investment necessary to substantially improve these communities.

For example, the municipality of Juárez has three phases of five years in its upgrading program for informal settlements. The first phase extends water and secures the household's property tenure. The second consists largely of drainage and green areas. The third involves provision of local schools and other community facilities. Thus, the municipality seeks to move every informal settlement to the next phase every five years, resulting in a fifteen-year goal for completion of upgrading.

Other approaches to the extension of infrastructure to informal settlement in developing countries may also prove useful for U.S. colonias. Some developing countries and cities start with providing infrastructure first to those informal settlements with the lowest per-capita upgrading costs. Typically, these lower-cost settlements have the most favorable characteristics (location nearer existing infrastructure lines, more regular and less chaotic settlement pattern, flatter topography, etc.). This strategy also effectively communicates the message to those thinking of settling in or starting colonias that more appropriate settlements will receive more immediate and fuller attention. The jurisdiction then moves to upgrading settlements requiring higher per-household expenditures as resources permit. Especially when the threat of new informal settlement is high, countries and cities also tend to invest first in the oldest settlements and refuse to make any investments in recent ones—with the objective of discouraging new settlement.

A fundamental principle now practiced throughout the developing world in informal settlement concerns the participation of the community. Essentially, the residents of these communities must provide resources (usually labor and/or materials) in some form to earn complementary public investments, particularly in housing and infrastructure. Sometimes, governments prioritize their investments based on the counterpart resources provided by these communities. Thus, settlements that commit more receive attention first. In comparison, the traditional approach of giving without requiring a counterpart effort—called paternalism or assistentialism[17] in Latin America—has fallen into disrepute for many good reasons. Together, these basic principles can help create the framework now lacking in the efforts of local, state, and federal government for providing collective services to existing U.S. colonias.

Improving and expanding individual houses. The focus of this chapter—housing microfinance (HMF)—is the best sustainable solution for improving and expanding individual houses in U.S. colonias. HMF in the U.S., as in developing countries, would consist of relatively small loans at market interest rates for short periods of time. As in developing countries, a series of such loans can finance the upgrading and expansion of a house over time—through adding a septic system, building a bedroom, and remodeling a kitchen, etc.—at monthly payments that families can afford.

Right across the border from El Paso in Juárez, the Ford Foundation has helped fund a housing microfinance program, called FUNHAVI, that for six years has successfully provided such small loans to upgrade houses in this city's informal settlements and is now expanding to Tijuana and other cities on the Mexican side of the border. These methods could be adapted and applied on the U.S. side of the border. Indeed, more such reverse technology transfer in housing and urban development could help the U.S. border as a whole.

Some differences between HMF in the United States and that in developing countries are immediately apparent. Loans would be larger in absolute amount. A small U.S. HMF loan would range from $5,000 to $15,000 rather than $300 to $5,000 as in developing countries. The originators of these loans could be Community Development Finance Institutions (CDFIs)—the counterparts of developing country microfinance institutions (MFIs)—particularly at first when the methods of U.S. HMF were being developed and the viability of such lending remained to be demonstrated. However, other lenders including building material supply chains[18] would be likely to take over much of this business once it demonstrated profitability.

Contract savings could play a key role in qualifying low-income U.S. households for HMF, much as it does in SEWA Bank in India and most other Asian examples of HMF. Counseling to build a household's financial skills and credit, and information on how to improve their home would likely play as important a role as access to credit in U.S. HMF.

Government entities and foundations could usefully galvanize HMF in the United States for such niche markets as colonia upgrading along the border with Mexico through a number of steps. The first would be a pilot project that adapts the methods of HMF in one to three U.S. counties along the Mexican border.

A key psychological barrier, however, must be overcome in developing HMF in the United States: acceptance of significantly higher cost (interest rate and other charges) on these small loans to low- and moderate-income households. A fundamental axiom of the MFI industry in developing countries is that availability of credit is much more important than price to low-income households. This axiom and its corollary—that the MFI industry must increasingly access funds and extend credit at market rates—lies at the heart of this industry's remarkable expansion over the last three decades in the developing world.

The prevailing ethos of affordable housing in the United States is the reverse, that low- to moderate-income households should receive large per-unit subsidies, often in the form of below-market interest rates—a particularly pernicious type of subvention. This ethos condemns the U.S. affordable housing industry (CDCs, CDFIs, tax credit syndicators, intermediaries, federal/state/local government housing agencies, etc.) to small scale and modest relevance in solving the country's worsening housing and urban development problems.

Building a few relatively large, highly subsidized units—the current modus operandi of U.S. affordable housing—has obvious political appeal and provides great photo opportunities. It also can have strategic use in revitalizing urban neighborhoods. However, as a general rule, this approach leaves the immense majority of needy households without assistance. Faced with much greater problems, governments in developing countries have evolved from this traditional approach of high per-unit subsidies for large complete units to smaller subsidies, more effort on the part of the beneficiary household and community, and progressive housing. This is the meaning of the observation of John Turner—a seminal thinker on the topic—that "housing is a verb," not a noun.

Informed observers of affordable housing along the border are beginning to arrive at a similar view. The Texas Department of Housing and Community Affairs estimated in 1999 that its housing programs will serve less than 1 percent of those Texans qualified for and needing housing assistance. Hence, the Texas Comptroller of Public Accounts concluded that a new approach that "increases the number of homes workers can afford" rather than offering a "limited number of income subsidies . . . for some families . . . to obtain homes they otherwise could not afford."[19]

HMF would indeed require significant public investment to develop and expand in the United States. However, U.S. HMF can thrive and reach scale as has microfinance in developing countries only by making subvention the exception rather than the rule, focusing these resources on building sustainable institutions rather than injecting high per-unit subsidies into projects, and by driving down costs by honing methods in primary and secondary market lending.

IMPLICATIONS FOR RETRACKING
U.S. LOW- TO MODERATE-INCOME HOUSING

This action plan for production of new core housing and colonia upgrading on the U.S. border with Mexico is an example of a larger change required for home ownership to remain viable for two-thirds of Americans. Increases in housing costs have substantially exceeded household incomes for most U.S. families, which have remained stagnant in real terms for the bottom half of the population over the last three decades. The mitigating factors that have allowed home ownership rates to hold their ground over the

last three decades—favorable mortgage financing and the entry of
women into the workforce—have gone as far as they can. They are
unlikely to come to the rescue again.

U.S. affordable housing practice[20] has had as its main goal filling the relatively small gap left by private home builders during
much of the half century following World War II when housing
was relatively affordable. However, along the border with Mexico
(and increasingly elsewhere in the United States), a third or more
of households now face severe problems finding adequate shelter
at affordable rates, whereas a significant portion of the middle
class can no longer purchase entry-level housing in high-cost metropolitan areas. Providing a few highly subsidized units—the
modus operandi of U.S. affordable housing—no longer fits the
socioeconomic realities of many areas in this country.

Looking ahead, trends in U.S. demographics suggest that the
entry-level housing problem will worsen. Supposing that immigration and fertility maintain their current levels, demographers
project that the U.S. population will rise to around 550,000,000 by
2050 (The Economist 2000). In contrast to much of Western
Europe and Japan, which is experiencing a population bust, U.S.
population growth is accelerating. Most of this increase in U.S.
households will likely consist of lower-income households, whose
incomes have lagged furthest behind the rise in housing costs in
the last two decades. An unanswered question facing U.S. housing
and urban development is: Where will these new Americans live,
and how?

Like developing countries with high rates of population growth,
the United States requires a great expansion in a wide range of new
entry-level housing products to stay even. This change requires
thinking and acting outside of today's standard box—freehold ownership by the owner-occupant household of the detached single-
family home. Reform runs along three continuums: the unit type,
tenure and ownership, and the accompanying financial innovations
required to support these changes in type of unit and tenure.

The main alternative unit types currently in production are
townhomes in urban areas and manufactured/mobile homes in
semirural and rural areas. However, other unit types have potential.
This chapter has analyzed the commercial possibilities of core and
expandable housing along the border with Mexico. Other alternatives include serviced lots with the financial package necessary for

the household to build a unit and—most important—support (in the form of credit finance and streamlined processing by local governments) for creation of accessory units in the existing single-family detached housing stock in urban areas.

In statistical terms freehold tenure by one household is virtually the only form of U.S. home ownership. However, rising housing costs relative to family income suggest the need for much a greater mixture of alternatives. As in developing countries, forms of tenure could be created specifically to maintain the affordability of low- to moderate-income housing.

New financial arrangements must accompany these innovations in unit type and tenure if they are to prosper. The current hegemony of freehold ownership by the owner-occupant household of a detached single-family home comes in no small part from the tremendous liquidity on superior terms available to fund this type of housing solution. This chapter has suggested two financial innovations necessary to support affordable housing on the U.S. border: introducing contract savings as a means for underwriting loans to low- and moderate-income households; and supporting the upgrading of houses in colonias through creating a pilot project and markets for U.S. housing microfinance. Other innovations such as equity sharing arrangements may have particular usefulness in allowing middle-income households to gain a foothold on the housing ladder in high-cost metropolitan areas. These reforms will require financial leadership, particularly from the secondary mortgage market institutions.

The stakes involved in these innovations are high. Housing in modern economies functions not only as shelter but also as the main asset of the middle class. Residential mortgages are the ballast of the financial system that mitigate its overall risk and keep it solvent. As of 2000, U.S. households with a net wealth of $100,000 to $250,000 held 43 percent of their wealth—the largest single share—as equity in their homes. Given the fall of U.S. stock markets from 2000 to 2002 and the continued appreciation in-house values, home ownership has gained even more importance to the U.S. economy and financial system.

Making the innovations in unit type, tenure, and financing now necessary to maintain if not increase home ownership rates holds critical importance for the health of U.S. capitalism. The border with Mexico may be a good place to start.

NOTES

1. See "Half a Billion Americans?" *The Economist* (August 24, 2002): 20–21; 550 million is at the upper range of the likely U.S. population by 2050, with 400 million at the low end.

2. For quantitative and qualitative analysis of progressive housing, see Ferguson (1996) and Ferguson and Haider (2000).

3. In the sense of having legal rights to some type of housing in which the family is living.

4. In 1970, less than 26 percent of homes in the housing stock had six rooms or more. By 2000, 38 percent fell into this category. The share of small homes—with four rooms or less—declined from 19 percent in 1970 to 12 percent in 2000. As these figures refer to the housing stock as a whole, the flow—new building—was heavily in the "large home" category to achieve such a shift.

5. For example, the median number of rooms per home in the Washington, D.C. metropolitan area actually fell between 1990 and 2000. This occurred because the number of efficiencies (one-room rental units) jumped 52 percent. The number of one-bedroom units (also overwhelmingly rental) also rose 51 percent. Although the data do not permit determining how or why, this increase is likely to come partly from the creation of accessory units to and in existing single-family homes—the least-costly and easiest way to produce affordable housing. Source: "Housing by the Numbers," 2002.

6. The SMSAs of Boston, Chicago, Dallas, Denver, Houston, Los Angeles, Miami, New York, San Francisco, and Seattle.

7. Calculations based on data from HMDA 2000.

8. These Mexican planning officials included Dr. Luis Felipe Siqueiros of the Municipal Planning Institute of Juárez and Eduardo Varela, Director of Urban Development of the municipality of Juárez.

9. *Bordering the Future.* John Sharp, Texas Comptroller of Public Accounts, 1998, notes on p. 92: "In 1995, state lawmakers approved the Colonias Fair Land Sales Act in order to curb the use of the contract for deed (method of finance used in these settlements) by requiring developers to record these contracts in county registries and provide annual financial summaries for buyers regarding their land purchase. Developers must also document services provided. . . . Additional legislation expanded the Attorney General's authority to prevent colonia development and permits border counties to refuse approval of a subdivision judged likely to be developed without sufficient infrastructure." Despite these laws, new colonias continued to develop in Texas during the 1990s. Even if Texas were completely successful in prohibiting new colonias—an unlikely prospect—the accelerating expansion of low-income households in many parts of the state would result in other types of housing problems: overcrowding, creation of tenements as families divide into smaller and smaller existing housing, and densification of existing colonias.

10. Typically, these local governments subdivide and sell progressive lots to low-income families with water and sewer, drainage, and electricity. Community residents are expected to form neighborhood organizations to contribute for subsequent improvements including pavement, sidewalks, and public lighting. Local governments sell fully serviced lots to somewhat higher-income groups, which then use a variety of means including mortgage credit to build a core unit. Over the last few years, the main Mexican federal government housing finance agencies have funded private-sector developers to build about 11,000 units per year in Juárez—consisting mainly of core expandable units for low-income families but also including complete larger units for middle-income families. The production for the year 2000 consisted of 6,800 units financed by INFONAVIT, 4,000 by FOVI and SEDESOL (under the Vivah program), and 240 by FOVISSSTE for a total of 11,040 units. The core expandable units typically cost $16,000 and are affordable to the many maquiladora workers earning $350 per month (roughly the Mexican median family income).

11. See p. 116 in *City of El Paso, 2000*. In its reliance on HOME and CDBG federal programs and in its miniscule production of affordable housing units relative to need, El Paso is typical of most U.S. cities.

12. Rose Garcia, president of the affordable housing nonprofit developer Tierra del Sol, noted concerning the GEO-Beazer Oasis Ranch project: "Their design plan was good. It was a well planned PUD. We checked out GEO and vouched for them. That type of development is very feasible but the private sector won't do it." Ninfa Moncada, the head of the El Paso office of Fannie Mae, concluded concerning the Oasis Ranch Project: "They succeeded in developing very affordable housing. It looks like a first class gated community with a community center and basketball courts."

13. In addition to these two major problems, the joint venture experienced more minor but still troublesome difficulties. The joint venture reportedly alienated a portion of the local home builder and development industry, which put various roadblocks in the way of the development. The Mexican partner, GEO, was also surprised with the length and complexity of the U.S. local planning process. The Mexican vice president of the joint venture noted that approval for the first development took six months to secure versus one month in Mexico, and also mentioned the continuous inspections: "Before you pour any slab, you have to get an inspection from the city. Before you start the slab of the second floor, you have to have the first floor approved. It adds time to the process." Cited in "MiCasa es tu casa," 1999.

14. A high mortgage loan rejection rate can increase the costs of housing development and, thus, reduce its potential for commercial success by slowing down the rate of sales for a project and increasing the builder's carrying costs (investment in land, infrastructure, completed but unsold homes), thereby eroding a builder's profit margin. Soon after the model homes of the Oasis Ranch were completed and construction on sold homes had begun, sales agents reported 100 signups (i.e., written offers for homes to be built). On the strength of the signups, the builder commenced construction of the

homes only to discover that most of the offerees' mortgage loan applications had been rejected. At that point, construction on the homes came to a halt to allow actual sales to catch up.

15. For example, besides the anticipated cost savings, the joint venture had selected concrete block as a building material, believing that Mexican immigrants would prefer a home made of materials similar to those they demand in Mexico. In Mexico, stick-built homes (wood frame and dry wall) have time and again been rejected by the Mexican home buyer in favor of traditional concrete or concrete block homes, desired for their durability. The El Paso home buyers of Mexican origin, however, considered the brick-colored block homes to be "odd-looking" in a city where stick-built homes are the norm.

16. In 1999, Fannie Mae launched a five-year, $1.5 billion "House Border Region" Investment Plan to finance affordable housing for 18,000 families. This program followed on two others, House El Paso and House Laredo. These initiatives consisted of multipronged support including: (a) grants to housing nonprofits; (b) mortgages with low down payments and flexible income sources; (c) lines of credit for construction of various specific developments, including that of the Oasis Ranch; and (d) multifamily equity investments. See *Fannie Mae News Release* (www.fanniemae.com/new/pressreleases).

17. In Spanish and Portuguese, "paternalismo" and "asistencialismo." A related term, "clientelismo," conveys the political side of the bargain between traditional politicians and households, often involving the provision of basic infrastructure. Families receive benefits such as basic services (or other sorts of gifts such as money, often at election time) in return for their vote and political support.

18. Indeed, building materials chains such as Home Depot already extend credit for building materials and for specialized labor (which they also provide) to install their products, but for a higher income clientele than colonia households and only for their products and services rather than the construction project as a whole.

19. See Carole Rylander. "Housing: Homes of Our Own," www.window. state.tx.us/border/ch07/ch07.html

20. US. "affordable housing practice" here means the 2,500 housing nonprofits (most of them housing developers), nonprofit intermediaries, private-sector developers and housing managers, local and state governments housing agencies, tax syndicators, and others that join to produce and/or manage low- to moderate-income housing funded supported by government and foundation subsidies.

11

The Future of Housing Microfinance in the United States*

Sohini Sarkar and Katharine W. McKee

The very conditions under which housing microfinance emerged and flourished in developing economies raise questions about its relevance and transferability to United States, whose socio-economic and political environment in general and the housing finance system, specifically, are far more sophisticated compared to developing economies. Despite an economy emerging from its first recession in nearly a decade, rock-solid home prices and historically low mortgage interest rates retained consumer confidence in the housing sector. In fact home sales, production, and home improvement spending climbed to record levels by the end of 2001. *The State of the Nation's Housing 2002* report indicates that the number of U.S. householders owning homes hit a record 72.6 million in 2001 (67.8 percent of U.S. households). More important, between 1994 and 2000, the home ownership rate for individuals with incomes at or above the median experienced a 4 percent increase in home ownership, to 82 percent (Retsinas and Belsky 2002, 105).

The resilience of the overall housing market aside, the housing needs of the low- to moderate-income households in the United States are also better addressed than their counterparts in developing economies. While housing microfinance has yet to establish its roots in any significant manner, numerous U.S. institutions and policies support and encourage mortgage lending to low- to moderate-income (LMI) borrowers. Most of these efforts address income and credit issues that are the basis of housing microfinance programs across the world. Unlike developing countries, where specialized institutions play a critical role in providing housing finance for the LMI, in the United States, such efforts are typically spearheaded by mainstream institutions trying to move downmarket.[1]

The U.S. housing finance system is a highly efficient capital market, with appropriate incentive structures that allow large lenders to move downmarket, and a variety of customized mortgage products and underwriting standards that make it easier for traditionally underserved borrowers to qualify for mortgage credit.[2] Spurred by the strong economy, favorable interest rates, and innovations in mortgage finance,[3] the share of home purchase loans going to lower-income households and/or households living in lower-income communities have increased steadily over the past decade (Harvard Joint Center for Housing Studies 2002, 1). The efficiency of the market is aided and abetted by a supportive regulatory environment, including the Community Reinvestment Act (CRA)[4] and the Federal Housing Enterprises Financial Safety and Soundness Act (FHEFSSA) that creates pressures on lenders, and the Government Sponsored Entities (GSEs), such as Fannie Mae and Freddie Mac, to take more aggressive steps in their service of low- to moderate-income and minority families.

WHY DO WE NEED HOUSING MICROFINANCE?

What, if any, is the role of housing microfinance in the United States? Despite its relative efficacy, there are certain fundamental weaknesses that afflict the U.S. housing system—and many of these weaknesses can be best addressed through a systemic and customized application of housing microfinance.

Mainstream housing finance in the United States, while sophisticated, fails to address the needs of a large section of the population, especially those at the lower levels of the socioeconomic strata. Despite the rapid expansion in mortgage finance products for low-income households from the conventional finance market, LMI borrowers are often not able to take full advantage of the products available through the system (see Huh and Kolluri, chapter 9). Low-income working families are often not considered bankable by conventional market standards and are unable to access the mainstream financial markets. There are currently an estimated ten million households (over 9.5 percent of households) in the United States that have no relationship to a traditional financial institution. These unbanked households are disproportionately low-income and minority; 30 percent earn less than $15,000 annually and another 10 percent earn between $15,000 and $30,000 annually (D'Amours 2000, 20–22, Kim 2001). Further, fewer than half the households with income below 80 percent of the area median have a credit card. This chasm between the mainstream financial markets and certain sections of the LMI borrowers dampens the overall prospect of wealth-building and also prevents many from becoming home owners—since having a well-documented credit history (including capacity to manage checking accounts and credit cards) increasingly influences mortgage terms and lending standards. Typically, the home ownership financing that can be accessed, if at all, by this segment, is limited and at times predatory in nature.[5]

A recent study acknowledges that the spur in home ownership is largely a function of a dual mortgage delivery system, in which new types of lending organizations provide distinctly different mortgage products to lower-income markets than those commonly offered in higher-income markets. In fact, government-backed loans and lending by subprime (many of whom are predatory) and manufactured housing specialists account for almost two-thirds of recent increases in lower-income neighborhoods. Conventional prime lending—mortgages with the lowest rates and most favorable terms—account for just 37 percent of the growth in lower-income lending, compared with 81 percent of loans to higher-income borrowers in higher-income neighborhoods (Harvard Joint Center for Housing Studies 2002, 1–2).

Thus, for all practical purposes the United States seems to have a dual housing finance market—a sophisticated array of products and services for the well-to-do and bankable population, and a more constricted range of options often marked by predatory conditions for the LMI population, especially those considered unbankable. The key role and contribution of housing microfinance in the United States will be to serve as the eraser of this dualism and the catalyst for a more equitable housing finance system.

POTENTIAL MARKETS
FOR HOUSING MICROFINANCE

The underserved LMI population, no doubt, provides a viable market for housing microfinance products and strategies. This

market is being increasingly captured by fringe lenders or subprime lenders, who have succeeded in identifying the market
demand and customizing loan products, services, and delivery
channels that uniquely target the so-called unbankable or high-
risk clients. LMI borrowers use subprime lending for a diverse
range of spending including buying or improving homes, debt
consolidation, and as an alternative source of consumer credit.
The recent growth in subprime lending[6] clearly indicates the pent
up demand in this market. Housing microfinance can play a significant role within this market by identifying targeted products,
strategies, and methodologies that will cater to the housing needs
of this population. Irrespective of the delivery services chosen to
supply microcredit, it can introduce a new dimension of competition and positively impact the overall vibrancy of these markets.

The dominant paradigm of single-family detached homes
(SFH), which are typically expensive in the United States for a
variety of reasons, constitutes a significant challenge for the LMI
population aspiring to become home owners.[7] Financing solutions
alone are inadequate. There is a need to look into diversifying the
housing products and construction processes available in the market so that they can be built and acquired for less money.

While the broad parameters of the primary population that
can benefit from housing microfinance is easily discernable, it is
not so clear exactly what kind of housing needs can be efficiently
addressed through microfinancing. In developing economies,
housing spans a wide range of physical housing solutions and legal
rights to property, thereby allowing LMI households to get on the
home ownership ladder near the bottom at low cost and move up
as their financial condition improves and housing needs expand.
In contrast, in the United States, the choices for aspirant home
owners, including LMIs, are fairly limited. "The economic and cultural dominance of freehold ownership by the owner-occupant
household of a detached SFH has largely eclipsed other types of
tenure and housing in the US." (Ferguson and Marez, this volume,
204). The freehold ownership system, characterized by housing
that is relatively large, complete, and fully legal and thereby typically expensive makes the option of providing microcredit for such
products nonviable. Within this context, comprehending the
potential of the housing microfinance market requires identifying
parallel housing needs (of the LMI population) besides home ownership, and thinking beyond the SFH paradigm of home ownership

for products and processes that are more affordable[8]—an undertaking effectively executed by several authors in this volume.

Rehab as a Potential Market

Huh and Kolluri (see chapter 9) make a convincing argument to consider housing microfinance to address the acute rehab needs of the U.S. housing market. Home maintenance and improvement costs are essential to build equity and revitalize neighborhoods and yet they pose significant resource burdens for the LMI population. A recent HUD report, *Barriers to the Rehabilitation of Affordable Housing*, acknowledges that of the "$623 billion in rehab needed nationwide—a conservative estimate—$227 billion, or about one-third, is unaffordable without some measure of subsidy or other means of support (e.g., using "sweat equity" or staggering improvements over time)" (Listokin and Listokin 2001, iv).[9] An estimated 14 percent of low-income households live in units that are structurally inadequate and overcrowded (this includes the rental population as well). The need for affordable rehab financing is also acute for the small rental property owners' market (ten units or less). A deteriorating rental stock, nearly one-third of which was built prior to 1950, is an increasing problem for communities facing an affordability crunch in the rental housing markets, particularly when it is easier for small property owners to abandon their properties than to properly maintain them.

The limited nature of subsidies offered through CDBG, HOME, LIHTC, and historic rehab tax credits (HRTC) combined with nominal presence of private rehab financing, are typically available only at a premium, leaving a large section of the LMI population with little choice but to depend on the subprime market for refinance mortgage and home-improvement financing.[10] But the subprime market may not be the most beneficial source of funds for home improvements. While it is clear that subprime borrowers pay higher prices (in terms of interest rates, fees, and points) than those in the prime market, it is less clear whether the higher prices paid by individual borrowers accurately reflect their underlying risk or merely the inefficiencies of the market.

In the current environment, housing microfinance can bridge this affordability gap for LMI households and small rental property owners that need short-term, affordable home rehabilitation loans, especially nonmortgage-based loans but for a variety reasons lack appropriate financing options (see chapter 9). While not the sole panacea, housing microfinance especially in conjunction with well synchronized federal, metropolitan, local, and private efforts can help break the vicious cycle of poverty and distress by providing affordable financing that will transform the topography of distress and attract people and investment to reenter these markets.

Becoming a Renter

Yet another market for housing microloans can be the rental process itself—loans not for rehabbing or creating rental units but for actually allowing an individual to move into one. Rising costs and diminishing supply of low-cost rentals are posing a major challenge for the LMI population, many of whom do not yet have the purchasing capacity to become a home owner. Despite the economic slowdown and increasing unemployment, contract rents (excluding utilities) are at an all-time high of $481 per month. Almost fourteen million of the 34 million renter households spend 30 percent or more on housing, while seven million spend 50 percent or more (Harvard Joint Center for Housing Studies 2002, 19). However, within this overall affordability crisis, there is the specific issue of down payment for first month's rent and security deposit, which poses an additional burden for LMI households.[11] Housing microloans can be a viable option for the working poor, who can use the money to afford the necessary upfront expenditure, to save in the long run.

Accessory Units

Similarly, the creation of accessory units in existing single-family detached homes, especially in urban neighborhoods (albeit mainly as rental units) could also be considered as a potential microfinance-friendly innovation. Accessory units can be constructed at much cheaper costs than a stand-alone unit and can be an effective way to increase affordable housing stock in urban neighborhoods that typically resist introduction of multilevel, multifamily affordable units. These can be built through microloans, providing both an additional source of wealth-building to home owners as well as an option for renters to move into mixed-income neighborhoods, that otherwise would have been out of their reach.

Starter Homes, Progressive Housing, and the Self-Help Process

Several authors in this compilation (see chapters 9 and 10) show-case affordable product and process alternatives to the SFH model. They include core or starter units with limited finish; the progressive housing process, which allows for construction of entry-level units that can be predesigned for future expansion in accordance with household housing needs; and the self-help housing process.[12] Extending these practices to the LMI population in border areas dominated by immigrant LMI population, distressed rural areas, Native American reserves, or inner city in-fill development can substantively enhance the depth of LMI housing options in the United States.

Manufactured Homes

Another crucial product that needs to be kept in mind as an affordable alternative that can be serviced through microloans is manufactured housing.[13] Manufactured homes are rarely considered decent, affordable shelter or valuable real estate capable of providing wealth-building opportunities. And yet 8 percent of home owners nationwide live in manufactured homes, 83 percent of them own their own homes, and it provides the path to first-time home ownership for approximately 14 percent of the U.S population (U.S. Census 2000). The fundamental challenge of focusing on manufactured housing is its problematic nature as a tool for wealth building. While site-built homes are always treated as real estate, manufactured homes are typically treated as personal property, because the latter is often sited on leased land. As Skillern (2002) notes, the consequences of this difference affect how manufactured housing is sold, appraised, financed, sited, and regulated—in a negative way.

With regard to financing, the difference between real property and personal property has led to the evolution of parallel financing systems for manufactured and site-built housing. Unlike site-built homes, manufactured housing buyers have less access to loans that are bought by GSEs like Fannie Mae and Freddie Mac, given that they are asset-backed instead of real-estate backed. In addition, relatively fewer lenders operate within this niche, thus, interest rate advantages engendered through market competition are difficult to come by. The financing operates under a reactive regulatory structure, triggered primarily by consumer complaints as opposed to a proactive federal banking regulatory structure. Also, there are fewer consumer protections in the purchasing process because the consumer loans used to finance manufactured home purchases are not covered under real estate loan antikick-back laws. Consequently, manufactured home buyers are faced with a lending environment characterized by higher interest rates, more risk of predatory or unfair loans, and fewer avenues for redress of grievances.

Efforts are already underway to make manufactured homes a part of the mainstream menu for affordable home ownership,[14] and it will be useful for housing microfinance advocates to explore strategic alliances with the visionary elements within the industry. The success of these alternatives will of course have to be accompanied or preceded by substantive modifications of the current legal, financial, and construction-related regulatory barriers that currently impede their adoption on a viable scale. Success also depends on whether these alternatives are culturally accepted as desirable, or at least practical, first steps toward building home equity.

THE FACE OF HOUSING MICROFINANCE IN THE UNITED STATES

Trying to understand the potential market for housing microfinance in the United States engenders two parallel themes: that there is an existing market for housing microfinance products and services, and that the U.S. housing finance market is far more evolved than many of its counterparts in developing countries. Thus, the role housing microfinance plays would be more complementary, as opposed to the dominant and, at times, only avenue to provide housing options to the LMI population in developing economies.

Its primary role in the United States lies in introducing lending alternatives that will qualify the creditworthy yet undeserved LMI population that cannot access traditional mortgage or non-mortgage a fair opportunity to fulfill their housing needs. Exactly if and when it will evolve as a widespread lending practice, if at all, is difficult to speculate. However, it is certain that for housing microfinance to succeed in the United States, it should learn from the successes and challenges of the practice internationally but also be able to customize it to the unique context of the U.S. housing finance industry. The following section captures the likely profile of housing microfinance in the days ahead.

Loan Amount

First, any discussion or effort related to U.S. housing microfinance should carry with it an explicit understanding that the gross dollar amounts at stake are higher than in developing economies. While housing microfinance refers to relatively small loans at market interest rates (or at times higher, given the risk profile of the client groups served) for short periods of time, the size of these loans will be higher than in developing economies. A typical U.S. housing microfinance loan is likely to range from $5,000 to $15,000, depending on its use, as opposed to $300 to $5,000 in developing countries. The use of the term "micro" is purely contextual, and commitment to transfer the knowledge and experience of the praxis of housing microfinance from developing economies contains no ethical or practical obligation to narrowly define the loan amount.

Microfinance Loan Use

The use of housing microfinance loans can vary depending on the need of the LMI clientele, the specifics of the local and regional housing market, and the socioeconomic and political context within which lending and housing construction occurs. For instance, an area not discussed in this volume, but definitely worth exploring, is its use as bridge financing. Given the relatively higher costs of housing, even the affordable kind, U.S. housing microfinance loans can serve as bridge financing to enable the LMI borrower to access federal, state, or local housing subsidy programs for which they are eligible. In various developing economies, housing microfinance programs act as institutional and financial intermediaries between the LMI population and public resources. Examples include FUSAI's microcredit program that capitalizes on FONAVIPO, the national housing subsidy program in El Salvador, or Cobijo, in Chile, that allows the poor to save money and subsequently qualify to participate in the government sponsored Progressive Housing program; Fundacion de la Vivienda Popular, in Venezuela, which organizes communities and assists them in accessing public funds through the Barrio Improvement Program; and the CHF International in South Africa, which provides housing finance to members eligible for the National Housing Subsidy Program (Center for Urban Development Studies 2000, 14).

If the political and the sociocultural climate can move beyond looking at home ownership and single-family detached units as the primary vehicle for fulfilling housing needs, the chances of bringing scale and sustainability to housing microfinance efforts will be greatly enhanced.

Lending Methodology

In terms of lending methodologies, several practices hold promise for the U.S. housing market.

Underwriting the household. An underwriting practice relevant for housing microfinance is the notion of underwriting the household for assessing creditworthiness of an applicant. In a recent conference on *The Future of Microfinance in the United States: Research, Practice and Policy Perspectives,*[15] development practitioners highlighted international microenterprise programs that use underwriting standards that apply to the income of the entire household, rather than the potential revenue from specific entrepreneurial activities for which the loan is being taken (Talen, Weiss, and Sarkar 2002, 337). This approach can be adapted for housing microfinance as well. It will make a significant difference for hardworking LMI families in the United States if the overall household income from both formal and informal earnings can be taken into account for assessing creditworthiness. It is possible to contradict on grounds that the notion of joint liability, especially financial, as a cultural construct lacks popularity within a dominantly individualistic social environment. However, besides questioning how dominant individualism really is, it also needs to be kept in mind that a substantive section of the growing LMI population comes from cultural contexts where notions of shared liability and responsibility toward wealth-building are common and easily accepted.

Use of compulsory savings schemes in underwriting. A diverse range of savings schemes, serving both as underwriting requirements as well as collateral (for nonmortgage-based lending) has evolved in developing economies. Similar strategies (including the use of traditional rotating savings groups in sociocultural contexts where such groups are already in existence) can be adopted for U.S. housing microfinance that addresses their housing needs and offers an opportunity to build wealth. In addition, savings mechanisms can also serve as nonmortgage collateral, especially in cases of manufactured housing or other low-cost entry-level products, where the value of the home is either not very high or difficult to appraise. It can also be used to establish alternative credit history, which subsequently needs to be acknowledged through innovative underwriting requirements by mainstream financial institutions. Even the current structure of LMI lending can benefit from the introduction of savings mechanisms, which are likely to minimize the risk associated with their high loan-to-value loans.

Technical assistance. While not exactly a lending method, technical assistance is often provided as a credit-plus option by many microfinance institutions, including those offering small loans for housing. The variances in delivery methods for and client profile of housing microfinance worldwide makes it difficult to arrive at a consensus about the level of construction assistance (if any) that should be provided by housing microfinance institutions (MFIs) and how it should be priced (Cities Alliance 2002, 2). Some MFIs provide a substantial degree of technical oversight, with on-staff engineers and architects working with borrowers throughout the design and construction of the project. The pricing for the construction assistance is built into the loan process. In contrast, others view such technical assistance as stepping away from their core competency as financiers and, thus, provide limited to no construction assistance. Within the U.S. context, the need for technical assistance is likely to be somewhat significant. Overall the affordable housing sector is fairly well developed, with large numbers of public, private, and nonprofit entities that are well versed in construction technology involved in the construction process. Entry-level products are typically manufactured at mass scale to reduce costs or are site built by nonprofit, public, or private developers with know-how about construction processes. However, technical assistance will need to be considered when microloans are made to individuals for self-help housing or for rehab.

Appropriate pricing of such training will also need to be creatively dealt with. Servicing technical assistance costs through the loans is a controversial issue. Training markets are frequently fraught with shortcomings, especially involving risk assessment by both consumers and suppliers, which causes challenges in terms of determining pricing. On one hand, the pricing should not drive away clients, but on the other hand it should not incur losses for the lender.[16] Credit enhancements can be creatively used for such purposes. The need to subsidize technical assistance, at least partially and definitely in the formative stages of the industry, will have to be clearly established. An interesting example can be found in the microenterprise training voucher program in Paraguay, first financed by the Inter-American Development Bank (IDB) in 1997 (now deactivated by the Paraguayan government for a more ambitious voucher program). Under this program, customers paid a part of the training costs up front (which can, alternatively, be priced into the housing loan itself) and also handed over the voucher, which covered 40 to 80 percent of the cost of the course. The technical assistance provider could redeem the voucher if the consumer attended at least 75 percent of the classes, which was used as a measure of the quality of technical assistance provided (Goldmark and Botelho 2000). The program was designed to stimulate the market for short-term practical training by diminishing the risk for both consumers and providers, and by shifting more decision making power about the type of training to the consumers. Similar technical assistance is amenable for experimentation within the United States as well, the bottom line being that they are demand driven and not generically imposed either by government or lenders. In the long run, it may even be possible to reduce the subsidy, if the private benefits derived by the trainees are sufficient to sustain the market with little external support (Schor and Alberti 1996). Subsidies can also be reduced if, through outreach, the effective demand for such training can be expanded beyond the borrowing trainees, to attract customers willing to pay the market price for such services.

Funding Housing Microfinance

Charitable and government funds as credit enhancements. Use of donor, government, and charitable funds for credit enhancement is fairly common in the housing microfinance sector in developing economies and LMI lending in the United States, especially to keep interest rates low. In fact, unlike many developing economies, U.S.

credit enhancements are available even through financial intermediaries and the secondary mortgage market, including mortgage insurance, that reduce credit-risk exposure of investors in
financial instruments backed by mortgages.[17] However, with the
shift in the housing microfinance industry worldwide to more
market-priced lending, credit enhancements are being creatively
used for other purposes. In the United States, the viability of using
such enhancements for nonmortgage financial products, organizational capacity of the microlending organizations, or for technical assistance will likely be successful.

Tripartite approach. Merrill and Temkin (2002, 273) highlights the
tripartite approach used extensively in Chile, and on a smaller
scale in Brazil, as a possible model for U.S. housing microfinance.
The Chilean model is structured around three components: targeted subsidies by the public sector, household savings, and bank
loans. For the United States, the authors recommend integrating
a state or national direct-grant subsidy program, with a compulsory savings program, a loan program, and possibly an FHA insurance (Merrill and Temkin 2002, 287). Combining savings programs with subsidy to help low-income people gain assets is
becoming increasingly common, by way of Individual Development Accounts (IDA).[18] IDA programs are typically run by nonprofit organizations, public agencies, or community development
financial institutions. It is worth exploring if these existing programs can be morphed, especially the ones run by community
development financial institutions to add a housing microloan
component to them, given that a large majority either use or
intend to use it for housing needs anyway.[19]

TASKS AHEAD

While a scan of the U.S. housing market, the people, the products,
and the current financial system clearly indicates a tangible niche
for microlending—why has it yet to catch up with the popular
imagination? If the real world were truly governed by liberal pre-
cepts of free-market economy, then the existing demand would
have been met through commensurate supply. But the real world
is much more than demand and supply. The market is embedded
within a dynamic environment where social, political, and economic

forces constantly interact with each other to define, shape, and govern it. The tools of understanding and analyzing provided to us by social science do not allow us to accurately identify and measure the diverse range of variables that shape the U.S. housing market. However, it is possible to identify at least some of the major areas where we need to focus our attention to make housing microfinance work.

Determining Pricing for Risk and Transaction Costs

Attracting mainstream lenders and reaching scale and sustainability, as mentioned earlier, are critically dependent on developing reliable mechanisms to deal with the potentially high-risk client population as well as minimizing transaction costs. In developing economies, housing microfinance increasingly relies on risk-based pricing as opposed to unsustainable dependence on subsidized interest rates and cross-subsidization (which are often mandatory and regulated). Risk-based pricing, however, is still at a nascent stage in the United States. Most of the U.S. affordable housing programs are predominantly subsidy driven. The latest generation of direct-demand subsidies, designed to leverage subsidies with market-rate loans, have been only moderately successful. Since a large portion of the LMI population fails to qualify for credit, such programs often end up providing larger subsidies to complete the financing of the units. The notion of risk-based pricing for the LMI population is a sensitive issue, because of its almost immediate association with the predatory lending practices in the subprime market.

Undoubtedly more research is needed to ascertain what constitutes legitimate risk within the context of the U.S. market and its appropriate pricing. Also, unlike traditional LMI lending which is mortgage based, housing microfinance can be done with non-mortgage collaterals, which in turn increases the challenges of analyzing risk. However, it must be remembered that microfinancing by definition reduces the overall risk compared to high loan-to-value traditional mortgages to begin with. As for the question of fair and viable high interest rates, a large section of the LMI population is already conducting financial transactions with predatory lenders, for a wide range of reasons including housing finance needs. There is an increasing realization that, for the underserved LMI population, the primary obstacle is not price but access to credit.[20] To that end, even if the pricing for microloans is at market rate or slightly above, as long as rates do not reach those charged by predatory lenders and are combined with saving schemes, training, and other wealth-building tools, they will constitute an acceptable option for the LMI population in this country.

Deciding and Developing Appropriate Delivery Channels

The universe of housing microfinance delivery mechanisms defies easy classification, being contingent on whether it is defined from a product-based or a provider-based perspective (see chapter 1). However, if both perspectives are taken into account, housing microfinance delivery mechanisms can be divided into two broad categories: delivery mechanisms or providers that make housing microfinance available on a stand-alone basis to all eligible clients, including first-time clients; and delivery mechanisms or providers that extend such financing on a linked basis, and only to those who have a prior financial relationship with the provider. The key players involved in developing economies are typically microfinance institutions, niche banks, and nongovernmental/nonprofit organizations. Mainstream financial institutions have mostly abstained from entering this market, and the secondary market for funding housing microfinance loans is typically underdeveloped.

In the United States, however, strategies for delivering microfinance need to be considered within the context of a highly sophisticated housing finance system, whose capacity to reach downmarket has improved significantly since 1990s.[21] Mainstream lenders, along with GSEs, are increasingly investing to amplify the housing opportunities for the LMI population. In addition, since the 1980s, the country's community development industry, replete with community development corporations (CDCs), financial intermediaries, and a whole host of private foundations have directed their resources toward affordable housing, if not housing microfinance per se. Also gaining popularity are alternative private sector financial institutions with a social mission, commonly referred to as community development financial institutions (CDFIs). CDFIs essentially make loans and investments that are considered unbankable by conventional industry standards and serve clients (including LMI individuals or nonprofit housing and business developers) who are underserved by mainstream financial institutions.[22]

Strategically speaking, attaining economies of scale for housing microfinance would be more viable if the efforts are concentrated on optimal utilization and enhancements to the existing housing finance infrastructure, rather than reinventing a parallel one. It is possible to include a housing microfinance component to existing operations of CDFIs, especially those involved with microenterprise development or IDAs. It is similarly possible to conceive of private lenders partnering with CDFIs, or community development corporations, that already have a presence in LMI communities to reach downmarket through housing microloans. Similarly, CDCs already in the business of providing affordable housing might consider either converting themselves into CDFIs or creating separate for-profit entities with depository powers to do housing microfinance.

Most important, the capacity of mainstream lenders in generating economies of scale for almost any kind of financial services should not be overlooked. The pro-LMI mandate of the CRA and FHEFSSA regulations already serves as an incentive for federally regulated lenders and GSEs to maintain a substantive presence in the LMI markets. This regulatory environment can be leveraged even further. Lack of systematic information about the characteristics, depth, and potential profitability of the LMI markets constitutes a core supply-side barrier that prevents mainstream lenders from considering housing microfinance, despite CRA and FHEFSSA regulations. Thus, it might be cost effective to focus on generating accurate and reliable market information, products, services, and lending methodologies that will reduce transaction costs, credit risks, and pricing dilemmas—to attract more mainstream lenders into the housing microfinance market.

Role of the Public Sector and Philanthropic Organizations

Most successful housing microfinance programs rely on both public and private sources of capital to run their programs, but there is an emerging consensus about moving away from heavily subsidy-dependent or donor-supported operations (Angel 2001, UNESCAP 2001). The focus instead is on strengthening the capital base through expansion of membership, minimization of default and arrear rates, and better capitalization on public and private contributions (The Center for Urban Development Studies 2000, 24). However, the role of public sector and philanthropic organizations should not be underestimated, especially within the United States, where housing microfinance is still at a nascent stage and can benefit from such capital for credit enhancement or as part of tripartite arrangements. Public and philanthropic funds can also play a critical role in sponsoring pilot projects that would demonstrate the viability of microloans for housing, and to make available reliable data on transaction costs, risks, impact, and long-term commercial sustainability.

Federal, state, and local governments, and federal agencies like HUD can play a key role in creating incentive structures and regulatory frameworks that allow and promote smaller units, greater lot coverage, shorter setbacks, and automatic approval of preplanned expansion of units and construction of new in-fill units, which are all amenable to be microfinanced (Lowry and Ferguson 1992). Philanthropic organizations and government research agencies can take an active role in facilitating research on both housing microfinance as well as affordable housing alternatives to reach the LMI population.

Building the Policy Network

The success of U.S. housing microfinance depends on a supportive policy environment. Thus, it is critical that advocates start building strategic alignments with innovative and sympathetic organizations and networks that are working not only on housing microfinance but microfinance networks in general, affordable housing networks, the Smart Growth network, and existing poverty reduction networks. Groups like Association for Enterprise Opportunity, the Smart Growth Network, or the National Affordable Housing Network—which have already started making significant impact on national policy agenda—can serve as potential allies through strategic collaborations. It is also critical to embed the U.S. housing microfinance movement within the larger international network to ensure that the domestic industry does not keep reinventing the wheel. Cities Alliance, for example, is partnering with Accion International, CHF International, and Frontier Finance to improve shelter finance for the poor. They are involved in documenting best practices and analyzing possible replications, adaptations, and further entry into shelter finance by commercial financial institutions. In addition, the Consultative Group for the Assistance to the Poorest, the International Finance Corporation, the World Bank, the Inter-American Development Bank, Plan International, the U.S. Agency for International Development, and the Urban Management Programme for Latin America and the Caribbean are also heavily invested in the arena, in terms of both program and research dollars. Knowledge and experience generated by such organizations within the international arena should be effectively leveraged.

Research

Viability of housing microfinance within the United States is fundamentally dependent on research. The chapters included in this volume are a crucial first step in that direction. While it is beyond the scope of this project to come up with a comprehensive research agenda, certain broad directions are worth proposing.

First, it is critical that we effectively capture existing and emerging research based on housing microfinance praxis abroad, especially those evolving from industrialized nations. Existing research on innovations and best practices, lending methodologies, risk analysis, pricing, and mainstreaming efforts need to be systematically identified and analyzed for viability within the U.S. context.

Second, it is also necessary to capture research that exists or is emerging on LMI lending, housing affordability, and technological innovations to reduce transaction costs for servicing the LMI population within the United States. Home ownership research (including affordable home ownership) has a long lineage, and the knowledge gained through that research needs to be captured for better analysis of how housing microfinance may fit—or doesn't fit—within the larger framework of LMI lending for housing.

Third, serious investments are needed to explore new ground. The question of effective demand for housing microfinance and its unintended consequences requires thorough investigation. We have very little systematic quantitative assessment of the socioeconomic profile or the housing needs of the LMI population that are underserved by LMI lending mechanisms. While certain niche markets have been identified and case studies and anecdotal evidences are available, the information is yet to reach a level of reliability that can attract mainstream lenders. Further, a critical methodological nuisance that needs to be addressed because of its strong policy and practice implications is the constant merging of data on the LMI population with data on minorities. Although a large section of minorities indeed fall under the LMI category, contrary to popular stereotypes two-thirds of households with the lowest incomes are non-Hispanic whites (Harvard Joint Center for Housing Studies 2002, 24). Generation of disaggregated data is absolutely imperative for a real assessment of the realities.

In addition, it is important to consider the unintended consequences of providing microloans loans to borrowers who are already income constrained, lack credit history, or are credit impaired. What are the risks involved in relaxing underwriting polices for home ownership loans, specifically in terms of delinquency and default, given that new LMI home owners can be especially vulnerable to unexpected home repairs, medical costs, or even loss of employment in the face of economic downturn? How well can compulsory savings serve to buffer these risks? Is there a trade-off between microloans focused on housing as opposed to income generation? Should public monies be used for this purpose, and if so, to what extent? Do the benefits of owning a starter unit outweigh the costs of its limited resale value? What are the trade-offs between focusing on supply-side issues as opposed to the demand-side barriers?

While there is a lot of ground to cover, the reassurance evolves from the fact that housing microfinance research in the United States can literally leapfrog to an advanced state, given current availability of knowledge on the issue internationally, and the strength of housing research in general on the domestic front.

CONCLUSION—SHIFTING ATTITUDES

The most resilient obstacle that stands between the United States and housing microfinance is the general perception about microfinance per se. So far, microfinance has been mainly marketed as a tool for developing economies, which harbor the majority of the world's poor. There is a common consensus that, in comparison, the financial systems in the United States and most of the G-8 nations are far more sophisticated and have effective mechanisms embedded in them to reach downmarket. However, the consensus becomes self-destructive when it translates into a false sense of confidence or even denial of persistent poverty within the so-called developed economies. If we step beyond the realm of comparative statistics, it is impossible to miss the ugly face of poverty that besets millions within these economies. In fact, in a sense, the tribulations of poverty are more acute within affluent economies, which are characterized by high living costs and psychosocial notions of what constitutes a decent quality of life, that are quite formidable when compared to developing economies. It is time to question the dominant perceptions of poverty as a pathology that afflicts "others."

It is also important to acknowledge that transfer of knowledge does not necessarily have to occur from the core to the periphery—in other words from North to South. Every so-called core nation has a periphery embedded within it and can benefit from learning and adopting strategies from the so-called developing economies to address the concerns of the periphery.

At a different level, we need to address the issue of affordability from a holistic perspective. Financing, product, and process innovations geared toward affordability addresses only one part of the equation. A fundamental axiom that the U.S. housing finance system and affordable housing practitioners leave largely unexamined is that a country's housing reflects in large part its level of income and income distribution. The U.S. income distribution has worsened substantially over the last thirty years, and the basic ratio of housing cost to household income has worsened for the population as a whole, particularly the bottom half. Efforts and deliberations on housing finance are likely to fall short or be unsustainable if this larger issue fails to be addressed meaningfully.

Finally, we need to view housing microfinance not as a subsidy-driven, boutique solution for the underserved LMI population but as a vibrant market mechanism that, if appropriately designed, can be commercially sustainable and generate positive externalities. Failure to do so might run the risk of creating housing microfinance initiatives that spatially confine the LMI population to housing submarkets offering less access to quality public services, job opportunities, and benefits of house price appreciation that occur in vibrant markets.

NOTES

*The opinions expressed in this chapter are those of the authors and should not be attributed to the Fannie Mae Foundation.

1. Based on information from a working draft prepared by Kenneth Temkin, 2002.

2. A case in point is the national home-buying capacity, which under the standard (or historical) mortgages that were available during 1970s and 1980s, stood at approximately $314 billion. However, in response to innovations and improvements, in 2000, that capacity ranged between $500 and $600 billion. Affordability, as measured by home-buying capacity, also saw phenomenal growth. Under the standard mortgage only 3.8 percent of renter families (approximately 1 million) could afford to buy their "dream house." In contrast, in 2000, about 8 percent of renter families (approximately 2 million) could afford to do so (Listokin, Wyly, Schmitt, and Voicu 2000).

3. A large part of these gains are due to the efforts of the housing finance industry to adopt more flexible underwriting standards, efforts by GSEs to create more affordable loan products, underwriting experiments to encourage greater home ownership, loan partnerships with community-based organizations to penetrate markets and assist with transactions, and guarantees and credit enhancements to sell to the secondary market to increase liquidity for affordable lending.

4. While the CRA of 1977 has increased the lending commitments of banks to underserved communities, it is difficult to draw explicit causal links, given that 50 percent of all mortgages are originated by mortgage banks not subject to CRA.

5. The Coalition for Responsible Lending recently estimated that predatory lending costs U.S. borrowers $9.1 billion annually (Stein 2001). Between 1990 and 1998, when interest rates were dropping, the home foreclosure rate increased by 384 percent. *See* United States Census Bureau, Statistical Abstract of the United States, Banking, Finance and Insurance, Table No. 823, "Mortgage Delinquency and Foreclosure Rates: 1980 to 1998" (1999). The bulk of these foreclosure actions involved borrowers who had subprime—including predatory—loans (Mansfield 2000).

6. Carr and Schuetz (2002, 11) highlights a recent U.S. Department of Housing and Urban Development study that between 1993 and 1998, the dollar volume of subprime loans grew sevenfold, from $20 billion to $150 billion, and the number of subprime refinance loans increased tenfold, from 80,000 to 790,000 loans.

7. The rapidly appreciating housing market further exacerbates the situation. Continuing a seven-year surge, inflation-adjusted home prices in 2001 were up 5.7 percent from 2000, as more than 70 million home owners continued to build home equity at astounding rates. While this can benefit some existing home owners, it poses significant challenges for LMI households looking to become first-time home buyers (*The State of the Nation's Housing* 2002).

8. Purchasing power of a small housing loan in the United States would be much lower compared to developing economies. In the United States, even basic manufactured units constructed with affordability in mind can cost as much as $46,500. In contrast, in developing economies like Mexico, the average two-room starter house for low- to moderate-income households sells for $12,000–$15,000, with substantial subsidies from the government conveyed in

below-market interest rates on loans for 80 percent of the amount (Ferguson and Haider 2002, 323).

9. It is important to remember that the challenges are not limited to lack of appropriate financing. It includes a wide range of obstacles including development stage barriers (acquiring properties, estimating costs, obtaining insurance, obtaining financing, land use restrictions), construction stage barriers (codes/regulations, trades etc.), and occupancy stage barriers (rent control, property tax increases) (Listokin and Listokin 2001, 39–138).

10. In 1998, subprime loans accounted for a little more than one-half of refinance loans originated to low- and moderate-income borrowers, about 16 percentage points more than the proportion of LMI borrowers receiving refinance mortgages in the prime, conventional market (Scheessele, Randall 1999). Subprime borrowers also tend to live in poorer census tracts: a little more than two-thirds of subprime loans originated in 1998 were in the lower- and moderate-income census tract compared to only 58 percent of prime loans. Based on information from a working draft by Kenneth Temkin. 2002.

11. An incisive account of this crisis is showcased by essayist and cultural critic Barbara Ehrenreich, in *Nickeled and Dimed*. Ehrenreich's real life stories about a wide range of Americans who work full-time, year-round for poverty-level wages, indicate that many are spending exorbitant amounts of their salary, in some cases as high as $1,800 a month, to stay in motels or similarly ill-priced accommodations, simply because they did not have enough savings to afford the down payment on security and first month's rent. Ehrenreich, in comparison, staying within the same housing market, could live in a $500 per month efficiency, in light of the fact that she could pay the $1,000 up front (Ehrenreich 2001, 25–28).

12. There is a long history of self-help programs in the United States. Informally, the concept dates back to community home and barn raisings. The modern incarnation of the self-help process was initiated by the American Friends Service Committee to house western Pennsylvania coal miners in 1937, and later refined by AFSC in serving farm worker households in California's San Joaquin valley in the early 1960s. The U.S. Department of Agriculture's Rural Housing Service (RHS, formerly the Farmers Home Administration or FmHA) began funding self-help housing efforts in 1963. From then through 1996 it has supported the development of over 26,000 self-help homes. http://www.ruralhome.org/pubs/selfhelp/selfhelp/selfhelp.htm.

13. The average sales price of a manufactured home in 2000 was $46,500 (cost of land excluded), compared to $207,000 for a site-built home (including land price) and $ 153,425 (excluding land price). US Census Bureau Manufactured Housing Survey at http://www.census.gov/const/www/mhsindex. html. The *1999 American Housing Survey* indicates that almost 40 percent of manufactured home owners cited financial considerations as the driving force that influenced their home ownership decision.

14. Notable public sector efforts include HUD's Partnership for Advancing Technology in Housing (PATH) program. PATH is exploring innovative designs for manufactured housing as part of an ongoing effort to increase affordable housing opportunities (*Innovations at the Cutting Edge—New Ideas in*

Manufactured Housing). HUD is also collaborating with Steven Winter Associates, Inc., to develop the NextGen project that uses technology to develop products, systems, and designs that can be adopted by the mainstream in the coming decade. Various programs and initiatives are now focusing on removing zoning and other regulatory obstacles to manufactured housing. One example of a very successful program currently underway is the manufactured housing Urban Design Demonstration Project (http://www.ndmha.com/industry.htm). Progress is also being made as new laws are adopted that mandate longer lease terms and redefine tax categories, which will likely have a positive impact in boosting investor confidence and lender competition for financing. Private secondary market initiatives, like Freddie Mac's new land lease mortgage product that allows for conversion of manufactured housing to real property even when a unit is placed on leased land, promises better financing options for those interested in manufactured homes. For details see http://www.freddiemac.com/sell/expmkts/mhle.html.

15. Hosted by the Fannie Mae Foundation and Woodrow Wilson International Center for Scholars on October 11, 2001 in Washington, D.C.

16. On the demand side, consumers have great difficulty in gauging the benefits of training before doing a course. Therefore, they may opt to either consume suboptimal amounts that they can afford or nothing at all, even if it leads to negative externalities in terms of poor quality construction, unanticipated costs, and ballooning financial requirement. This is particularly true with income- and time-constrained LMI population, who might not find it cost effective to spend additional dollars in training and might not have the time to do so. On the supply side, microloan providers may not want to invest in and supply training before receiving payment because they fear that customers will renege on their payments once the good is consumed, and thereby need to price in the cost of training into the loan from the beginning.

17. For a detailed analysis of credit enhancement usage by the secondary mortgage market in the United States see HUD's Office of Policy Development and Research report, *Study of the Use of Credit Enhancements by Government Sponsored Enterprises,* 2001. According to this report, in 1999, Fannie Mae sustained approximately $400 million in single-family and multifamily credit losses. Of this amount, Fannie Mae bore approximately $125 million ($118 for single-family and $7 million for multifamily), with the remaining $275 million assumed by risk-sharing partners, primarily mortgage insurers. An interesting example is Freddie Mac's credit enhancement program for fixed-rate and floating-rate multifamily housing bonds. Freddie Mac collaborates with state and local housing authorities to provide credit enhancements for tax-exempt bonds issued by the localities. The credit enhancement allows the bond issuers to receive or maintain a high "AAA" credit rating, thereby reducing the cost of their borrowing and the rents on financed homes more affordable.

18. IDAs are matched savings accounts that allow low-income families to accumulate a few thousand dollars for high return on investments. The monthly savings by individuals are matched by funds from foundations, financial institutions, community organizations, churches, or state/federal agencies. Currently, there are more than 400 community-based IDA programs in 49 states. Also, a

bipartisan bill pending in Congress provides a federal commitment to IDAs. If enacted into law, it will allow participating financial institutions to receive a full tax credit for savings match contributions up to a certain threshold, and a small reimbursement for administrative costs.

19. As of June 30, 2000, 13 percent of IDA participants made matched withdrawals. About 24 percent made a home purchase, with another 20 percent using their matched withdrawal for home repair. In terms of intended use, 57 percent reported that they intend to buy a home with the savings. (Center for Social Development 2001).

20. Contrary to popular belief, the upper limit of consumer tolerance for high interest rates is not necessarily shaped by credit card rates. Interest rates for certain alternative "fringe" consumer financial services can range from 400 percent to more than 1,000 percent annually, and in some extreme cases up to more than 2,000 percent annually (Carr and Schuetz, 2001).

21. See Merrill and Temkin 2002, 278–281 for a synopsis of the institutional structure for low-income lending in the United States.

22. A wide range of organizations that fall under the rubric of CDFIs include community development banks, community development credit unions, community development loan funds, community development venture capital funds, and microenterprise development loan funds. See http://www.cdfi.org/cdfitype.html. Accessed on 11/23/02.

12

Taking Housing Microfinance to Scale: Advice for Governments and Donors

Mohini Malhotra

The preceding chapter discussed the future of housing micro-finance in the United States. Here we focus on what government, donors, and relevant decision makers can do to help housing microfinance achieve scale and financial viability in developing economies. This chapter has four central arguments:

- there is demand from poor people for housing finance services tailored to the way they build;
- the lessons for how best to respond to this demand can be drawn in large part from the microfinance revolution that started in the 1970s;
- a key constraint at this stage is retail institutional capacity, but converging interests are creating the conditions for a rapid ramp-up; and
- there is huge potential for achieving scale, provided policy makers in governments, donor agencies, and financial institutions work in concert toward achieving that goal.

This chapter makes specific recommendations for policy makers in government and in donor agencies to take supportive actions to nurture those financial institutions that have the vision, strategy, competence, track record, and realistic plans to achieve scale and sustainability in providing shelter finance services to the poor. It complements chapters 3, 4, 5, 6, and 7, which guide financial institutions on how to reach scale and commercial viability.

DEMAND FOR HOUSING FINANCE SERVICES
IS HIGH AND RISING

By 2030, there will be an additional two billion people living in urban areas, driven by similar trends across all continents:

- Sub-Saharan Africa's population is projected to triple by 2030 as it did in the preceding twenty-five years.
- Asia's urban population is projected to double over the next thirty years.
- In the countries of Eastern Europe and Central Asia, 300 million (of 450 million) people are living in urban areas, and the urban poor are twice as numerous as the rural poor.
- Latin America and the Caribbean will be 81 percent urban by 2030, up from today's 75 percent.
- The Middle East will be 72 percent urban by 2030, up from 42 percent in 1970.[1]

An unfortunate corollary to this continued trend is the urbanization of poverty and extreme poverty. This is particularly stark in Latin America, the most urbanized of all regions and most likely the harbinger of what may occur in other regions as they reach similar levels of urbanization. Twenty-five percent of Latin America's urban population, or 90 million people, live in slums. UN-Habitat estimates that 600 million urban dwellers worldwide live in life- and health-threatening environments as a result of poor sanitation and housing (Gelbard, Haub, and Kent 1999). Demand for housing and housing finance will increase, particularly from the poor, as illustrated by the following examples:

- *Peru:* 82 percent of the eight million people living in greater Lima are classified as poor. At least half of poor households and 60 percent of the poorest households express a strong desire to expand or improve their home within the next twelve months. Only 10 to 15 percent are borrowing from formal or informal sources. The potential market in metropolitan Lima for housing finance loans is estimated at 110,000 projects annually (Brown and Garcia 2002).
- *Indonesia:* In 2000, the country's urban population of 85 million already represented 40 percent of the total. By 2010 the country's urban dwellers will represent 50 percent of the

total population, with 120 million people. Annual projections for housing needs for the next ten years are approximately 735,000 new units and an additional 420,000 in need
of improvement. An estimated 70 to 80 percent of all housing in Indonesia is constructed informally and incrementally, with minimal access to formal financial markets.[2]

- *Morocco:* Two surveys found that 88 percent of households
  have or are planning a productive activity in the home, and
  more than 83 percent of households are willing to take a
  loan to finance their home improvement projects. Ninety-
  two percent of urban and 94 percent of rural households
  constructed their own homes without access to formal
  finance (Davis and Mahoney 2001).

- *Mexico:* Approximately 3.5 million families need housing
  improvements and 1.1 million need homes in Mexico. More
  than 56 percent of new housing and home improvement
  demand comes from families earning less than three minimum salaries. Alternatives to home ownership, such as
  affordable renting, are very limited for poor households in
  Mexico, due to unfavorable tax treatment and the legacy of
  rent controls. The housing finance system's bias is toward
  new housing units, thus, limiting financing for progressive
  housing (World Bank 2002).

Poor urban residents identify their most important needs as
lack of jobs, inadequate housing, and water supply, in that order.
In terms of their second priority of housing, most lack access to
formal sources of finance.

AN EMERGING FINANCIAL SECTOR
RESPONSE THAT BUILDS ON EARLIER
MICROFINANCE LESSONS

In response to the housing problems of the poor and their
demand for housing finance, innovations in providing shelter
loans on commercial terms to poor people are emerging largely
from private financial institutions, many of which originated as
microfinance institutions (MFIs). These institutions are a heterogeneous set of players comprising private commercial banks,
credit unions, nonbank financial intermediaries, housing finance

companies, and nongovernment organizations (NGOs). Their basic lending methodology is to offer small working capital loans and reward good repayment behavior with access to larger and longer-term loans. The clients of the first generation of such institutions are investing significant portions of their longer-term and larger loans into home improvement. For example, SEWA Bank, a cooperative bank in India, discovered that roughly 40 percent of its loan funds were invested in home improvements such as building toilets, expanding rooms, and getting water connections. These same institutions are venturing into new product and service delivery, such as housing finance, to retain their existing clients and attract new ones. The following points are illustrated with examples in most part from case studies of SEWA Bank in India; FUNHAVI, a Mexican NGO; and MiBanco, a regulated financial institution in Peru that Cities Alliance commissioned.

The Clients

A concern of governments and donors is whether services they fund actually reach the poor they are intended for. These financial institutions describe their clients as the economically active poor in the informal sector as the following examples illustrate:

- MiBanco, a commercial, regulated bank in Peru, has housing finance clients whose income hovers around and below the poverty line. The poverty line indicator of gross national income per capita was $175 per month in 2000 (Brown and Garcia 2002).
- FUNHAVI, a Mexican NGO focused exclusively on housing finance, serves clients who earn between two and eight times the local minimal wage, but less than one percent had accessed formal finance prior to borrowing from FUNHAVI (Daphnis et al. 2002).
- SEWA Bank's clients are all self-employed women. Urban members are predominately vendors, laborers, or home-based workers. In 1998, an estimated 76 percent of SEWA borrowers had annual household incomes below U.S.$415 and half of these had annual incomes below U.S.$276 (Center for Urban Development Studies 2000).
- Fifty-eight percent of the clients of FADES, an NGO in Bolivia, live in a one-room house, with the majority having families of

four or more persons, and 38 percent of the houses with mud or dirt walls, roofs, and floors (Plan International 2001).

- Fifty-seven percent of the clients of Genesis, an NGO in Guatemala, live in one-room houses made of sheet metal or plastic. The monthly household income of 75 percent of borrowers is less than U.S.$250.
- Ninety-five percent of the clients of CARD, a commercial bank in the Philippines, were below the poverty line, with a weekly income not exceeding U.S.$13 (Center for Urban Development Studies 2000).

The Product

The shelter finance loan product offered by MFIs is distinct from mortgages in that it is typically for housing improvement rather than to purchase or build a new home. It also is distinct but not remarkably different from the typical working capital loan technology that most microfinance institutions use, as illustrated below:

- MiBanco's loan product differs from its microenterprise loan in the following four ways: a lower annual interest rate, longer terms (up to thirty-six months compared with twenty-four months), slightly larger amount ($916 on average), and available to low-income salaried workers. Legal title is not required to obtain a loan, and the guarantees used are traditional microenterprise collateral such as cosigners and household assets.
- CARD's average housing loan amount is U.S.$349 compared with its average microenterprise loan of U.S.$103. The term for microenterprise loans ranges from twenty-five to fifty weeks, whereas its housing loans are set at fifty weeks.
- Grameen's loans are available to clients with a good repayment track record, and loans are available for a range of activities such as home repair, home construction, or land purchase. Loan amounts and terms are larger than for the microenterprise loans, interest rates are lower, and a member must provide legal documentation of land ownership when a house is to be built. Grameen recommends a prototype house for its clients (Center for Urban Development Studies 2000).

Scale—Small but Growing

The number of institutions involved in shelter finance provision is increasing. While overall numbers are not available, a study funded by the International Finance Corporation (IFC) identifies 141 institutions providing shelter finance loans to the poor.[3] And while the scale of operations is small for most of these institutions, it is a growing portion of the portfolio. Among the twenty-seven financial institutions in the Accion network, seven have housing portfolios totaling almost 10,000 active clients and $20 million in outstanding balances. SEWA Bank's outstanding housing loan portfolio as of January 2002 was 40 percent of its total portfolio. Shelter loans account for approximately 7 percent of BancoSol's portfolio in Bolivia. They are six percent of MiBanco's current portfolio but are expected to grow to as much as half in a few years. The percentage of Grameen Bank's portfolio in housing loans is 6.7 percent, with a total dollar portfolio of more than $620 million. Grameen disbursed 317 housing loans in its first year (1984) and by May 1999 had given out 506,680 housing loans. As of February 1999, CARD's total amount of loans outstanding was U.S.$2.2 million, of which 18.4 percent were housing loans (Center for Urban Development Studies 2000). For these institutions, and for the majority entering this market, shelter loans are a growing segment of their service mix.

Financial Sustainability

Very little is known about the profitability of shelter finance to the providers at this point (see chapter 2). Given the novelty of these loans as a specific product line, the scale of operations of service providers has yet to be sufficiently documented or analyzed. While many financial institutions recognize that an increasing proportion of their loan portfolios are being invested in housing, very few maintain disaggregated portfolio data. The Cities Alliance case studies of MiBanco in Peru, FUNHAVI in Mexico, and SEWA Bank in India are the first to use an analytical framework of scale and sustainability for shelter finance operations. Although the sample is small, these three case studies indicate that financial institutions can provide this service on commercially viable terms:

- *MiBanco.* The institutional impact of MiCasa (MiBanco's housing loan program) after twelve months has been positive, with almost 3,000 clients, a high quality (albeit young) portfolio, with the portion at risk greater than thirty days of 0.6 percent. MiCasa broke even on a cash flow basis, including the initial investment in adjusting the management information system within nine months, and, if performance continues at present levels, is expected to generate a return on loan portfolio of between 7 and 9 percent, compared with its overall return on loan portfolio of 3.4 percent.

- *FUNHAVI*. After six years in operation, FUNHAVI is operationally self-sufficient and moving toward full financial sustainability, which would include covering the full cost of capital. FUNHAVI earns 11 percent of revenues from selling construction materials to clients.

- *SEWA*. SEWA Bank is profitable and has been every year since 1998, with small operating losses reported in 2001. It has had a correspondingly positive return on assets except for 2001 (these figures include SEWA's total portfolio, since the portfolio was not disaggregated for shelter loans; an estimated 40 percent of the total portfolio).

More such analysis and evidence is necessary in order to attract the institutions and investors necessary to take this concept to scale.

Impact

The issue of client impact is critical to governments and donors, in terms of how to expend scarce funds to achieve the greatest developmental return. The few impact evaluations of shelter finance point to positive results for the poor. An evaluation of Plan International's Credit for Habitat programs in Bolivia and Guatemala showed that clients invested their $200 to $5,000 loans in roofing, walls, floors, tiling, water, sewage, and electrical connections, and additional rooms. Seventy-eight percent of clients said that home improvements improved family health (Plan International 2001). Clients with Grameen homes, equipped with Grameen's construction standards of cement pillars and sanitary latrines, had 50 percent fewer incidences of illnesses than those without Grameen houses (Center for Urban Development Studies 2000). An impact assessment of SEWA's slum upgrading program, which included progressive housing loans, reports increases in literacy (school children enrollment), productivity (increase in number of working hours), income, health (lower incidences of illness and, thus, lower health expenditures), increased marriage opportunities, and higher status and respect in the community (SEWA 2002).

CREATING CONDITIONS FOR RAPID RAMP-UP

The practice of shelter finance for the poor is at a stage similar to where financial institutions were ten to fifteen years ago in terms of microfinance or working capital loan provision. The pattern of evolution is likely to be a similar one, except that the ramp-up and take-off phase will be much shorter for the following converging developments:

- *Product innovation in shelter finance by a generation of MFIs* that has supported delivery of other financial services to the same clientele and that is institutionally and financially stronger now than fifteen years ago. MiBanco illustrates this trend. When it decided to offer its MiCasa housing finance loans in August 2000, it had already established itself as one of the largest MFIs in Latin America, with nearly 70,000 active clients, an outstanding portfolio of $45 million, and a profitable net income of $1.2 million. Having the strong institutional foundation to build on meant that it could demonstrate results on its MiCasa (housing) portfolio within the first twelve months.
- *Product innovation in low-cost housing construction at scale,* engineered by community-based organizations such as SPARC in India and the South African Homeless People's Federation, where poor communities are building homes at a fraction of the cost of comparable houses in the local market.
- *Joint ventures between housing institutions and financial institutions,* as illustrated by Intermediate Technology Development Group (ITDG), an international NGO, and NAHECO, a group of community-based organizations, working together in Nakuru's informal settlements in Kenya, where ITDG has developed a low-cost house and NAHECO provides business and housing loans for acquisition of these homes (Brown et al. 2002). One

of the most significant breakthroughs in shelter finance for the poor will likely come from marriages between developers of low-cost housing (Grameen's low-cost prototype house, for example) and financial institutions that provide shelter finance loans to the poor.

- *Entry of traditional commercial banks and credit unions* that find the longer terms, larger amounts, and some form of collateral backing the loan closer to their comfort zone than traditional microenterprise loans. Examples include Mutual La Primera in Bolivia, Capital Bank in Haiti, and Caja Social in Colombia.

- *Governments seeking solutions to chronic housing problems* and a dearth of public finance to perpetuate the social housing model of subsidy provision per each fully constructed unit, as well as disenchantment with the limited scale and mistargeting of such efforts.

- *Entry of private developers* such as Argoz in El Salvador that are buying plots of land in city peripheries, building homes, servicing them, and extending loans to poor households for home purchase (Ferguson and Haider 2000).

- Most important, *client demand for services* and *demonstration that they are creditworthy* and a potentially profitable large segment of the population.

WHAT ROLE FOR GOVERNMENTS AND DONORS TO HELP SHELTER FINANCE REACH SCALE?

The stage is set for a potentially rapid ramp-up of housing finance institutions around the world with entry by a larger and more heterogeneous array of providers than entered microfinance at a similar stage of development. The success of the microfinance industry is showing the way for governments and donors who want to support and accelerate the development of a vibrant shelter housing industry. The most successful microfinance institutions were started by social entrepreneurs with locally raised funds, typically from private sources and often including their own. Once they seed promising institutions, governments and their donor partners can play a facilitative role and help nurture such institutions to achieve their goals of scale and sustainability.

Recommendations to Governments: Setting the Policy and Regulatory Framework

Governments play a unique role to create a facilitative policy and regulatory environment for shelter finance institutions. There will simply be no demand for housing finance if the poor are not allowed to build, or live in fear of their homes being razed to the ground or taken away. There will be no supply of housing finance services if potential institutions are restricted by legal constraints or fail to innovate because there is no competition in the market. Policy debates regarding the enabling environment for micro-enterprise finance focus on the financial services legislation and regulation adopted by the national government. Issues such as minimum capital requirements, depositor protection, usury laws, degrees of intermediation allowed, ownership structures, and institutional soundness and sustainability are seen as the key policy levers available to government to influence and control the development of the sector. All of these issues are relevant for housing finance. But in addition the enabling environment also encompasses issues that affect poor people's ability to buy land, obtain legal rights to that land, and build a home upon it.[4] Specifically, governments should focus on the following steps to set the proper policies:

1. Help set a conducive macroeconomic, and financial policy and regulatory framework for progressive build finance.

   Macroeconomic stability and sound financial sector policy remain important preconditions for the development of sound and sustainable financial institutions, and this is equally true for those focused on the poor. Governments should follow the Bolivian model that enabled the rapid growth of sustainable microfinance (i.e., closing down competing state run banks operating on an unequal playing field, removing interest rate ceilings, and regulating providers *after* their formative stage when regulations are appropriate).[5] Kenya illustrates how overregulation has stunted the development of housing finance despite there being a relatively mature set of interested MFIs.

2. Recognize that "progressive build" is the paradigm for how poor people build, and set policies and regulations in accordance.

Building codes and financial laws are often based on the assumption that people acquire homes through purchase of a fully constructed unit. For example, in Kenya, building codes were designed for the construction of complete homes, thus, making progressive building illegal, despite it being the most common form of home construction for the poor. They are based on the English code, which, in the Kenyan context means using expensive or imported materials and European-design standards (such as roofs that can withstand minimum snow loads). These codes limit the poor's demand for financial services—they fear that their out-of-code structures will be destroyed and so prudently limit investment in them. The Banking and Building Societies Act requires mortgage finance companies and building societies to lend only against mortgaged properties, which means borrowers need legal land title that is up to code, and explicitly forbids lenders to lend for a plot of land with no or a partial housing structure on it. While these examples come from Kenya, the point can be generalized to many developing countries. As notable exceptions, the governments of Indonesia and South Africa have developed comprehensive housing policy strategies that support commercially based housing microfinance programs as one of the principal tools for housing finance expansion.

3. Do not subsidize interest rates to the poor—it will constrain shelter finance provision.

MiBanco, FUNHAVI, and SEWA demonstrate that interest rate subsidies to the poor are not necessary and that competent financial institutions can deliver shelter finance loans on commercial terms. Interest rate ceilings, subsidies, or "debt forgiveness" policies by national governments distort overall financial sector policy and constrain the development of viable institutions. The Donde Act in Kenya, which regulates loan terms and conditions with the intent of making loans more affordable to poor households, is having the opposite effect with banks reducing their lending to higher-risk populations and investing in safer treasury bills instead.

Another argument for not subsidizing interest rates to the poor is that housing is a productive asset, capable of generating the income necessary to service the loan. Thirty to 60 percent of shelter finance clients are engaged in a home-based, income-generating activity. A survey of clients participating in SEWA's slum upgrading program reported a 35 percent average increase in weekly earnings, due in large measure, to loans for home improvements and water and electrical connections (Center for Urban Development Studies 2000). Most important, as the growing portfolios of microfinance institutions attest, the poor are voting with their feet, and their message is loud and clear—it is *access* to quality financial services and not *cost* that is important to them.

4. Provide secure tenure for the poor.

Improving tenure rights is the key to increasing security and stimulating improvements in housing and living standards. As property owners, households are willing to invest more than 30 percent of their income to acquire land, build, or improve their loans (Center for Urban Development Studies 2000). Conversely, they will not spend more than 15 percent of their income on shelter without some assurance about security of occupancy as owners or renters.

While granting individual legal titles (freehold) is a long-term goal to work toward, MFIs providing shelter finance loans do not rely on hard collateral or mortgages to issue shelter loans. Despite the significant land titling program in Peru, which issued four million deeds in four years, MiBanco only uses mortgages for loans higher than $5,000, due to the high cost, and poor clients are understandably reluctant to use title as collateral for loans that average less than $1000. Instead MiBanco relies on the guarantees that it has successfully used for its microenterprise loans—household assets and coguarantors.

Governments need to provide secure tenure, as an intermediate step toward ultimately providing full legal titles. There are many examples of intermediate tenure systems that increase security and facilitate investment in housing. Examples include the Ahmedebad Municipal Corporation granting slum dwellers ten year security of tenure, which led to significant investments in housing and infrastructure; addressing (naming streets and numbering dwellings) in informal settlements in Sao Paolo, and temporary occupation licenses allocated annually on a renewable basis to promote investment in small businesses in Kenya (Payne 2002).

Recommendations to Donors

To complement sound government policies and promote a vibrant shelter finance industry, donors should focus on picking the right partners, providing them with appropriate financial instruments and capacity building support, and helping develop and disseminate knowledge to inspire adaptation and replication. Donors should:

1. Select a few financial institutions with a proven track record to partner with, emphasizing financial sustainability and portfolio quality as key criteria for selection.

   It could be argued that the most important factor for the creation of microfinance industries in Bangladesh, Indonesia, and Bolivia was the power of demonstration by Grameen Bank, BRI, and BancoSol in those respective countries—they spawned industries in their nations and inspired action abroad. As a strategic choice, there is more to be gained by investing limited funds in a select few potential winners and demonstrating impact than spreading resources indiscriminately across many. Nothing spreads like success.

2. Provide funds for building institutional capacity, not just for on-lending.

   Help the start-up costs of experimentation and knowledge spread across financial institutions. Accion International is planning to pilot test a housing microfinance loan product through four affiliated institutions, and then disseminate the results throughout its network of twenty-seven institutions in twenty-one countries to scale-up the experience. Such activities merit funding. Grants or subsidized funds should be used for initial start-up costs and operating expenditures for a limited time, based on the performance of retail financial institutions. Financial institutions' loan funds should typically not be subsidized.

3. Fund pilots with existing institutions that have a track record.

   The industry is at the early stage of requiring more experimentation, and donors would be well-placed to assist institutions that wish to market-test and refine their product offerings and fund pilot efforts. As an example, The World Bank is offering a small loan ($5 million) that will provide medium-term capital and technical assistance to established MFIs in Indonesia wishing to experiment with housing finance loans.

4. Not place conditions on donor financing of microfinance institutions which can (inadvertently) reduce ability to experiment with housing finance.

   Donor funding agreements with MFIs often restrict support to micro*enterprise* loans and restrict institutions from providing a wider array of services to their poor clients in response to client demand. Practitioners are urging donors to assist in building their institutions and their capacity to deliver a wide array of financial services to the poor, and to not predetermine or restrict the service mix they offer.[6]

5. Help fund or establish facilities that provide medium-term capital to financial institutions.

   Financial institutions offering shelter finance loans need access to three- to five-year sources of capital to match their asset and liability term structures. While public policy makers need to continue to focus on overall capital market development, in the interim, institutions providing shelter finance will need access to this medium-term capital to allow them to expand their portfolios in this area and reduce their greater term mismatch and risk from shelter loans. DFID (a U.K. development agency) has just financed such a facility to provide a mix of grants, loans, and guarantees, initially to Indian institutions specialized in provision of urban shelter and related infrastructure to the poor.

6. Promote and fund applied research and its dissemination.

   Donors work in multiple countries and are well placed to transfer knowledge. In particular, further knowledge is needed on:

   • the profitability of housing finance. More analysis and greater financial transparency of institutions providing shelter finance will be needed to make the case for its commercial viability, which is so necessary to stimulate the entry of more institutions. Achieving significant scale will not happen without their participation;

   • the range and forms of security of tenure that MFIs can use in lieu of mortgage guarantees for the provision of housing loans;

- the points of intersection between mortgage finance technology and microfinance lending technologies to improve product offerings and to reach a wider segment of the low-income population;
- the links between housing finance institutions and local and national government initiatives—what public sector/ municipal level service provision can do to support and facilitate the development of housing by the poor, and housing finance institutions that enable them to do so;
- exploration of construction of prototype homes that are affordable to the poor, linked with financial service provision.

Very preliminary analysis of the emerging housing finance industry for the poor demonstrates the same lesson that microfinance has taught us: the poor are reliable clients who are willing to pay the full cost for *cost-effective* services tailored to their need. Pioneer financial institutions are continuing to build on their strengths and innovate with new product offerings such as shelter finance to retain and expand their clients. The initial round of innovations in this area is likely to come from the existing generation of microfinance institutions. But with proven success, as is happening with the commercialization of microfinance, they will be paving the path for a whole new set of players—commercial banks, mortgage finance companies, private builders, and others that typically shy away from poor people. It is our hope that they will soon be vying side by side for poor people's attention and purchasing power.

NOTES

The opinions expressed in this chapter are those of the author and should not be attributed to the Fannie Mae Foundation.

1. Adapted from Population Division of the Department of Economic and Social Affairs of the United Nations Secretariat "World Urbanization Prospects: the 1999 Revision," United Nations, 1998.

2. Indonesia: Housing Microfinance Project Idea Note, 2002.

3. Database prepared by MEDA under contract to IFC/Cities Alliance.

4. Cities Alliance, Kenya, 2002. This study focused on the enabling environment for shelter finance for the poor, using Kenya as a focus country. Given the availability of this recent study, this chapter draws heavily on examples from

Kenya to illustrate points; however, the points are quite applicable to many countries around the world.

5. See Elisabeth Rhyne 2001 for more information on the Bolivian government's role in mainstreaming microfinance.

6. Cities Alliance, Kenya, 2002; Daphnis; FUNHAVI presentation at World Bank, March 2002.

Bibliography

Adams, D. W., D. H. Graham, J. D. Von Pischke, and Economic Development Institute (Washington D.C. 1984). *Undermining Rural Development with Cheap Credit.* Boulder, Colo.: Westview Press.

African Population and Health Research Center. "Population and Health Dynamics in Nairobi's Informal Settlements" (Nairobi: APHRC, 2002), 256.

Avery, Robert, Raphael Bostic, Paul Calem, and Glenn Canner. 1996. "Credit Risk, Credit Scoring, and the Performance of Home Mortgages." *Federal Reserve Bulletin:* 633. July.

Balamir, Murat, and Geoffrey Payne. 2001. "Legality and Legitimacy in Urban Tenure Issues" Abstract Paper submitted to the ESF/N-AERUS Conference. Belgium, May 23–26.

Balkenhol, Berd, and Haje Schütte. 1995. *Collateral, Collateral Law, and Collateral Substitutes.* Geneva: ILO.

Basle Committee in Banking Supervision. [July 1988]. "International Convergence of Capital Measurement and Capital Standards," (Introduction, Section 8). Available at Bank for International Studies site: www.bis.org/publ/bcbs04a.htm.

Baumann, Ted. 2000. "Bridging the Finance Gap in Housing and Infrastructure." Case Study. South Africa: People's Dialogue.

Baydas, Mayada. 1993. *Capital Structure Determinants and Asset Portfolio Choice among Micro, Small, and Medium Scale Enterprises in the Gambia,* Ph.D. Dissertation, Ohio State University.

Baydas, Mayada, Douglas Graham, and Liza Valenzuela. 1997. "Commercial Banks in Microfinance: New Actors in the Microfinance World." Microenterprise Best Practice paper. U.S. Agency for International Development.

Belsky, Eric S. 2002. "Rehabilitation Matters: Improving Neighborhoods One Home at a Time." *Bright Ideas* 21, no. 3, 3–7.

Boomgard, J. J., S. P. Davies, S. J. Haggblade, and D. C. Mead. 1992. "A Subsector Approach to Small Enterprise Promotion and Research." *World Development* 20, no. 2: 199–212.

Bostic, Raphael W. and Brian J. Surette. 2000. *Have the Doors Opened Wider?: Trends in Home Ownership Rates by Race and Income.* Working Paper.

Washington, D.C. See www.federalreserve.gov/pubs/feds/2000/200031/
200031pap.pdf
Brown, Warren, and Angel Garcia. 2001. "MiCasa: Financing the Progressive
Construction of Low-Income Families' Homes at MiBanco." Shelter for
the Poor Series, Mohini Malhotra, ed. Washington, D.C.: Cities
Alliance.
Cabannes, Yves. 1996. "From Community Development and *Mutirao* to Hous-
ing Finance and *Casa Melhor* in Fortaleza, Brazil." London: International
Institute for Environment and Development.
Canner, Glenn B., and Wayne Passmore. 1999. "The Role of Specialized
Lenders Extending Credit to Low-Income and Minority Home Buyers."
Federal Reserve Bulletin. Washington, D.C.: Federal Reserve.
Capital Advisors Ltd. 1997. "Border Financial Institutions—Feasibility Study."
Mimeo. Washington, D.C.: Capital Advisors Ltd.
Carr, James, and Jenny Schuetz. 2001. "Financial Services in Distressed Com-
munities: Framing the Issue, Finding Solutions." In *Financial Services in
Distressed Communities: Issues and Answers.* Washington, D.C.: Fannie Mae
Foundation.
Carr, James H., and Zhong Yi Tong (eds.) *Replicating Microfinance in the United
States.* Washington, D.C.: Woodrow Wilson Center Press.
Center for Policy Priorities. 1999. "Congressional Budget Office as analyzed
by the Center of Policy Priorities." *New York Times* (September 5).
Center for Social Development. 2001. Savings and Asset Accumulation in
IDAs—Down payments on the American Dream. Washington, D.C.: Cen-
ter for Social Development.
Center for Urban Development Studies. Harvard University Graduate School
of Design. 2000. *Housing Microfinance Initiatives: Synthesis and Regional
Summary: Asia, Latin America, and Sub-Saharan Africa with Selected Case
Studies.* Bethesda, Md.: Development Alternatives, Inc.
Chen, Martha Alter, and Donald Snodgrass. 1999. "An Assessment of the
Impact of SEWA Bank in India: Baseline Findings." Cambridge, Mass.:
Harvard Institute for International Development.
Cities Alliance. 2002. *Shelter Finance for the Poor.* Available at www.citiesalliance.
org/citiesalliancehomepage.nsf/Attachments/shelter/$File/Shelter+
Finance.pdf. Accessed November 25, 2002.
City of El Paso. 2000. *Consolidated Plan for the City of El Paso, Texas, 2000–2005.*
———. 1998. *El Paso Economic Summit.*
Consultative Group to Assist the Poorest (CGAP). 1996. "Microenterprise Inter-
est Rates." CGAP Occasional Paper no. 1, revised. Washington, D.C.: CGAP.
———. *Financial Transparency: A Glossary of Terms.* Washington, D.C.: CGAP.
Full-text pdf: www.cgap.org/docs/Glossary_Transparency.pdf.
———. 2002. "Microfinance in World Bank Projects: Twelve Questions About
Sound Practice." Donor Brief no. 1. Washington, D.C.: CGAP.
Cohen, Monique. 2002. *Journal of International Development* 14, no. 3, 335–
350.
Collier, David. 1976. *Squatters and Oligarchs.* Baltimore, Md.: John Hopkins
University Press.

Cooperative Housing Foundation (CHF n.d.). *Incorporating a Home Improvement Loan Program: A Feasibility Assessment Guide for Microfinance Institutions.* Silver Spring, Md.: CHF.

D'Amours, Norman E. 2002. "The Battle to Increase Access and Ensure Fair Pricing." *The Neighborhood Works Journal,* Winter, 20–22.

Daphnis, Franck, and Kimberly Tilock. 2001. *So You Want to Do Housing Microfinance?* Silver Spring, Md.: CHF International.

Daphnis, Franck, Kimberly Tilock, Mathew Chandy, and Ingrid Fulhauber. 2002. "Assessment of SEWA Bank's Housing Microfinance Program." Shelter Finance for the Poor Series, ed. Mohini Malhotra. Washington, D.C.: Cities Alliance.

Daphnis, Franck, Kimberly Tilock, Thea Anderson, and Ingrid Faulhaber. 2002. *Assessment of FUNHAVI's Housing Microfinance Program.* Shelter Finance for the Poor Series, ed. Mohini Malhotra. Washington, D.C.: Cities Alliance.

Davis, Geoff, and Eliza Mahoney. 2001. *Housing Microfinance: Building the Assets of the Poor, One Room at a Time.* Master's Thesis. John F. Kennedy School of Government, Harvard University, Cambridge, Mass.

DeLiban and Lancaster 1995. "Agricultural Rural Development Policy in Latin American New Directions and Challenges" (FAO Agricultural Policy and Economic Development Series 2). Food and Agricultural Organization of the United Nations (FAO), Rome, 1997.

De Janvry, Alain, Nigel Key, and Elizabeth Sadoulet. Rome: FAO, 1997.

De Soto, Hernando. 1989. *The Other Path.* New York: Harper and Row.

———. 2000. *The Mystery of Capital.* New York: Basic Books.

Diamond, Douglas, and Ritu Nayyar-Stone. 2001. "India: Heading Towards A Liberalized and Integrated Housing Finance System." *Housing Finance International,* 2001, 15, no. 3, 42–50.

Durand-Lasserve, Alain, Edesio Fernandez, Geoffrey Payne, and Martin Smolka. 2002. "Secure Tenure for the Urban Poor." Presentation from Roundtable seminar organized by Cities Alliance, World Bank, May 23.

Ehrenreich, Barbara. 2001. *Nickeled and Dimed: On (Not) Getting By in America.* New York: Henry Holt.

Enterprise Research Institute for Latin America. 1997. "An Exploration of Issues Related to Land Titling Programs." ERILA Special Report.

Erb, Debra L. 2000. "Home Financing Where It's Never Been Done Before. Putting the "Real" in Real Estate for Aspiring Home Owners in Countries with no Mortgage Systems." *The World Paper,* Boston, Mass.

Escobar, Alejandro. 2002. *Shelter Finance: Literature Review and State of Practice.* MEDA Consulting Group, Lancaster, Pennsylvania (Draft) for International Finance Corporation (IFC).

Fannie Mae. 1997.

———. 1999. *Fannie Mae News Release.* May 16. Available *at* www.fanniemae.com/new/pressreleases.

Federal Reserve Board. 2000.

Ferguson, Bruce. 1994. "The Community Development Financial Institutions Initiative" in Economic Development Commentary. *Journal of the*

National Council for Urban Economic Development. Washington, D.C., Summer 1994.

———. 1996. "The Environmental Impacts and Public Costs of Unguided Informal Settlement: The Case of Montego Bay." *Environment and Urbanization* 8, no. 2:172–193.

———. 1999. "Microfinance of Housing: A Key to Housing the Low or Moderate Majority." *Environment and Urbanization* 11, no. 1: 185–199.

Ferguson, Bruce, and Elinor Haider. 2000. "Mainstreaming Microfinance of Housing." *Housing Finance International,* 2000, 15, no. 1, 3–17.

———. 2002. "Microfinance of Progressive Housing: Can Techniques from Developing Countries be Adapted in the United States?" In Carr, James H. and Zhong Yi Tong (eds.) *Replicating Microfinance in the United States.* Washington, D.C.: Woodrow Wilson Center Press.

Feshbach, Dan and Pat Schwinn. 1999. "Tactical Approach to Credit Scores." *Mortgage Banking.* February.

FFIEC. 1997. *Community Reinvestment Act Examination Procedures for Large Retail Institutions.* Mimeo

Finnish Ministry of the Environment. 2001. *Housing Statistics in the European Union.* Helsinki: FME.

Fleisig, Heywood. 1997. *Secured Transactions: The Power of Collateral.* Washington, D.C.: Center for the Economic Analysis of Law.

Freddie Mac. 2000. *Freddie Mac Releases Automated Underwriting Factors used by Loan Prospector.* Press Release, June 7.

Gelbard, Alene, Carl Haub, and Mary Kent. 1999. "World Population Beyond Six Billion." *Population Bulletin* 54, note 1 (March 1999): 3–44.

Glover, Christine, 1997. "Broadening Access to Affordable Housing." *Housing Finance International* (December).

Glover, Christine. 1995. "The Group Credit Company History from 1987 to the Present." Unpublished mimeo.

Gold, Jane, et al. 2002. "Collective Action and the Urban Poor: The Principles of Local Agenda 21" in Windhoek: Collective Action and the Urban Poor, series working paper 9. Jane Gold and Anna Muller with Diana Mitlin, 2002, 58. Can be found at International Institute for Environment and Development, http://www.iied.org/docs/urban/local21s_wp09.pdf.

Goldmark, Lara, and Caren Addis Botelho. 2000. *Paraguay Vouchers Revisited: Strategies for the Development of Training Markets.* USAID's Microenterprise Best Practices. Bethesda, Md.: Development Alternatives, Inc.

Gosling, John. 1995. "Affordable Housing Development in Mexico." *Urban Land* 54, no. 2 (February 1995): 34.

Haider, Elinor. 2000. "Credit Bureaus: Leveraging Information for the Benefit of Microenterprises." *Microenterprise Development Review.* Washington, D.C.: Inter-American Development Bank.

"Half a Billion Americans?" 2002. *The Economist,* August 24: 20–21.

Hardoy, Jorge, and David Satterthwaite. 1989. *Squatter Citizen: Life in the Urban Third World.* London: Earthscan Publications.

Henneberger, John. 2000. "Affordable Housing on the Border." *Borderlines* 65 (3): 8.

Hirad, A. & Zorn, P. M. 2001. *A Little Knowledge is a Good Thing: Empirical Evidence of the Effectiveness of Prepurchase Home Ownership Counseling.* Working Paper. McLean, VA: Freddie Mac. www.federalreserve.gov/communityaffairs/national/CA_Conf_SusCommDev/pdf/zornpeter.pdf.

Home Mortgage Disclosure Act, 2000.

Hoek-Smit, Marja, Douglas Smit, and Claude Bovet. 1998. *Housing Finance and Housing Subsidies in Barbados.* Report prepared for the Government of Barbados under a contract of the International Development Bank.

Holsten, M., Pacholek, L., and Naboa, M. 1999. Evaluation of the PLAN/Tarija, FADES home improvement loan program. PLAN International, Arlington, VA.

"Housing by the Numbers." *Washington Post,* June 15, 2002. H01 staff database editor Dan Kouting contributed to this report.

Hulme, D. 2000. "Impact Assessment Methodologies for Microfinance: Theory, Experience and Better Practice. *World Development* 28, no. 1:79–98.

Immergluck, Daniel, and Marti Wiles. 1999. *Two Steps Back: The Dual Mortgage Market, Predatory Lending, and the Undoing of Community Development.* Chicago: The Woodstock Institute.

Inter-American Development Bank. 2000. "El Salvador Housing Program: Profile II." Internal Document. Washington, D.C.: Inter-American Development Bank.

Lowry, Ira S., and Bruce Ferguson. 1992. *Development Regulations and Housing Affordability.* Washington, D.C.: The Urban Land Institute.

Joint Center for Housing Studies, Harvard University. 2002. *The State of the Nation's Housing 2002.* Cambridge, Mass.: Harvard University.

JSP Associates Management Consultants. 1993. "Baseline Financial Profiles of Housing Finance Companies in India." Prepared for Indo-U.S. Housing Finance Expansion Program (USAID), New Delhi, India: ABT Associates, Inc.

Kennickell, Arthur, et al. 2000. "Recent Changes in U.S. Family Finances: Results from the Survey of Consumer Finances." *Federal Reserve Bulletin* 86, no. 1: 1–29.

Kim, Anne. 2001. *Taking the Poor into Account: What Banks Can Do to Better Serve Low-Income Markets.* Washington, D.C.: Progressive Policy Institute.

Klinkhamer, Madeleine. 2000. "MicroFinance Housing Products and Experience with Land Title as Collateral." GHIF Report.

Listokin, David, and Barbara Listokin. 2001. *Barriers to Rehabilitation of Affordable Housing, Volume 1, Findings and Analysis.* Washington, D.C.: U.S. Department of Housing and Urban Development.

Listokin, David and Elvin Wyly, et al. 2000. *Innovative Strategies to Expand Lending to Traditionally Under-Served Populations: Approaches and Case Studies.* Report Submitted to the Fannie Mae Foundation. March.

Listokin, David, Elvin Wyly, and Joan Voicu. 2002. *The Potential and Limitations of Mortgage Innovation in Fostering Home Ownership in the United States.* Washington, D.C.: Fannie Mae Foundation.

Lloyd, Peter. 1990. *The Young Towns of Lima.* Cambridge: Cambridge University Press.

Louie, Josephine, et al. 1998. "The Housing Needs of Lower-Income Home Owners." Working paper 98–8. Cambridge, Mass.: Joint Center for Housing Studies, Harvard University.

MacDonald, Heather. 1995. "Secondary Mortgage Markets and Federal Housing Policy." *Journal of Urban Affairs* 17, no. 1: 53–79.

McAuslan, Patrick. 1985. *Urban Land and Shelter for the Poor.* London: Earthscan.

McCarthy, George and Roberto Quercia. 2000. *Bridging the Gap Between Supply and Demand: The Evolution of Home Ownership Education and Counseling Industry.* Washington, D.C.: The Research Institute for Housing America. Report. May.

McLeod, Ruth. 2000. "Bridging the Finance Gap in Housing and Infrastructure, India: SPARC—A Case Study." *Homeless International.* Phase I Report to the Department for International Development.

———. 2001. "Bridging the Finance Gap in Housing and Infrastructure." *Homeless International.* Phase 2 Report to the Department for International Development.

Mahoney, Peter and Peter Zorn 1996. "The Promise of Automated Underwriting." 1996 *Mortgage Trends.*

Mansfield, Cathy L. 2000. *The Road to Subprime 'HEL' Was Paved with Good Congressional Intentions: Usury Deregulation and Subprime Home Equity Market.* 51 SCL Rev. 473.

Marez, Michael. 2000. "Case Study: Adapting Risk Management Practices to the Realities of the Mexican Mortgage Market." *International Journal of Real Estate Finance* 1, no. 2.

Mead, D. C. 1994. "The Contribution of Small Enterprises to Employment Growth in Southern and Eastern Africa." *World Development* 22, no. 12: 1881–1894.

Mead, D. C., and Liedholm, C. 1998. "The Dynamics of Micro and Small Enterprises in Developing Countries. *World Development* 261: 61–74.

Mehta, Meera. 1994. "Analysis: Down Marketing Housing Finance Through Community Based Financial Systems." Prepared for Indo-U.S. Housing Finance Expansion Program (USAID). New Delhi, India: ABT Associates, Inc.

Merrill, Sally. 2001. "Innovations in Microfinance for Housing in the United States and Emerging Markets: Can We Transfer Methodologies?" *Housing Finance International,* 2001, 15, no. 3: 3–16.

———. 2001. "Low- and Moderate-Income Housing Finance in South Africa: Making Progress in a Troubled Environment." *Housing Finance International,* 2001, 15, no. 3: 51–64.

Merrill, Sally R., and Kenneth Temkin. 2002. "Microfinance and Low-Income Lending for Housing in Emerging Markets and the United States." in James H. Carr and Zhong Yi Tong (eds.) *Replicating Microfinance in the United States.* Washington, DC: Woodrow Wilson Center Press, 257–98.

Merrill, Sally, Jim Griffin, and Peter Richardson. 1994. "South Africa: A Review of the Policy Framework and Roles of Traditional and Non-Traditional Retail Lenders and Wholesale Fund Mobilization." Proposal for a

Private/Public Partnership for Low-Income Housing, National Housing Forum.

Merrill, Sally, Kenneth Temkin, Claudio Pardo, Douglas Diamond, Ritu Nayyar-Stone, and Michael Lea. 2000. "Housing Finance for Low- and Moderate-Income Households: Innovations in the United States and around the World." Prepared for the U.S. Department of Housing and Urban Development (HUD). Washington, D.C.: The Urban Institute.

"MiCasa es tu casa." 1999. *Latin Trade Magazine,* (July).

Mitlin, Diana. 1997. "Reaching Low-income Groups with Housing Finance." Housing Finance Report 3. London: International Institute for Environment and Development.

Moser, Caroline. 1998. "The Asset Vulnerability Framework: Reassessing Urban Poverty Reduction Strategies." *World Development* 26, no. 1: 1–19.

Navajas, S., M. Schreiner, R. L. Meyer, C. Gonzalez-Vega, and J. Rodriguez-Meza. 2000. "Microcredit and the Poorest of the Poor: Theory and Evidence from Bolivia." *World Development* 28, no. 2: 333–346.

Noudehou, Alain. 2002. *Evaluation: LAFTO Low-Income Housing Area Improvement Program.* Silver Spring, Md.: Cooperative Housing Foundation.

———. (2002). *A Housing Microfinance Program for Indonesia.* Prepared for the World Bank. Silver Spring, Md.: Cooperative Housing Foundation.

Office of the Comptroller of the Currency. 1997. *The Single-Family Affordable Housing Market: Trends and Innovations: A National Symposium Convened on July 23, 1997 by the Office of the Comptroller of the Currency.* Report.

Office of Policy Development and Research. 2001. *Study of the Use of Credit Enhancements by Government Sponsored Enterprises.* Washington, D.C.: U.S. Department of Housing and Urban Development.

OFHEO. 2000. *2000 Report to Congress.* Washington, D.C. Report.

Pachura, Stanley. 1996. "Up and Running: How Three Lenders on the Front Lines of the Automated Revolution are Reducing Costs, Adding Customers, Energizing Loan Processors and Getting a Competitive Head Start on the 21st Century." Mortgage Banking. May.

Palmer David, and John McLaughlin. 1996. "Integrated Land Administration: Institutional and Technical Challenges." A special issue of the ITC Journal for the Habitat II Conference.

Pardo, Claudio. 1996. "The Chilean Tripartite Approach: Loans, Family Savings, and State Subsidies." *Housing Finance International,* 2001, 15, no. 3: 32–41.

Park, A., and C. Q. Ren. 2001. Microfinance with Chinese characteristics. *World Development* 29, no. 1: 39–62.

Payne, G. 2002. *Land, Rights, and Innovation.* "Chapter One: Introduction." London: ITDG Publishing.

Penington-Cross, Anthony, Anthony Yezer, and Joseph Nicols. 2000. *Credit Risk and Mortgage Lending: Who Uses Subprime and Why?* Washington, D.C.: Research Institute for Housing America.

Phillips, Kevin. 2002. *Wealth and Democracy.* New York: Broadway.

Plan International. 2001. "Credit for Habitat Program Evaluation." Summary Report.

Porteous, David. "Coming Second? Secondary Market Development in Developing Countires: A Case Study of South Africa." *Housing Finance International,* 2000, 15, no. 3: 18–25.

Renaud. *Housing and Financial Institutions in Developing Countries: An Overview* (Washington, D.C.: World Bank, 1984, 111).

Renaud, Bertrand. 2001. *Access to Housing Finance Bank Operations.* Infrastructure Forum. Unpublished document. World Bank.

Retsinas, Nicolas P., and Eric S. Belsky. 2002. "Examining the Unexamined Goal." In Retsinas, Nicolas P., and Eric S. Belsky (eds.) *Low-Income Home Ownership: Examining the Unexamined Goal.* Washington, D.C. and Cambridge, Mass.: Brookings Institution and Joint Center for Housing Studies.

Rhyne, Elisabeth. 2001. *How Lending to the Poor Began, Grew, and Came of Age in Bolivia.* Bloomfield, Conn.: Kumarian Press.

Rhyne, Elisabeth, and M. Otero. 1992. "Financial Services for Microenterprises—Principles and Institutions." *World Development* 20, no. 11: 1561–1571.

Rylander, Carole. "Housing: Homes of Our Own." Available at www.window.state.tx.us/border/ch07/ch07.html.

Scanlon, Edward. 1996. "Home Ownership and its Impacts: Implications for Housing Policy for Low-Income Families." Working Paper no. 96–2. Center for Social Development, Washington University.

Scheessele, Randall. 1999. "1998 HMDA Highlights." Working Paper no. HF-009. Washington, D.C.: U.S. Department of Housing and Urban Development, Office of Policy Development and Research.

Schor, G. 1999. *Estrategia para Mejorar la Situacion Habitacional de la Poblacion de Bajos Ingresos en El Salvador.* Washington, D.C.: IPC.

Schor, G., and J. P. Alberti. 1996. *Training Voucher Schemes for Microenterprises in Paraguay: Benefits of a Demand-Driven Approach to Government Intervention in the Training Market.* Internationale Projekt Consult GmbH (IPC) Working paper no. 12, Frankfurt, Germany.

SEWA. 2002. *Parivartan and its Impact: A Partnership Programme of Infrastructure Development in Slums of Ahmedabad City.* SEWA, India.

Sharp, John. 1998. *Bordering the Future: Challenge and Opportunity in the Texas Border Region* (Austin, Tex.: Texas Comptroller of Public Accounts, 1998) iii, 233.

Shidlo, Gil. 1994. "Housing Regulatory Reform in Mexico." Report for the World Bank Report, Urban HS-8, Department of Transportation, Water and Urban Development.

Skillern, Peter. 2002. "The American Dream for Less and Less of the American Dream: Manufactured Housing Home Ownership." Draft paper, Community Investment Association of North Carolina.

Smolka, Martim, and Laura Mullahy. 2000. "Land Policy Issues in Latin America." *Land Lines.* Lincoln Institute of Land Policy (September).

Stegman, Michael. 1999. *State and Local Affordable Housing Programs: A Rich Tapestry.* Washington, D.C.: Urban Land Institute.

Stein, Eric. 2001. *Quantifying the Economic Cost of Predatory Lending.* Available at http://predatorylending.org/research/Quant10-01.pdf. Accessed January 25, 2003.

Szalachman, Raquel. 2000. *Perfil de deficit y politicas de vivienda de interes social: Situacion de algunos paises de la region en los noventa* (Santiago, Chile: UN Economic Committee for Latin America).

Talen, Ayse Can, Marc A. Weiss, and Sohini Sarkar. 2002. "The Future of Microfinance in the United States: Research, Practice, and Policy Perspectives." In Carr, James H. and Zhong Yi Tong (eds.) *Replicating Microfinance in the United States.* Washington, D.C.: Woodrow Wilson Center Press.

Temkin, Kenneth. 2002. "Emerging Issues in Housing Microfinance in the US." Unpublished Manuscript.

Temkin, Kenneth. 2001. "The U.S. Housing Finance System for Low-Income Families: A Review of Recent Innovations and Changes." *Housing Finance International* 15(3):17–31.

Temkin, Kenneth, Roberto Quercia, George Galster, and Sheila O'Leary. 1999. *A Study of the GSEs' Underwriting Guidelines. Report prepared for the U.S. Department of Housing and Urban Development, Office of Policy Development and Research.* Washington, D.C.: Report.

Temkin, Kenneth and Jennifer Johnson. 2000. *An Assessment of Recent Innovations in the Secondary Market for Low- and Moderate-Income Lending. Report submitted to U.S. Department of Housing and Urban Development, Office of Policy Development and Research.* Washington, D.C.: Report.

Texas Department of Human Services. 2001. *Colonias Factbook.* Austin, Tex.

Tomilinson, Mary R. 1998. "The Role of the Banking Industry in Promoting Low-Income Housing Development." *Housing Finance International* 12, no. 4.

———. 1998. "South Africa's Housing Policy: Lessons from Four Years of Delivery." Prepared for The Banking Council of South Africa.

———. 1999. "International Union for Housing Finance Sourcebook: South Africa." Chicago, Ill.

———. 2000. "Extending Appropriate Financial Services to Low-Income Communities." The Banking Council of South Africa, Discussion paper.

Tucker, R. S. 1999. "The Retail Dimension: Rethinking the Provision of Retail Banking Services to Low-Income Communities." *Housing Finance International* (December).

Turner, John. 1963. "Lima Barriadas Today." *Architectural Digest* 33, no. 8: 375–380.

———. "Barriers and Channels for Housing Development in Modernizing Countries." *Journal of the American Institute of Planners* 33: 167–181.

United Nations Department of Economic and Social Affairs. 1998. *World Urbanization Prospects: The 1999 Revision.* New York: United Nations Secretariat.

United Nations Centre for Human Settlements. 1996. "Global Campaign for Secure Tenure: Implementing the Habitat Agenda: Adequate Shelter for All" (Rio de Janeiro, Brazil: UNCHS (Habitat) Regional Office for Latin America and the Carribbean, 2000).

UNCHS. 2000. "The New Face of Urbanization in the Cities of Latin America and the Caribbean." Paper given at the LAC-Regional Conference on Habitat, Los Angeles, October 25–27, 2000.

U.S. Bureau of the Census. 1999. *Statistical Abstract of the United States. 1999.* Washington, D.C.: U.S. Department of Commerce.

———. 2000. "2000 Selected Characteristics of New Manufactured Homes Placed for Residential Use, by Region." Available at www.census.gov/const/www/mhsindex.html.

———. 2000. "America's Families and Living Arrangements." *Current Population Reports.* Washington, D.C.: U.S. Department of Commerce.

U.S. Department of Housing and Urban Development (HUD). 2000. *Curbing Predatory Home Mortgage Lending.* Washington, D.C.: HUD.

———. 2000. *Unequal Burden: Income and Racial Disparities in Subprime Lending.* Washington, D.C.: HUD.

U.S. National Association of Realtors, May 2002.

Vora, P. P. December 1999. "The Indian Housing Finance System." *Housing Finance International* 14, no. 2.

Ward, Peter. 1998. Abstract Paper presented at International Forum on Regularization and Land Markets. *Land Lines.* Lincoln Institute of Land Policy.

Wattanasiritham, Paiboon. December 1997. "Broadening Access for More Affordable Housing: Housing Finance for Thailand's Poor." *Housing Finance International.*

Westley, Glenn, and Brian Branch, eds. 2000. *Safe Money: Building Effective Credit Unions in Latin America.* Washington, D.C.: Johns Hopkins University Press.

Williams, Richard. 1999. *The Effects of GSEs, CRA, and Institutional Characteristics on Home Mortgage Lending to Underserved Markets.* Washington, D.C.: U.S. Department of Housing and Urban Development, Office of Policy Development and Research. Report.

Wolff, Edward N. 1998. "Recent Trends in the Size Distribution of Household Wealth." *Journal of Economic Perspectives* 12, no. 3: 131–150.

World Bank. 2002. *Mexico Low-Income Housing: Issues and Options.* Washington, D.C.: World Bank.

World Health Organization (WHO). 1992. "Our Planet, Our Earth." WHO Commission on Health and the Environment. Geneva: WHO.

Wright, Graham, Mosharrof Hossain, and Stuart Rutherford. 1997. "Savings: Flexible Financial Services for the Poor and Not Just the Implementing Organization." Prepared for the International Workshop on Poverty and Finance in Bangladesh.

About the Contributors

Mayada Baydas is the General Manager of Access to Microfinance and Enhanced Enterprise Niches (AMEEN), the largest microfinance provider in Lebanon. Ms. Baydas is an experienced researcher, consultant, and project manager and a recognized expert in microfinance market assessments. She has conducted housing microfinance and microenterprise-focused market research in more than twenty countries around the world.

Franck Daphnis is the Director of Field Program Operations for CHF International where he has directly overseen the design and implementation of microfinance programs in more than twenty countries and played a key role in the creation and management of seven local microfinance institutions. Mr. Daphnis was trained as an architect and urban planner at Cornell University and the University of Wisconsin.

Alejandro Escobar is a Global Business Analyst at DuPont Nonwovens , based in Wilmington, Delaware. Previously, he worked for several years for Mennonite Economic Development Associates (MEDA). As a Senior Consultant in Microfinance and Business Development, Mr. Escobar helped in the formation of MEDA's private investment fund, which targets microfinance retail institutions and small and medium size enterprises in Latin America. He is also an adjunct professor at Eastern University's International Economic Development Program.

Bruce Ferguson, who joined the World Bank in 2003, spent the last decade focused on designing housing and urban programs, mainly for the Inter-American Development Bank, where he led a housing group for Central America, Mexico, and the Dominican Republic. He has worked in housing, urban, and economic development in the United States and internationally. Dr. Ferguson was trained as an urban planner at University of California, Berkeley and UCLA.

Kil Huh is currently the Manager of Housing Policy and Programs in the Financial Innovations, Planning and Research division at the Fannie Mae Foundation in Washington, D.C. Prior to that, he worked at Asian Americans for Equality, a community development corporation located on Manhattan's Lower East Side.

Lopa Purohit Kolluri is Director of Policy, Planning and Community Development at the Housing and Mortgage Finance Agency in New Jersey. She has also worked for the Fannie Mae Foundation and at CHF International.

Mohini Malhotra currently works at the World Bank Institute. She has also served as Advisor in Financial Services at the Cities Alliance Secretariat at the World Bank. She has fifteen years of experience working with microfinance institutions worldwide, including the creation and management of the Consultative Group to Assist the Poorest (CGAP), a microfinance program, for its first four years.

Michael Marez is Senior Vice President for Latin America for Pulte Mortgage, LLC, a subsidiary of Pulte Homes. He has worked in the area of low-income housing finance in the United States and Latin America for twenty years and through his work at Pulte, he has participated in the development of the modern housing finance industry in Mexico.

Katharine W. McKee is the Director of the Microenterprise Development Program at USAID. She has also worked at Self Help, one of the largest U.S. community development lenders serving local home buyers, small businesses, and nonprofit organizations.

Sally Roe Merrill is a senior associate with the Urban Institute, specializing in housing finance, housing policy, and microfinance for housing. She has worked in numerous countries in Central and Eastern Europe, Asia, and Africa.

Sohini Sarkar is manager for Financial Innovations and Community Investment at the Fannie Mae Foundation, where she is responsible for the development of knowledge, tools and programs to support market-based community revitalization. She also serves as Managing Editor for "Building Blocks: A Practitioner's Guide to Planning and Financing Community Revitalization."

Kimberly Tilock is CHF International's Microfinance Manager in Iraq. She also served as CHF's credit manager for four years prior to her current assignment. Ms. Tilock is the co-author of *So, You Want to Do Housing Microfinance? A Guide to Incorporating a Home Improvement Loan Program into a Microfinance Institution.*

Kenneth Temkin is a task manager at Kormendi/Gardner Partners, a Washington, D.C. investment banking firm, where he participates in the development and execution of a variety of structured transactions. Prior to joining Kormendi/Gardner Partners, he was a Senior Research Associate at the Urban Institute, responsible for leading housing finance research within the Center on Metropolitan Housing and Communities.

Irene Vance is an external consultant to the Swedish International Development Agency's(SIDA) housing and local development program in Nicaragua, which channels funds to microfinance institutions for housing microfinance and microenterprise. Previously, she worked for the United Nations Centre for Human Settlements-Habitat, in Bolivia and throughout Latin America, specializing in the development of low-income housing programs.

Index

 Also from Kumarian Press...

Microfinance

The Commercialization of Microfinance: Balancing Business and Development
Edited by Deborah Drake and Elisabeth Rhyne

Defying the Odds: Banking for the Poor
Eugene Versluysen

Mainstreaming Microfinance
How Lending to the Poor Began, Grew and Came of Age in Bolivia
Elisabeth Rhyne

The New World of Microenterprise Finance
Building Healthy Financial Institutions for the Poor
Edited by María Otero and Elisabeth Rhyne

Pathways Out of Poverty: Innovations in Microfinance for the Poorest Families
Edited by Sam Daley-Harris

Conflict Resolution, Environment, Gender Studies, Globalization,
International Development, Political Economy

Confronting Globalization
Economic Integration and Popular Resistance in Mexico
Edited by Timothy A. Wise, Hilda Salazar and Laura Carlsen

Nation-Building Unraveled? Aid, Peace and Justice in Afghanistan
Edited by Antonio Donini, Norah Niland, and Karin Wermester

Promises Not Kept
Poverty and the Betrayal of Third World Development, Sixth Edition
John Isbister

Reinventing Government for the Twenty-First Century
State Capacity in a Globalizing Society
Edited by Dennis A. Rondinelli and G. Shabbir Cheema

Rethinking Tourism and Ecotravel Second Edition
Deborah McLaren

Southern Exposure
International Development and the Global South in the Twenty-First Century
Barbara P. Thomas-Slayter

Worlds Apart: Civil Society and the Battle for Ethical Globalization
John D. Clark

Visit Kumarian Press at **www.kpbooks.com** or
call **toll-free 800.289.2664** for a complete catalog.

Kumarian Press, located in Bloomfield, Connecticut, is a forward-looking, scholarly press that promotes active international engagement and an awareness of global connectedness.